HOMEMADE is BETTER

from Tupperware® Home Parties

Pictured on the cover, clockwise from bottom left: Pizza Roll-Up, Carrot Cake, Turkey Biscuit Ring, Whole Wheat Butterhorns, and Easy Lemon-Blueberry Muffins.

This seal assures you that every recipe in HOMEMADE is BETTER from Tupperware® Home Parties is tested and approved by the Better Homes and Gardens Test Kitchen. Each recipe is tested for family appeal, practicality, and deliciousness.

TUPPERWARE is a registered trademark of DART INDUSTRIES INC.

Produced by Meredith Publishing Services, 1716 Locust St., Des Moines, IA 50336

TABLE
of
CONTENTS

**HOMEMADE
IS BETTER**

HOMEMADE is BETTER

It's a real challenge to make sure your family is getting a well-balanced diet, especially when you have to compete with on-the-go schedules and rising food costs. That's why Tupperware® Home Parties created this book especially for you.

Homemade is Better is a collection of the best time- and money-saving recipes you'll ever find. The goodness of homemade flavor is combined with the convenience of short-cut cooking for great-tasting, nutritious, everyday family meals.

Create hearty main dishes from homemade mixes that short-cut traditional "scratch" cooking — at considerable savings over commercial convenience products. Included are nutritious, practical food ideas for on-the-go eating — an attractive alternative to high calorie, high cost snacks. Make-ahead casseroles, salads, and desserts have been designed to keep on hand for easy, low-cost family meals — a bargain compared to commercial frozen foods. And the skip-a-step recipes for home-baked breads and desserts make oven-fresh goods a practical, wholesome addition to any meal. And, this book is packed with fresh ideas and helpful hints to make all your home cooking easier and more economical. So turn the page — you'll discover *Homemade is Better*.

Pictured clockwise from bottom left are: Ham And Pasta, Ad-Lib Antipasto, and Orange-Sauced Pears. (See Index for recipe pages.)

A WELL-STOCKED KITCHEN

WHERE GOOD COOKING BEGINS

Whether you've been captaining a galley for years, or you're setting up shop for the first time, equipping a kitchen properly is the key to preparing quick and easy meals. Here's a rundown of basic equipment you'll need from preparation and cooking utensils, bakeware, and top-of-the-range cookware, to food storage and serving items.

The variety available can be overwhelming, but remember it isn't necessary to have everything. Concentrate first on the basic utensils — and buy good quality products that will stand up to frequent usage.

MEASURE IT!

A **measuring cup set** enables you to make accurate measurements of recipe ingredients to insure success. Tupperware® makes a 6-piece set of cups that stack compactly for space-saving cabinet storage. And, this set includes ⅔ cup and ¾ cup measures not usually included in other sets.

A **measuring spoon set** usually consists of four common measures — ¼ teaspoon, ½ teaspoon, 1 teaspoon, and 1 tablespoon. The Tupperware set adds three more spoons that really aid the cook — ⅛ teaspoon plus two spoons designed to measure liquids without spilling.

A **liquid measuring cup** is generally a glass or opaque container marked with standard and/or metric measures for accurate eye level liquid measurements. Tupperware offers a large and small Mix-N-Stor® pitcher that lets you mix, pour, and store batter all in one container. Its tight-fitting cover helps protect the freshness and flavor of the contents during storage so you can bake some of the batter now and save the remaining for later use.

MIX IT!

Mixing bowls are great for stirring batters, frostings, fillings, mixing meat loaves or stuffings, and tossing fruits or vegtables. Tupperware Mixing Bowls serve a dual purpose. A virtually airtight Seal allows you to use them for storage as well as mixing.

A **colander** is a real must for washing salad greens, fresh fruits and vegetables, or for draining foods such as hot cooked vegetables or pasta. A **strainer** can help you wash and drain smaller quantities of foods, too. The 1-qt. Strainer is easy to use with an easy-grip handle and twin pouring lips that make transferring food from strainer to preparation, serving, or storage container easy.

A **shredder/grater** has several surfaces with varying textures for grating, fine shredding, and shredding. Tupperware makes the Grater Bowl — a multi-use product. It's a 3-piece set, with a capacity of 8 cups or 2 quarts, that can be used for preparing, storing, and serving food. The 2-cup capacity Handy Grater is useful for tackling little jobs and storing foods, too!

Kitchen scissors are handy for snipping parsley and herbs. Slice bread or tomatoes with a **serrated knife**. A **chef's knife** makes quick work of chopping, dicing, and cubing many fruits and vegetables. Wash and dry knives by hand and store them in a divided rack or drawer to protect the blade edge.

A **rotary beater** is handy for beating light mixtures. For heavy-duty mixing or long mixing times, an **electric mixer** on a stand is best. Follow the recipe directions for mixer bowl size and mixing speed.

Wooden spoons are best for beating and mixing since they're silent against a glass or metal mixing bowl. And, wooden spoons stir hot mixtures without scratching pans or burning fingers.

Prevent damage to knives and countertops by doing all your cutting chores on a **cutting board**. The Chop-N-Pour® Set is a chopping disc and tray that takes care of small food chopping jobs.

Use a **rolling pin** to help you work with pastry, cookie, biscuit, and yeast doughs successfully. The unique Tupperware brand Rolling Pin can be filled with ice water or warm water to make rolling out different types of dough a cinch.

A **pastry sheet** is the surface used for rolling out pie crusts, cookies, biscuits, and other doughs. Tupperware has designed one specifically for this purpose with concentric circles to indicate the exact size you need.

BAKE IT!

Fruit pies, cream pies, and frozen pies — all are made in a **pie plate**. You can also bake round loaves of bread in a pie plate.

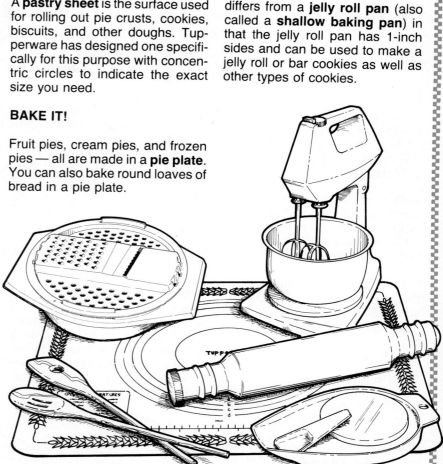

differs from a **jelly roll pan** (also called a **shallow baking pan**) in that the jelly roll pan has 1-inch sides and can be used to make a jelly roll or bar cookies as well as other types of cookies.

Baking pans come in several shapes and many sizes. Layer cakes are baked in 8- or 9-inch round pans. Popular rectangular pans are the 11x7½ x 2- and 13x9x2-inch sizes. Bar cookies are often baked in 15x10x1½-, 8x8x2-, or 9x9x2-inch pans. Bake yeast and quick bread loaves in 9x5x3- or 8x4x2-inch loaf pans. A **muffin pan** can be used to bake yeast rolls and cupcakes, too. For muffins and cupcakes, you may want to use paper cups in the muffin cups to save on clean up.

A **baking sheet** or **cookie sheet** is a flat metal pan that may have a raised edge on one or two sides. It

Use a **wire rack** for cooling finished baked products. It allows air to circulate so food cools without becoming soggy from the steam remaining in it.

A **casserole dish** differs from a baking dish in that it is deeper and may be of any shape, but is usually round or oval. It is made of glass or ceramic materials. To find its volume, fill to the top with water, measuring as you fill.

A **broiler pan** is a shallow pan with a fitted rack designed to keep meat out of the drippings while broiling.

A WELL-STOCKED KITCHEN

COOK IT!

Saucepans are basic for top-of-the-range cooking. It's best to use about ⅔ of their capacity, so select a small (1- to 1½-quart), a medium (2- to 2½-quart), and a large (3- to 4-quart) covered saucepan when choosing your cookware.

Skillets are wider and more shallow than saucepans. Small (6-inch), medium (8-inch), and large (12-inch) skillets with covers will suit most needs.

You'll need a **kettle** or **Dutch oven** for larger quantities. Saucepans and kettles differ in that the latter have two handles for easy carrying.

STORE IT!

For storing uncooked and cooked fresh meats and produce, you'll need assorted **refrigerator-freezer dishes**. Tupperware® lets you freeze with ease in Square Rounds® containers. They come in three capacities — 16-, 30-, and 48-oz. containers. Refrigerator bowls and food storage containers are also available in a variety of shapes and sizes.

The **bread box** may be old-fashioned, but storing baked products to preserve freshness is just as important today as ever. Tupperware provides storage containers for yeast and quick bread loaves, sheet cakes, tube cakes, pies, muffins, cupcakes, and cookies.

Canisters mean convenience when it comes to storing such food staples as flour, sugar, biscuit mix, coffee, or tea. Storage for these frequently used items must be handy and guarantee freshness.

And canister containers are a smart storage investment for powdered sugar, dried beans, marshmallows, oatmeal, popcorn, rice, and brown sugar, too.

Tupperware offers a wide variety of virtually airtight containers in sizes and styles to fit most every need.

When serving foods at any meal, always serve hot foods hot and cold foods cold. And Tupperware makes the perfect container to do just that. The Multi-Server™ container can be filled with hot liquid or crushed ice with the food placed in the strainer insert. And, the Multi-Server can poach fish fillets, parboil green peppers, and drain cooked pasta, too. On the table or in the refrigerator, the Multi-Server container can be used for serving or storing.

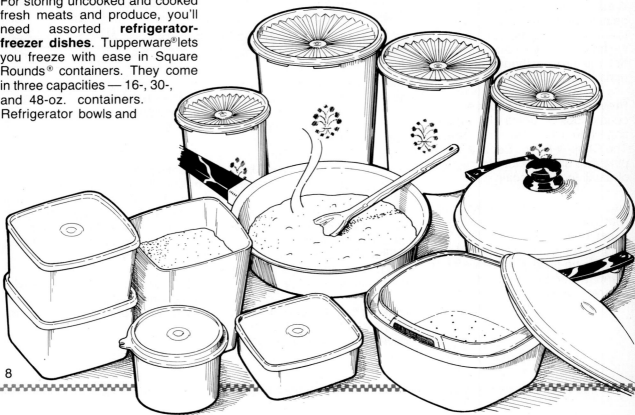

EMERGENCY SUBSTITUTIONS

For best results, use the ingredients
specified in the recipe. But when you're
in a bind, this chart can help you find
an acceptable substitute.

If you don't have:	Substitute:
1 cup cake flour	1 cup minus 2 tablespoons all-purpose flour
1 tablespoon cornstarch (for thickening)	2 tablespoons all-purpose flour
1 teaspoon baking powder	¼ teaspoon baking soda plus ½ cup buttermilk or sour milk (to replace ½ cup of the liquid called for)
1 package active dry yeast	1 cake compressed yeast
1 cup granulated sugar	1 cup packed brown sugar *or* 2 cups sifted powdered sugar
1 cup honey	1¼ cups granulated sugar plus ¼ cup liquid
1 cup corn syrup	1 cup granulated sugar plus ¼ cup liquid
1 square (1 ounce) unsweetened chocolate	3 tablespoons unsweetened cocoa powder plus 1 tablespoon butter or margarine
1 cup whipping cream, whipped	2 cups whipped dessert topping
1 cup sour milk or buttermilk	1 tablespoon lemon juice or vinegar plus enough whole milk to make 1 cup (let stand 5 minutes before using) *or* 1 cup whole milk plus 1¾ teaspoons cream of tartar
1 cup buttermilk	1 cup plain yogurt
1 cup whole milk	½ cup evaporated milk plus ½ cup water *or* 1 cup reconstituted nonfat dry milk (plus 2 teaspoons butter or margarine, if desired)
1 cup light cream	2 tablespoons butter plus 1 cup minus 2 tablespoons milk
1 whole egg	2 egg yolks (for most uses)
2 cups tomato sauce	¾ cup tomato paste plus 1 cup water
1 cup tomato juice	½ cup tomato sauce plus ½ cup water
1 clove garlic	⅛ teaspoon garlic powder or minced dried garlic
1 small onion	1 teaspoon onion powder or 1 tablespoon minced dried onion, rehydrated
1 teaspoon dry mustard	1 tablespoon prepared mustard
1 teaspoon finely shredded lemon peel	½ teaspoon lemon extract

Short-Cut COOKING

Time saved is time earned. Use today's extra minutes to prepare a basic homemade mix. Each mix turns into a delicious homemade meal on a day when there is no extra time. This chapter includes eight basic mixes with quick and easy recipes to make a variety of tempting main dishes. Economy and taste, as well as your precious time, are all preserved with short-cut cooking.

Pictured clockwise from bottom left are: Zippy Stuffed Franks, Meat Loaf-In-A-Blanket with dill sauce, Spinach-Meatball Toss, Hot Mexican Beef Bake, and Curried Turkey Open-Faced Sandwiches. (See Index for recipe pages.)

START WITH ITALIAN SAUCE

ITALIAN SAUCE

Once you discover how easy and delicious this sauce is, you'll never settle for less than homemade again—

- 6 medium carrots, shredded
- 3 large onions, chopped
- 3 garlic cloves, minced
- ⅓ cup cooking oil
- 6 28-ounce cans tomatoes
- 1 tablespoon sugar
- 1 tablespoon salt
- 1 tablespoon dried basil, crushed
- 2 teaspoons dried oregano, crushed
- ⅛ teaspoon pepper
- 2 bay leaves

In an 8- to 10-quart Dutch oven, cook carrots, onion, and garlic in hot cooking oil till onion is tender but not brown. Add undrained tomatoes, sugar, salt, basil, oregano, pepper, and bay leaves. Boil gently, uncovered, for 1¼ to 1½ hours.

Cool Italian Sauce. Remove bay leaves and discard. Place about one-quarter of the mixture at a time in blender container and blend till smooth.

Package Italian Sauce in four 1-cup and six 2-cup portions in 16 oz. Square Rounds® containers. Apply Seals. Label with contents, amount, and the date. Freeze.

MARINATED ITALIAN SHRIMP-ON-A-STICK

Use one pound of shrimp for 4 servings if you purchase the shrimp in shells —

- 12 ounces fresh or frozen shelled shrimp
- 1 13¼-ounce can pineapple chunks
- 1 1-cup container ITALIAN SAUCE, thawed
- 2 tablespoons brown sugar
- 1 teaspoon prepared mustard
- 1 medium green pepper, cubed
  Hot cooked rice

Thaw shrimp, if frozen. For marinade, drain the canned pineapple chunks using 1-qt. Strainer over Small Mix-N-Stor® pitcher, reserving ¼ cup of the syrup. To the syrup add Italian Sauce, brown sugar, and mustard. Place shrimp in Season-Serve® container; pour marinade over. Marinate in the refrigerator for 1½ hours, turning at least once.

Drain shrimp, reserving marinade. On each of four skewers, alternate marinated shrimp, pineapple chunks, and green pepper cubes. Broil on greased pan, 4 inches from heat, about 14 minutes, turning and brushing with sauce. Serve over rice. Heat and serve remaining marinade, if desired. Makes 4 servings.

SPICY MACARONI AND MEATBALLS

- 1 1-cup container ITALIAN SAUCE
- ¼ cup water
- 1 8-ounce can jellied cranberry sauce
- ¼ cup bottled barbecue sauce
- ½ teaspoon salt
- ½ teaspoon ground ginger
- ¼ teaspoon ground cinnamon
- 1 24-meatball container FREEZER MEATBALLS (see recipe, page 19)
  Hot cooked macaroni

Place Italian Sauce and water in a skillet and cook over low heat, covered, 15 minutes. Stir in the jellied cranberry sauce, barbecue sauce, salt, ginger, and cinnamon, breaking up cranberry sauce with a spoon. Add Freezer Meatballs.

Cook, uncovered, over medium-low heat for 20 minutes or till meatballs are heated through. Serve over hot cooked macaroni. Makes 4 servings.

MARINATING TIP

Use the Season-Serve container to marinate meats, poultry, fish, or vegetables. Family and guests will enjoy the special flavor a marinade adds to food. This container is designed specifically for marinating food, and it's extra easy because you simply invert the Season-Serve container to distribute the well-seasoned liquid.

Marinate the shrimp in the Season-Serve container, skewer, and grill. Marinated Italian Shrimp-On-A-Stick makes an easy entertaining entree.

START WITH ITALIAN SAUCE

CORNY SAUSAGE CASSEROLE

- 1 pound bulk pork sausage
- 1 cup chopped onion
- 1 16-ounce can tomatoes, cut up
- 1 1-cup container ITALIAN SAUCE, thawed
- 1 4-ounce can sliced mushrooms, drained
- ¾ cup all-purpose flour
- ¾ cup cornmeal
- ¾ cup grated Parmesan cheese
- 1 tablespoon sugar
- 1 tablespoon baking powder
- ¾ teaspoon salt
- ¾ cup milk
- 3 tablespoons cooking oil
- 1 well-beaten egg
- 4 ounces shredded cheddar cheese (1 cup)
- 2 tablespoons snipped parsley

In saucepan, cook sausage and onion till meat is brown and onion is tender; drain off excess fat. Stir in undrained tomatoes, Italian Sauce, and mushrooms. Bring to boiling. Simmer, covered, for 5 minutes.

Meanwhile, in a Large Mix-N-Stor® pitcher, stir together flour, cornmeal, Parmesan cheese, sugar, baking powder, and salt. Make a well in center of dry ingredients. Add milk, cooking oil, and egg all at once, stirring till combined. Spread batter in bottom of an ungreased 13x9x2-inch baking dish. Spoon tomato mixture on top. Bake in 400° oven for 20 minutes. Sprinkle shredded cheddar cheese and parsley atop. Bake 5 minutes more. Makes 8 servings.

PORK CHOP AND PASTA DINNER

- 1½ cups corkscrew macaroni or elbow macaroni
- 6 pork rib chops, cut ½ inch thick
- 2 tablespoons cooking oil or shortening
- 1 2-cup container ITALIAN SAUCE, thawed
- ¼ cup chopped onion
- ¼ cup grated Parmesan cheese

Cook macaroni in boiling salted water according to package directions; drain in 1-qt. Strainer. Place macaroni in 12x7½x2-inch baking dish.

In a large skillet, brown chops in hot cooking oil or shortening; drain off excess fat. Season with a little salt and pepper. Arrange browned pork chops over macaroni in baking dish. Combine Italian Sauce and chopped onion; pour over chops and macaroni. Sprinkle with Parmesan cheese. Cover and bake in 350° oven for 1 to 1¼ hours or till meat is tender. Serve with additional Parmesan cheese, if desired. Makes 6 servings.

SHORT-CUT ITALIAN-STYLE LASAGNE

- 8 ounces bulk Italian sausage or other ground meat
- 4 ounces lasagne noodles or other wide noodles
- 1 beaten egg
- 1 cup cream-style cottage cheese
- ¼ cup grated Parmesan cheese
- 6 ounces mozzarella cheese, shredded (1½ cups)
- 1 2-cup container ITALIAN SAUCE, thawed

In a skillet, brown meat; drain off fat. Cook noodles in boiling salted water according to package directions; drain in 1-qt. Strainer. In Small Mix-N-Stor pitcher, combine egg, cottage cheese, Parmesan cheese, and the cooked meat. In a 10x6x2-inch baking dish, layer, in order, half the noodles, half the meat mixture, half the mozzarella, and half the Italian Sauce. Repeat layers.

Place baking dish on baking pan to catch any juices that may bubble over. Bake, uncovered, in 375° oven for 50 minutes or till bubbly and golden. Let stand 10 minutes before serving. Sprinkle with additional Parmesan cheese, if desired. Makes 4 to 6 servings.

PASTA STORAGE

There are many advantages to storing pasta in Ultra Clear™ Counterparts™ containers. Like all Tupperware products they're practical because they keep the contents fresh. The Ultra Clear series allows the contents to be seen, so preparing your shopping list is easy. And, they're an attractive addition to any kitchen decor.

RAVIOLI ROLL-UPS

EASY EGG PASTRY for Single-Crust Pie (see recipe, page 57)
- 1 egg
- 1 tablespoon water
- 1 8-ounce can spinach, well drained
- 1 4½-ounce can deviled ham
- ⅓ cup grated Parmesan cheese
- 1 1-cup container ITALIAN SAUCE

On lightly floured Pastry Sheet, roll Pastry to 10-inch circle. Cut into 8 wedges. Slightly beat egg; mix in water. Brush dough lightly with some egg mixture.

In a Small Mix-N-Stor pitcher, combine spinach, deviled ham, and Parmesan cheese; mix well. Place 2 tablespoons spinach mixture in center of wide end of each pastry wedge. Roll up, starting at wide end. Arrange rolls, point side down, on greased baking sheet. Brush again with egg-water mixture. Bake in 375° oven for 25 minutes.

Meanwhile, in saucepan, heat Italian Sauce, covered, over low heat; stir to break up sauce. Spoon over hot ravioli rolls. Makes 4 servings.

SPAGHETTI PIE

- 6 ounces spaghetti
- 2 tablespoons butter or margarine
- 2 beaten eggs
- ⅓ cup grated Parmesan cheese
- 1 cup cream-style cottage cheese
- 1 pound bulk pork or Italian sausage
- ½ cup chopped onion
- ¼ cup chopped green pepper
- 1 1-cup container ITALIAN SAUCE, thawed
- 1 6-ounce can tomato paste
- 2 ounces shredded mozzarella cheese (½ cup)

In a large saucepan, cook spaghetti in a large amount of boiling salted water for 10 to 12 minutes or till just tender; drain in a 1-qt. Strainer. Transfer drained spaghetti to a Large Mix-N-Stor pitcher. Stir butter or margarine into hot spaghetti; stir in beaten eggs and Parmesan cheese. Form spaghetti mixture into a "crust" in a greased 10-inch pie plate. Spread with cottage cheese.

In a skillet, cook sausage, onion, and green pepper till meat is browned and vegetables are tender. Drain off fat. Stir in Italian Sauce and tomato paste. Heat through.

Turn meat mixture into spaghetti crust. Cover edges with foil. Bake in 350° oven for 20 minutes. Sprinkle with shredded mozzarella cheese; bake about 5 minutes more or till cheese is melted. Cut into wedges. Makes 6 servings.

ASSEMBLING SPAGHETTI PIE

1. Grease a 10-inch pie plate. Pour in spaghetti and shape to an even depth on the bottom and sides of the pie plate.

2. Spread cottage cheese evenly on the bottom of the spaghetti "crust." Fill with Italian Sauce mixture.

3. Cover edges with foil to keep spaghetti soft and moist. To give the spaghetti crust a crunchy texture, remove foil when adding mozzarella cheese.

15

START WITH ITALIAN SAUCE

ITALIAN PIZZA

- 1 pound bulk Italian sausage
- ¼ cup chopped onion
- 1 2-cup container ITALIAN SAUCE , thawed
- ½ teaspoon salt
- 8 ounces provolone or mozzarella cheese Pizza Crusts

In skillet, cook sausage and onion till meat is browned; drain off fat. Stir in Italian Sauce and salt. Cover; simmer about 10 minutes. Shred cheese on Grater Bowl. Spread desired pizza crusts with meat mixture. Top with cheese. Bake as directed in crust recipe.

SOMBRERO PIZZA

- 1 pound bulk pork sausage or bulk Italian sausage
- ½ cup chopped onion
- 1 2-cup container ITALIAN SAUCE , thawed
- 1 cup sliced pitted ripe olives
- 1 4-ounce can green chili peppers, rinsed, seeded, and chopped
- 1 teaspoon dried parsley flakes
- 8 ounces cheddar cheese
- 2 tomatoes, sliced Shredded lettuce Pizza Crusts

In skillet, cook sausage and onion till meat is browned; drain off fat. Stir in Italian Sauce, olives, chili peppers, and parsley. Cover; simmer about 10 minutes. Grate cheese on Grater Bowl. Spread desired pizza crusts with meat mixture; top with cheese. Bake as directed in crust recipe. Just before serving, top with tomato slices and shredded lettuce.

PIZZA CRUSTS

- 2½ to 3 cups all-purpose flour
- 1 package active dry yeast
- 2 tablespoons cooking oil

In Large Mixing Bowl, combine 1¼ cups of the flour, the yeast, and 1 teaspoon *salt*. Stir in 1 cup warm *water* (115° to 120°) and oil. Beat at low speed of electric mixer for ½ minute. Beat 3 minutes at high speed. Stir in as much remaining flour as you can mix in with a spoon. On lightly floured Pastry Sheet, knead in enough remaining flour to make a moderately stiff dough that is smooth and elastic .

Thin pizza crusts: Cover dough and let rest 10 minutes. Divide dough in half. On lightly floured Pastry Sheet, use Rolling Pin to roll each half into a 13-inch circle. Transfer circles of dough to greased 12-inch pizza pans or baking sheets. Build up edges slightly. Bake in 425° oven about 12 minutes. Add desired pizza topping. Bake for 10 to 15 minutes more. Makes two 12-inch pizzas.

Pan Pizza Crusts: Return dough to a clean, greased Large Mixing Bowl; apply Seal and let rise in warm place till double (about 1 hour). Punch down. Divide in half. Cover; let rest 10 minutes. Pat dough onto bottom and halfway up sides of two greased 11x7x1½-inch or 9x9x2-inch baking pans. Cover; let rise till nearly double (30 to 45 minutes). Bake in 375° oven for 20 to 25 minutes. Add desired pizza topping. Bake 20 to 25 minutes more. Makes two.

SPAGHETTI WITH PEPPERONI SAUCE

- 1 medium onion
- 1 clove garlic
- ½ cup pitted ripe olives
- 1 4- or 5-ounce package pepperoni
- 2 tablespoons cooking oil
- 5 cups ITALIAN SAUCE , thawed
- 1 6-ounce can tomato paste
- 1 cup water
- ¼ cup parsley, snipped
- 1 teaspon dried basil, crushed
- ¼ teaspoon dried thyme, crushed
- 1 bay leaf
- 4 quarts water
- 1 tablespoon salt
- 1 teaspoon cooking oil
- 16 ounces spaghetti

Chop onion; mince garlic; slice olives and pepperoni. In Dutch oven, cook onion and garlic in 2 tablespoons oil till tender, but not brown. Add pepperoni, olives, Italian Sauce, tomato paste, 1 cup water, parsley, basil, thyme, and bay leaf. Simmer, uncovered, 30 to 45 minutes, stirring occasionally. Remove bay leaf.

Meanwhile, bring the 4 quarts water, salt, and 1 teaspoon oil to a boil; add spaghetti and cook till tender but firm. Drain immediately in Multi-Server strainer insert, allowing ¾ inch hot water to drain into serving dish. Place spaghetti in strainer over hot water and cover to keep warm. Serves 5 to 6.

Start with the basic Italian Sauce and serve Spaghetti With Pepperoni Sauce spooned over your favorite hot cooked pasta; sprinkle lavishly with grated Parmesan cheese.

16

START WITH FREEZER MEATBALLS

FREEZER MEATBALLS

If you like, substitute ground lamb or ground pork for some of the ground beef—

- **3 eggs**
- **½ cup milk**
- **3 cups soft bread crumbs (4 slices)**
- **½ cup finely chopped onion**
- **2 teaspoons salt**
- **⅛ teaspoon pepper**
- **3 pounds ground beef**

In Large Mixing Bowl, beat eggs. Stir in milk, bread crumbs, chopped onion, salt, and pepper. Add ground meat and mix well. Chill.

With wet hands, shape meat mixture into 6 dozen (72) 1-inch meatballs. Bake meatballs in two 15½x10x1-inch baking pans in 375° oven for 25 to 30 minutes. Place meatballs on another baking pan. Cool. Place meatballs in freezer just till frozen.

Package 24 meatballs in each of three 30-oz. Square Rounds® containers; apply Seals. Label with contents, amount, and date. Freeze. Makes 3 packages of 24 meatballs each. (*Or,* for a smaller number of packaged meatballs, place 12 meatballs into each of six 16-oz. Square Rounds containers.)

RICE RING TIP

1. Prepare quick-cooking rice in the Multi-Server™ container by adding 2¾ cups boiling water to the amount already called for on the package. Pour over rice in insert strainer. Cover and let stand for 5 minutes.

2. Pack the rice into the ring while piping hot, then turn out onto a serving platter.

If you prefer the economy and flavor of regular rice, buy the medium grain variety for rice rings. It's less expensive than long grain rice and has a stickier consistency that's ideal for molding. (Cook according to package directions.)

MEATBALLS IN CONFETTI RICE RING

- **2½ cups quick-cooking rice**
- **5 cups water**
- **1 10-ounce package frozen mixed vegetables**
- **¼ teaspoon salt**
- **1 cup CREAMY SAUCE MIX (see recipe, page 50)**
- **2 cups cold water**
- **¼ cup catsup**
- **1 teaspoon minced dried onion**
- **1 teaspoon Worcestershire sauce**
- **4 ounces American cheese, shredded (1 cup)**
- **1 24-meatball container FREEZER MEATBALLS**

For rice ring, place rice in Multi-Server strainer insert and place strainer in dish. In a saucepan, combine the 5 cups water, mixed vegetables, and salt. Bring to a boil and pour over uncooked rice; cover immediately. Let stand for 5 minutes while preparing sauce.

In large skillet, thoroughly combine Creamy Sauce Mix and the 2 cups cold water. Stir in catsup, onion, Worcestershire sauce, and the shredded cheese. Cook and stir till thickened and bubbly and cheese has melted. Add meatballs; heat through.

Stir rice mixture, then press into an ungreased Jel-Ring® mold. Unmold at once on a bed of cooked spinach on a hot platter. Fill center with meatballs and some of the sauce. Pass remaining sauce. Makes 6 servings.

Freezer Meatballs and Creamy Sauce Mix team up for Meatballs In Confetti Rice Ring. This colorful rice mold is a tasty alternative to serving noodles or potatoes at dinner time.

19

START WITH FREEZER MEATBALLS

SWEET AND SOUR MEATBALLS

- 1 20-ounce can pineapple chunks
- ¾ cup maple-flavored syrup
- ½ cup vinegar
- 1 24-meatball container FREEZER MEATBALLS
- 1 large red or green pepper
- 2 tablespoons cornstarch
- ½ teaspoon salt
- ¼ cup cold water
- 1 11-ounce can mandarin orange sections, drained
- Chow mein noodles or hot cooked rice

Place 1-qt. Strainer over medium saucepan and drain pineapple. Set pineapple aside. To pineapple syrup in saucepan, add the maple-flavored syrup and vinegar. Add Freezer Meatballs; bring to boiling. Simmer, covered, 15 minutes or till meatballs are hot. Chop green pepper into ¾-inch pieces. Add chopped pepper to meatball mixture. Stir together cornstarch and salt. Stir in water. Blend into mixture in saucepan. Cook and stir till thickened and bubbly; cook 1 to 2 minutes longer. Add drained pineapple and mandarin orange sections; cook till heated through. Serve over chow mein noodles or hot cooked rice. Serve in Get-Togethers™ Buffet Tray. Turn meatball mixture into one section and noodles or rice into other section of tray. Makes 4 to 6 servings.

SPINACH-MEATBALL TOSS

Pictured on page 10—

- 1 24-meatball container FREEZER MEATBALLS
- ½ cup water
- 10 ounces fresh spinach (7 cups)
- 3 hard-cooked eggs
- 1 8-ounce can water chestnuts, drained
- 2 cups fresh bean sprouts
- ¼ cup sugar
- 1 tablespoon cornstarch
- ⅓ cup catsup
- ¼ cup vinegar
- 2 tablespoons finely chopped onion
- 1 tablespoon Worcester-shire sauce

In large saucepan, place Freezer Meatballs in a single layer. Add water and cover. Cook over low heat for 15 minutes or till meatballs are heated through. Meanwhile, tear spinach into bite-size pieces in the large Decorator Salad Bowl. Quarter eggs and slice water chestnuts; add to spinach with bean sprouts.

In a Small Mix-N-Stor® pitcher, stir together sugar and cornstarch. Blend in catsup, vinegar, onion, and Worcestershire sauce. Add catsup mixture to saucepan; cook and stir over medium heat till thickened and bubbly. Cook and stir 1 to 2 minutes more. Pour over vegetables in Salad Bowl. Toss. Serve in individual Decorator Salad Bowls. Makes 6 servings.

SPAGHETTI AND MEATBALLS

- 1 24-meatball container FREEZER MEATBALLS
- 1 15-ounce can tomato sauce
- 1 teaspoon dried oregano, crushed
- 1 teaspoon Worcestershire sauce
- ½ teaspoon sugar
- ½ teaspoon dried basil, crushed
- ¼ teaspoon garlic powder
- ¼ teaspoon salt
- ⅛ teaspoon pepper
- Hot cooked spaghetti or other pasta
- Grated Parmesan cheese (optional)

In a large saucepan, combine Freezer Meatballs, tomato sauce, oregano, Worcestershire sauce, sugar, basil, garlic powder, salt, and pepper. Bring to boiling.

Simmer sauce, uncovered, for 30 minutes, stirring occasionally. Serve over hot spaghetti. Pass Parmesan cheese, if desired. Makes 4 servings.

SPEEDY SPAGHETTI

For a quick-fixing spaghetti sauce, all you need are 4 cups of the basic Italian Sauce (see recipe, page 13) and one 24-meatball container Freezer Meatballs. Combine the sauce and meatballs in a large saucepan. Bring to boiling. Simmer, uncovered, till heated through. Serve over hot cooked spaghetti.

MEATBALL MEXICALI BAKE

1 16-ounce can tomatoes, cut up
½ teaspoon salt
½ teaspoon ground coriander
1 5-ounce jar American cheese spread
1 24-meatball container FREEZER MEATBALLS
1 16-ounce can hominy, drained
2 to 3 tablespoons canned green chili peppers, rinsed, seeded, and chopped
2 cups corn or tortilla chips, coarsely crushed

In a blender container, combine undrained tomatoes, salt, and coriander. Cover; blend till smooth. Add cheese spread. Cover; blend till smooth. Pour tomato-cheese mixture into oven-going skillet; add Freezer Meatballs, hominy, and chopped green chilies. Bring to boiling, stirring occasionally. Transfer to a 350° oven. Bake, uncovered, for 30 to 35 minutes. Sprinkle with crushed corn chips. Makes 4 to 6 servings.

SPICY ITALIAN MEATBALL ROLLS

Here's a hearty meatball sandwich that's a special hit with teenagers. Next time the "school crowd" gathers at your house, let the kids take over the kitchen and fix this easy meal for friends —

1 24-meatball container FREEZER MEATBALLS
1 2-cup container ITALIAN SAUCE (see recipe, page 13) or one 15½-ounce jar meatless spaghetti sauce
1 medium onion, sliced
1 medium green pepper, cut into strips
1 tablespoon butter or margarine
6 individual French rolls or hoagie rolls, split and toasted
¼ cup grated Parmesan cheese

In a medium saucepan, combine Freezer Meatballs and the Italian Sauce or spaghetti sauce. Simmer, covered, for 20 to 25 minutes. Meanwhile, in a small skillet, cook onion and green pepper in butter or margarine till tender. To serve, place four meatballs on each roll bottom. Spoon some of the onion mixture over meatballs. Spoon tomato sauce atop; top with Parmesan cheese. Add roll tops. Makes 6 sandwiches.

QUICK MEATBALL MINESTRONE

Ladle up this robust soup after a fall afternoon outing. Serve a crusty loaf of Italian bread alongside, or sprinkle buttered bread slices with grated Parmesan and toast under the broiler —

1 24-meatball container FREEZER MEATBALLS
1 15-ounce can great northern beans or navy beans
1 tablespoon instant beef bouillon granules
1 tablespoon minced dried onion
1 teaspoon dried basil, crushed
1 large bay leaf
4 cups water
½ of a 7-ounce package spaghetti, broken into 2-inch lengths
1 16-ounce can tomatoes, cut up
1 16-ounce can mixed vegetables, drained, or one 10-ounce package frozen mixed vegetables, thawed
1 teaspoon sugar
  Grated Parmesan cheese

In a 4-quart Dutch oven, combine Freezer Meatballs, undrained beans, bouillon granules, onion, basil, bay leaf, and water. Bring to boiling. Add spaghetti. Cover; simmer about 20 minutes or till meatballs are heated through. Stir in undrained tomatoes, the mixed vegetables, and sugar. Heat through. Remove bay leaf. Ladle into Stacking Bowls. Sprinkle individual servings with Parmesan cheese. Makes 6 to 8 servings.

BLENDER TIP

Your blender container will be easier to wash if you don't allow food to dry and harden. Immediately after using, place about a cup of water and a few drops of dish washing liquid in the container. Cover; turn on blender for a few seconds. Rinse with clear water.

START WITH FREEZER MEATBALLS

CHILI MEATBALL SUPPER

Let each family member sprinkle cheddar cheese and corn chips atop their bowl of chili —

- 1 medium onion
- ½ of a medium green pepper
- 1 16-ounce can tomatoes, cut up
- 1 16-ounce can red kidney beans, drained
- 1 8¾-ounce can whole kernel corn
- 1 1-cup container ITALIAN SAUCE (see recipe, page 13) or one 8-ounce can tomato sauce
- 1 teaspoon salt
- 1 to 2 teaspoons chili powder
- 1 bay leaf
- 1 24-meatball container FREEZER MEATBALLS
- 4 ounces sharp cheddar cheese, shredded (1 cup)
- Crushed corn chips

Chop onion and green pepper. In saucepan, combine onion, green pepper, undrained tomatoes, kidney beans, undrained corn, Italian Sauce or tomato sauce, salt, chili powder, and bay leaf. Bring to boiling. Add Freezer Meatballs. Cover and simmer for 45 minutes, stirring occasionally. Remove bay leaf.

Ladle hot chili into Stacking Bowls. Serve shredded cheddar cheese and crushed corn chips to sprinkle atop individual servings of chili.

SAUCY MEATBALLS WITH BISCUITS

- Biscuit Topper
- 1 24-meatball container FREEZER MEATBALLS
- 1 10¾-ounce can condensed cream of celery soup
- 2 tablespoons all-purpose flour
- ½ teaspoon paprika
- ½ cup water
- 1 3-ounce can chopped mushrooms

Prepare Biscuit Topper; set aside.

Place Freezer Meatballs in a 10-inch skillet. Combine canned celery soup, flour, and paprika. Stir in water and undrained mushrooms. Pour mixture over meatballs in skillet; bring to boiling. Reduce heat and simmer 10 minutes. Pour boiling mixture into 1½-quart casserole; top immediately with Biscuit Topper. Bake, uncovered, in 400° oven for 15 minutes. Serves 4.

BISCUIT TOPPER

- ½ cup all-purpose flour
- 1 teaspoon baking powder
- ⅛ teaspoon celery salt
- ¼ cup milk
- 2 teaspoons cooking oil
- ¾ cup soft bread crumbs
- 2 tablespoons butter or margarine, melted

In a Small Mix-N-Stor® pitcher, combine flour, baking powder, and celery salt. Combine milk and cooking oil. Stir into flour mixture just till blended. Combine bread crumbs and butter. Divide dough into 8 portions; drop into buttered crumbs. Turn to coat all sides; place atop hot meat mixture. Continue as directed in recipe.

MEATBALLS STROGANOFF

To keep sour cream from curdling, stir a small amount of the hot mixture into it. Then add the "warmed" cream to the hot mixture all at once. Don't let the mixture return to a boil —

- 1 24-meatball container FREEZER MEATBALLS
- 2 teaspoons instant beef bouillon granules
- 1 cup water
- 1 4-ounce can mushroom stems and pieces, drained
- ¼ teaspoon salt
- ¼ cup all-purpose flour
- ½ cup cold water
- 1 cup dairy sour cream
- Hot cooked noodles
- Snipped parsley (optional)

In a 10-inch skillet, combine Freezer Meatballs, beef bouillon granules, and the 1 cup water. Cover; simmer for 20 minutes. Remove meatballs from skillet.

Add mushrooms and salt to juices in skillet. In Small Mix-N-Stor pitcher, combine flour and ½ cup cold water; add to skillet. Cook and stir till thickened and bubbly. Cook and stir 1 to 2 minutes more. Stir about ½ cup of the hot mixture into sour cream; return to skillet. Add meatballs. Heat through over low heat; do not boil. Serve over hot cooked noodles. Garnish with snipped parsley, if desired. Serves 4.

SAUERBRATEN-STYLE MEATBALLS

- 2 cups water
- 1 cup unsweetened pineapple juice
- 2 teaspoons instant beef bouillon granules
- 8 gingersnaps
- ⅓ cup packed brown sugar
- ¼ cup raisins
- 2 tablespoons lemon juice
- 1 24-meatball container FREEZER MEATBALLS
  Hot cooked rice or noodles

In a medium saucepan, bring water, pineapple juice, and beef bouillon granules to boiling. Use Pastry Sheet and Rolling Pin to coarsely crush gingersnaps. Add gingersnap crumbs, brown sugar, raisins, and lemon juice to saucepan; cook and stir till gingersnap crumbs are almost dissolved. Add Freezer Meatballs. Cover and simmer about 20 minutes or till meatballs are heated through, stirring occasionally. Serve over hot cooked rice or noodles. Makes 4 to 6 servings.

SAUERBRATEN WITH SPATZLE

For a change serve Sauerbraten-Style Meatballs over Spatzle instead of over rice or noodles. Prepare Spatzle batter as directed on page 30. In a large saucepan, bring 3 quarts water and 1 teaspoon salt to a boil. Force dough through the 1-qt. Strainer as directed. Cook for 5 minutes; drain and keep warm in Multi-Server™ container.

MEATBALL CURRY

- 1 cup chopped onion
- 1 clove garlic, minced
- 1½ to 2 teaspoons curry powder
- 2 tablespoons butter or margarine
- 1 24-meatball container FREEZER MEATBALLS
- ½ cup water
- 2 medium tomatoes, peeled and chopped
- 1 medium apple, peeled, cored, and chopped
- 1 teaspoon instant beef bouillon granules
- ½ teaspoon ground ginger
- ¼ teaspoon salt
- ¼ cup cold water
- 1 tablespoons all-purpose flour
  Parslied Rice (see recipe at right)
  Assorted condiments (see tip box below)

In a 10-inch skillet, cook onion, garlic, and curry powder in butter or margarine till onion is tender. Add Meatballs and the ½ cup water; cook, covered, over medium heat for 10 minutes. Stir in chopped tomatoes, apple, beef bouillon granules, ginger, and salt. Cover and simmer for 5 to 10 minutes or till apple is tender.

Combine the ¼ cup cold water and flour; stir into meat mixture. Cook and stir till thickened and bubbly. Cook and stir 1 to 2 minutes more. Serve over hot Parslied Rice. Serve with a variety of condiments for garnishing. Makes 4 servings.

PARSLIED RICE

For an occasional change of pace, serve this easy meal accompaniment in place of potatoes —

- 1⅓ cups quick cooking rice
- 3½ cups water
- 1 teaspoon salt
- ¼ cup snipped parsley
- 1 tablespoon butter or margarine

Place rice in Multi-Server strainer insert and place insert in the serving dish. In a saucepan, combine water and salt. Bring to a boil and pour over rice; immediately cover. Let stand for 5 minutes. Remove cover; add butter and parsley. Use a fork to distribute parsley and butter and fluff rice. Makes 4 servings.

CURRY CONDIMENTS

Enhance the flavor of spicy curry with a sprinkling of something sweet, sour, salty, or crunchy. The obvious choice to serve a selection of condiments is the Condimate® set. Fill bowls ahead of time and lock in the flavor while avoiding last-minute hassle. We've listed several ideas for topping the Meatball Curry, but you can try some new ones of your own, too!

Serve any combination of: shredded or flaked coconut, sieved hard-cooked egg, crumbled crisp-cooked bacon, sliced green onion, raisins, chutney, salted peanuts, and chopped cucumber.

START WITH COOKED CHICKEN

FORMING POTATO PATTIES

1. *Apply salad oil to inside of Hamburger Press ring, bottom of keeper, and underside of press. Measure ⅓ cup potato mixture into press ring with a Measuring Cup. Use moderate pressure with press in a twisting motion. Lift off press and gently remove ring.*

2. *Turn keeper upside down and press gently with thumbs, if necessary, to remove patty.*

Make evenly shaped Potato Patties with the Tupperware Hamburger Press. Fry the patties till golden brown and top with Creamed Chicken.

COOKED CHICKEN

- 2 **3-pound broiler-fryer chickens, cut up, or one 6-pound stewing chicken, cut-up**
- 1¼ **pounds chicken wings or backs**
- 4 **stalks celery with leaves, quartered**
- 1 **small carrot, peeled and quartered**
- 1 **small onion, cut up**
- 2 **sprigs parsley**
- 2 **teaspoons salt**
- ¼ **teaspoon pepper**

In a large Dutch oven or skillet, place chicken pieces, celery, carrot, onion, and parsley. Sprinkle with salt and pepper. Add 2½ quarts *water*. If necessary, add additional water to cover. Bring mixture to boiling. Reduce heat; cover and cook over low heat for 1 hour (1½ to 2 hours for stewing chicken) or till tender. Use tongs to lift chicken pieces; cool. Remove vegetables and discard. Refrigerate broth or chill in a bowl placed in a larger container of ice water. When chicken pieces are cool enough to handle, remove the meat from bones; discard skin and bones. Cube meat; chill.

Skim fat from broth. Strain broth in 1-qt. Strainer over Large Mixing Bowl. Pack four 1½-cup portions chicken meat and five 2-cup portions chicken broth into 16-oz. Square Rounds® containers. Apply Seals. Label with contents, amount and date. Freeze.

CREAMED CHICKEN ON POTATO PATTIES

- ¾ **cup CREAMY SAUCE MIX (see recipe, page 50)**
- 1⅓ **cup water**
- 1 **1½-cup container COOKED CHICKEN**
- 1 **cup fresh or frozen peas**
- 1 **2-ounce can chopped mushrooms, drained**
  Potato Patties (see recipe below)

In a saucepan, combine the Creamy Sauce Mix and water; cook and stir till thickened and bubbly. Cook and stir 1 to 2 minutes more. Stir in Cooked Chicken, peas, and drained mushrooms; heat through. For each serving, place a Potato Patty on serving plate; ladle some of the chicken mixture over top. Makes 6 servings.

POTATO PATTIES

- 2 **cups cold mashed potatoes**
- 1 **beaten egg**
- ¼ **cup finely chopped onion**
- ¼ **cup finely chopped celery**
- ½ **teaspoon salt**
- ⅛ **teaspoon pepper**
- 2 **tablespoons butter or margarine, melted**

In Medium Mixing Bowl, combine mashed potatoes, beaten egg, onion, celery, salt, and pepper. Mix well. Measure about ⅓ cup of the potato mixture into well-oiled Hamburger Press, forming a uniform patty. Repeat to make 5 more patties. In large skillet, brown patties slowly in butter about 5 minutes or till golden brown on each side. Makes 6 patties.

START WITH COOKED CHICKEN

CHICKEN AND BROCCOLI CREPES

- 1 10-ounce package frozen cut broccoli
- 2 tablespoons butter or margarine
- 2 tablespoons all-purpose flour
- ¼ teaspoon salt
- ¼ teaspoon ground nutmeg
- 1½ cups milk
- 1 4-ounce can mushroom stems and pieces, drained
- 3 ounces shredded Swiss cheese (¾ cup)
- 1 1½-cup container COOKED CHICKEN, thawed
- 12 Main Dish Crepes (see recipe at right)
- Paprika (optional)

Cook broccoli according to package directions; drain in 1-qt. Strainer and set aside.

For cheese sauce, in medium saucepan, melt butter or margarine; blend in flour, salt, and nutmeg. Add milk all at once. Cook and stir till thickened and bubbly. Cook and stir 1 to 2 minutes more. Add mushrooms and Swiss cheese; stir till cheese is melted. Set aside.

For filling, combine thawed Cooked Chicken, broccoli, and 1 cup of the cheese sauce. Spoon about ¼ cup filling along center of unbrowned side of each crepe. Roll up crepes; place, seam side up, in 12x7½x2-inch baking dish. Pour remaining cheese sauce over crepes. Sprinkle with paprika, if desired. Cover; bake in 375° oven for 18 to 20 minutes or till heated through. Serve immediately. Makes 6 servings.

MAIN DISH CREPES

- 1 cup all-purpose flour
- 1½ cups milk
- 2 eggs
- 1 tablespoon cooking oil
- ¼ teaspoon salt

In a Small Mix-N-Stor® pitcher, combine the all-purpose flour, milk, eggs, cooking oil, and salt; beat with a rotary beater till blended.

Heat a lightly greased 6-inch skillet; remove from heat. Pour in about 2 tablespoons of the batter; lift and tilt skillet to spread batter evenly. Return to heat; brown crepes on one side only.

Invert skillet over paper toweling; remove crepe. Repeat with remaining batter to make 16 to 18 crepes, greasing skillet as necessary. Freeze any remaining crepes, referring to tip box below.

FREEZING CREPES

Crepes freeze well for later use. Why not double your recipe and get a head start on another meal. If you can spare your Grater Bowl, it is the perfect size for storing 6- or 8-inch crepes.

Alternate the crepes with two sheets of waxed paper. Apply the Classic Round Seal carefully to guard against freezer burn and keep the crepes fresh. Crepes keep in the freezer for two to four months.

CHICKEN AND STUFFING SCALLOP

- 2 cups HERB STUFFING MIX (see recipe, page 45)
- 1 1½-cup container COOKED CHICKEN, thawed
- ¼ cup butter or margarine
- ¼ cup all-purpose flour
- 1 2-cup container CHICKEN BROTH
- 3 beaten eggs
- Paprika
- ½ cup milk
- 1 10¾-ounce can condensed cheddar cheese soup
- 2 tablespoons chopped canned pimiento

Spread dry Herb Stuffing Mix in a greased 10x6x2-inch baking dish; top with thawed Cooked Chicken. In a saucepan, melt butter or margarine; blend in flour. Add Chicken Broth. Cook and stir till thickened and bubbly. Gradually stir a moderate amount of hot mixture into eggs; return to remaining hot mixture. Pour over chicken. Sprinkle with paprika; cover with foil. Bake at 325° for 25 minutes. Uncover. Continue baking till knife inserted halfway between center and edge comes out clean, about 20 minutes more. Let stand 5 minutes before serving. In saucepan, blend milk into soup; add pimiento. Cook and stir till heated through. Serve over chicken. Serves 6.

CHEESE-VEGETABLE CHOWDER

Chunks of melting cheese are a delicious surprise in this rich double-cheese chowder —

- 1 2-cup container CHICKEN BROTH
- 1 medium carrot, shredded
- 1 stalk celery, chopped
- ½ of a small onion, chopped
- 3 tablespoons butter or margarine
- ¼ cup all-purpose flour
- 2 cups milk
- 1 5-ounce jar process cheese spread
- 2 ounces cheddar, Swiss, or Monterey Jack cheese, cut into ¼-inch cubes (½ cup)

In saucepan, heat Chicken Broth to boiling; add carrots, celery, and onion. Cook, covered, for 7 to 10 minutes or till vegetables are tender. Remove from heat and set aside. In a large saucepan, melt butter or margarine; blend in flour. Add milk all at once; cook and stir till thickened and bubbly. Cook and stir 1 to 2 minutes more. Add cheese spread. Cook and stir over low heat till cheese melts. Add chicken broth with vegetables. Heat through. To serve, divide cheese cubes among four Stacking Bowls; ladle soup over. Makes 4 servings.

HOMEMADE NOODLES

- 1 egg
- 2 tablespoons milk
- ½ teaspoon salt
- 1 cup all-purpose flour

In a Small Mix-N-Stor pitcher, beat egg. Add milk and salt. Add enough of the flour to make a stiff dough. Let rest 10 minutes. On a floured Pastry Sheet, use Rolling Pin to roll dough very thin (about an 18x12-inch rectangle). Let stand 20 minutes. Roll dough up loosely; slice ¼ inch wide. Unroll, spread out, and let dry 2 hours. Makes 6 ounces of noodles or about 3 cups.

OVEN-STYLE CHICKEN HASH

- 1 1½-cup container COOKED CHICKEN, thawed
- 1 cup cubed cooked potato
- 1 5⅓-ounce can (⅔ cup) evaporated milk
- ¼ cup finely snipped parsley
- ¼ cup finely chopped onion
- 1 teaspoon Worcestershire sauce
- ½ teaspoon salt
- ¼ teaspoon sage
   Dash pepper
- 7 saltine crackers
- 1 tablespoon butter or margarine, melted

In Medium Mixing Bowl, stir together Cooked Chicken, potato, evaporated milk, parsley, onion, Worcestershire, salt, sage, and pepper; turn into lightly greased 1-quart casserole. Use Pastry Sheet and Rolling Pin to crush crackers. Toss together cracker crumbs and butter or margarine; sprinkle atop hash. Bake, uncovered, in 350° oven for 30 minutes or till heated through. Makes 4 servings.

CHICKEN AND NOODLE STEW

We've streamlined this old-fashioned favorite without short-cutting an ounce of homemade flavor—

- 1 1½-cup container COOKED CHICKEN
- 2 2-cup containers CHICKEN BROTH
- 1 5⅓-ounce can (⅔ cup) evaporated milk
- ½ cup chopped celery
- ½ cup chopped onion
- ½ cup chopped pimiento
- 1 teaspoon salt
- ½ teaspoon poultry seasoning
- ⅛ teaspoon pepper
   Homemade Noodles (see recipe at left)
- 2 tablespoons all-purpose flour
- ¼ cup cold water

In a large Dutch oven, place frozen Cooked Chicken and Broth. Add evaporated milk. Cook, covered, over medium heat for 15 to 20 minutes or till thawed. Add chopped celery, onion, pimiento, salt, poultry seasoning, and pepper. Bring to boiling. Add Homemade Noodles slowly to boiling broth. Boil, uncovered, 10 to 15 minutes. Combine flour and water. Stir into boiling broth. Cook, stirring constantly, till chicken broth mixture is thickened and bubbly. Makes 6 servings.

START WITH COOKED CHICKEN

CHICKEN CHOP SUEY

- 1 cup quick cooking rice
- ¼ teaspoon salt
- 3½ cups boiling water
- ½ cup onion slices
- 2 tablespoons butter
- 1 2-cup container CHICKEN BROTH
- 1 cup sliced celery
- 1 8-ounce can water chestnuts, sliced
- ½ cup sliced carrot
- 1 1½-cup container COOKED CHICKEN
- 2 tablespoons cornstarch
- 3 tablespoons soy sauce
- 1 16-ounce can bean sprouts, drained
  Chow mein noodles

Place rice and salt in strainer insert in Multi-Server™ container. Pour boiling water over. Cover and let stand while preparing chicken mixture. In a saucepan, cook onion in butter or margarine till tender but not brown; add the Chicken Broth, celery, water chestnuts, and carrots. Heat to boiling. Add frozen Cooked Chicken, stirring to break up cubes. In Small Mix-N-Stor® pitcher, combine cornstarch and soy sauce; stir into chicken mixture. Cook, stirring constantly, till thickened and bubbly. Cook and stir 1 to 2 minutes more. Add bean sprouts, cooking till just heated through. Pour into one rectangular section of Get Togethers™ Buffet Tray. Place chow mein noodles in a Square Server. Turn rice into remaining portion of Buffet Tray. Garnish with carrot curls, celery leaves, and almonds, if desired. Serves 4 to 6.

Serve Oriental-style Chicken Chop Suey in the Get Togethers Buffet Set. The saucy chicken mixture tastes great over chow mein noodles or rice. Pass additional soy sauce if you wish.

CHICKEN-MUSHROOM QUICHE

- 1 9-inch unbaked EASY EGG PASTRY SHELL, (see recipe, page 57)
- 1 1½-cup container COOKED CHICKEN, thawed
- 1 4½-ounce jar sliced mushrooms, drained
- 3 ounces shredded American cheese (¾ cup)
- 4 eggs
- 1 10¾-ounce can condensed cream of chicken soup
- ¼ cup milk

Line Pastry Shell with foil; place dry beans in bottom. Bake in 450° oven for 5 minutes. Remove beans and foil. Reduce oven temperature to 325°.

Arrange chicken and mushrooms in bottom of hot pastry shell; sprinkle with the shredded cheese. In a Small Mix-N-Stor pitcher, beat eggs. In a small saucepan, combine soup and milk; heat just to boiling, stirring constantly. Gradually stir into eggs. Pour soup mixture over cheese.

Bake, uncovered, in 325° oven for 40 to 45 minutes or till knife inserted near center comes out clean. Let stand 10 minutes before serving. Makes 6 servings.

CHICKEN-MACARONI MOLD

- 1 2-cup container CHICKEN BROTH
- 1 3-ounce package lemon-flavored gelatin
- ½ cup cold water
- 3 tablespoons vinegar
- 1 tablespoon chopped onion
- ⅔ cup mayonnaise or salad dressing
- 1 1½-cup container COOKED CHICKEN, thawed
- ½ cup cooked macaroni
- ¼ cup chopped celery
- ¼ cup pimiento-stuffed olives, sliced

In covered saucepan, heat Chicken Broth over medium-low heat till thawed, about 15 minutes, stirring occasionally to break up. Heat to boiling. In a Large Mix-N-Stor pitcher, dissolve gelatin in Chicken Broth. Stir in cold water, vinegar, and onion. Blend in mayonnaise or salad dressing till mixture is smooth. Chill till partially set, about 1 to 1½ hours. (Gelatin should mound slightly when spooned.) When mixture is partially set, fold in thawed Cooked Chicken, macaroni, celery, and olives. Assemble Jel-N-Serve® mold with design Seal. Turn gelatin mixture into mold. Apply large Seal; chill several hours or overnight or until firm. Leave mold at room temperature for 10 to 15 minutes or immerse mold in warm water for 15 to 20 seconds, taking care not to melt gelatin. Remove from water and peel off large Seal. Place Serving Tray over mold and invert. Slowly remove design Seal. Carefully lift off mold. Serves 4.

START WITH STEW MEAT MIX

STEW MEAT MIX

- ¾ cup all-purpose flour
- 1½ teaspoons salt
- 1 6- to 7-pound arm or blade pot roast
- ⅓ cup cooking oil
- 8 cups water
- 4 stalks celery with leaves, quartered
- 2 large onions, quartered
- 2 carrots, quartered
- 3 cloves garlic, minced
- 2 bay leaves
- 2 tablespoons instant beef bouillon granules

Combine flour, salt, and ⅛ teaspoon *pepper* in a Large Mixing Bowl. Cut meat from bones; trim and discard excess fat. Cut meat into 1-inch cubes. Add one-third of the meat cubes to flour mixture in Mixing Bowl; Apply Seal; shake bowl to coat. In a large Dutch oven, brown meat cubes in hot oil and remove. Repeat with remaining meat; return all to pan. Add bones, celery, onion, carrot, garlic, bay leaves, and enough water to cover. Bring to a boil; reduce heat. Simmer, covered, 1 hour or till meat is almost tender. Cool. Drain meat, reserving broth. Remove any meat remaining on bones; discard bones and vegetables. Measure broth only in Large Mix-N-Stor® pitcher; return to Dutch oven. Add enough water to make 14 cups total; stir in bouillon granules. Measure six 1½-cup portions of meat and seven 2-cup portions of broth; pack each into 16-oz. Square Rounds® containers. Apply Seals. Label with contents, amount, and date. Freeze.

AUTUMN STEW

- 1 1½-cup container STEW MEAT MIX
- 1 cup apple cider
- 1 cup water
- ¼ teaspoon dried thyme, crushed
- 2 carrots, peeled and quartered
- 2 potatoes, peeled and quartered
- 1 onion, sliced
- 1 stalk celery, sliced
- 1 apple, chopped
- ⅓ cup cold water
- 3 tablespoons all-purpose flour
- 1½ teaspoons salt
- ⅛ teaspoon pepper
- ¼ teaspoon Kitchen Bouquet (optional)

In large saucepan, combine Stew Meat Mix, cider, 1 cup water, and thyme. Cover and cook over low heat for 15 minutes. Break meat cubes apart with a fork. Add carrots, potatoes, onion, celery, and apple to meat mixture. Cook about 30 minutes or till vegetables are tender. In a small bowl, combine the ⅓ cup cold water and flour; stir into stew. Stir in salt, pepper, and the Kitchen Bouquet, if desired. Cook and stir till thickened and bubbly. Cook and stir 1 to 2 minutes more. Ladle stew into Stacking Bowls. Makes 4 servings.

SPEEDY BEEF-VEGETABLE SOUP

- 1 1½-cup container STEW MEAT MIX
- 2 2-cup containers MEAT BROTH
- 1 16-ounce can tomatoes, cut up
- 1 10-ounce package frozen mixed vegetables
- ½ cup chopped onion
- ⅓ cup sliced celery
- 1½ teaspoons seasoned salt
- 1 teaspoon Worcestershire sauce
- ⅛ teaspoon pepper
  Dash bottled hot pepper sauce
  Spatzle

In Dutch oven, combine first 10 ingredients. Cook over medium heat about 25 minutes or till broth is thawed. Bring to a boil. Reduce heat; cover and simmer 15 minutes. Prepare Spatzle; add to simmering soup as directed in Spatzle recipe. Ladle into Stacking Bowls. Serves 4 to 6.

SPATZLE

- 1 cup plus 2 tablespoons all-purpose flour
- 1 egg
- ½ cup milk

In Small Mix-N-Stor pitcher, stir together flour and 1 teaspoon *salt*. Blend egg and milk; stir into flour mixture. Place half of the dough in 1-qt. Strainer. Hold over soup kettle. With wooden spoon, press dough through Strainer to form spatzle. Repeat. Cook and stir 5 minutes.

Push the Spatzle dough through the Tupperware 1-qt. Strainer into the Speedy Vegetable-Beef Soup to make these curly noodles.

START WITH STEW MEAT MIX

SPOON BREAD MEAT PIE

- 1 2-cup container MEAT BROTH
- 1 tablespoon cornstarch
- 2 tablespoons cold water
- ⅔ cup mayonnaise or salad dressing
- 1 1½-cup container STEW MEAT MIX, thawed
- 1½ cups cubed, cooked, potatoes
- 1 cup sliced, cooked carrots
- ½ cup chopped onion
- 4 ounces shredded American cheese (1 cup)
- 1 tablespoon chopped pimiento
- ¼ teaspoon salt
  - Spoon Bread Topper (see recipe at right)

In a saucepan, heat Meat Broth, covered, till thawed. Measure 1 cup of the broth in a Small Mix-N-Stor® pitcher; set aside for use in Spoon Bread Topper. Combine cornstarch and water. Stir into broth remaining in saucepan. Cook and stir until thickened and bubbly. Blend in mayonnaise or salad dressing. Add Stew Meat Mix, potatoes, carrots, onion, cheese, pimiento, and salt. Heat through. Turn into a greased 2-quart casserole. Add Spoon Bread Topper. Bake in 400° oven for 40 minutes or till golden. Makes 4 to 6 servings.

SPOON BREAD TOPPER

This corn bread topping makes your meal complete —

- 1 cup yellow cornmeal
- 2 teaspoons baking powder
- ½ teaspoon salt
- 1 cup MEAT BROTH
- ½ cup milk
- 2 eggs
- 1 tablespoon butter or margarine, melted

In Medium Mixing Bowl, combine cornmeal, baking powder, and salt. Heat the Meat Broth to boiling and add to the cornmeal mixture in bowl; mix well.

Add milk, eggs, and melted butter or margarine; beat thoroughly using rotary beater. Pour the cornmeal batter over hot meat pie mixture. Bake as directed in recipe.

THAWING MEAT MIXES

To thaw your homemade meat mixes without heating, place sealed Square Rounds® container under running hot tap water for a few minutes, or until pieces of meat can be separated.

The Square Rounds container also can be set in the sink or another container filled with hot tap water until meat pieces can be broken apart.

SPEEDY GOULASH

- 2 1½-cup containers STEW MEAT MIX
- 1 2-cup container MEAT BROTH
- 1 16-ounce can mixed vegetables, drained
- ½ teaspoon dried basil, crushed
- ½ teaspoon salt
- ⅛ teaspoon pepper
- ¼ cup cold water
- 2 tablespoons all-purpose flour
- ½ cup dairy sour cream or plain yogurt
  - Hot cooked noodles
  - Snipped parsley

In a large saucepan, combine frozen Stew Meat Mix, Broth, mixed vegetables, basil, salt, and pepper. Simmer, covered, for 20 to 25 minutes, stirring occasionally, till heated through. Blend water and flour; add to meat mixture. Cook and stir till thickened and bubbly. Cook and stir 1 to 2 minutes more. Stir in sour cream or yogurt. Serve immediately over hot cooked noodles. Sprinkle with snipped parsley. Makes 4 to 6 servings.

SAVE LEFTOVER VEGETABLES

Keep a Classic Sheer™ Jr. Canister in your freezer for those dabs of leftover vegetables. When filled, create a soup with beef or turkey bones. If stews and meat pies are favorites, keep separate Classic Sheer Square Rounds containers of leftover cubed potatoes, peas, and sliced carrots in the freezer. Then you'll be ready to measure out the right amount for a recipe. Either way, you'll be able to see exactly what and how much you have.

BRONCO BUSTER SOUP

Here's a hearty stick-to-the-ribs soup that's a winner with the kids. Leftovers are ideal for school lunches —

- 1 1½-cup container STEW MEAT MIX
- 2 2-cup containers MEAT BROTH
- 1 15-ounce can pinto beans, drained
- 1 cup chopped onion
- ½ teaspoon dried thyme, crushed
- 2 medium potatoes, peeled and diced
- 2 medium carrots, sliced
- ¼ cup grated Parmesan cheese

In a large saucepan, combine Stew Meat Mix, Broth, pinto beans, onion, and thyme. Cook, covered, over medium heat till broth is thawed, 10 to 15 minutes. Mash beans slightly. Add potatoes and carrots to soup. Cover. Reduce heat and simmer about 30 minutes or till vegetables are tender, stirring occasionally. Season to taste. Ladle into Stacking Bowls. Sprinkle each serving with 1 tablespoon of the Parmesan cheese. Makes 4 servings.

FRESH GRATED PARMESAN

Keep a small wedge of hard Parmesan cheese in a sealed Handy Grater on your refrigerator shelf. Then when a recipe calls for Parmesan, grate just the amount you need. The fresh-grated flavor is something special!

BEEF AND MUSHROOM OVEN STEW

- 1 1½-cup container STEW MEAT MIX, thawed
- 1 16-ounce can sliced carrots, drained
- 12 pearl onions or frozen small whole onions
- 2 cups sliced fresh mushrooms
- 3 tablespoons quick-cooking tapioca
- 2 tablespoons prepared mustard
- 2 teaspoons instant beef bouillon granules
- 1 teaspoon sugar
- ½ teaspoon salt
- 2¼ cups tomato juice
- 1 cup water

Place Stew Meat Mix, carrots, onions, and mushrooms in a 2-quart casserole. In a Small Mix-N-Stor pitcher, combine tapioca, mustard, beef bouillon granules, sugar, and salt. Stir in tomato juice and water. Pour over meat and vegetables. Cover and bake in a 350° oven for 50 to 60 minutes or till heated through and slightly thickened. Stir once after 30 minutes and again before serving. Makes 4 to 6 servings.

STEW MEAT SAVINGS

Cutting stew meat cubes from a roast can mean savings especially if you shop sales. Try to keep the cubes uniform in size and shape so they'll cook evenly.

PASTA-FILLED TOMATOES

- ½ cup tiny shell macaroni
- 4 firm ripe tomatoes
- 1 1½-cup container STEW MEAT MIX, thawed
- ¼ cup bias-sliced celery
- ¼ cup chopped green pepper
- ¼ cup chopped onion
- ⅓ cup mayonnaise
- ⅓ cup shredded Swiss or cheddar cheese
- 1 tablespoon prepared mustard
- ½ teaspoon poppy seed (optional)
- ¼ teaspoon salt
  Dash pepper
  Lettuce
  Sliced pitted ripe olives (optional)

Cook macaroni according to package directions. Pour into 1-qt. Strainer. Rinse in cold water; drain. Place tomatoes stem end down. Make 5 to 6 wedges by cutting down to, but not through, base. Scoop out some of the center pulp; set aside. Sprinkle tomatoes with a little salt; invert in Thin-Stor® container, apply Seal, and chill.

In Medium Mixing Bowl, combine Stew Meat Mix, celery, green pepper, onion, tomato pulp, and drained macaroni. In Small Mix-N-Stor pitcher, combine mayonnaise, cheese, mustard, poppy seed, salt, and pepper. Add to meat mixture, tossing to coat. Seal and refrigerate at least 1 hour.

To serve, place each tomato, cut side up, on a lettuce-lined plate. Fill with meat mixture. Garnish with sliced pitted ripe olives, if desired. Makes 4 servings.

START WITH STEW MEAT MIX

PINEAPPLE-BEEF SALAD

Keep the biggest head of lettuce crackling fresh in a Super Crisp-It® container —

- ⅓ cup vinegar
- ⅓ cup salad oil
- 2 tablespoons chopped green onion
- 2 tablespoons snipped parsley
- 1 teaspoon dry mustard
- ¼ teaspoon salt
- ¼ teaspoon dried tarragon, crushed
- 1 1½-cup container STEW MEAT MIX, thawed
- 3 cups torn mixed salad greens
- 1 15¼-ounce can pineapple chunks, drained
- 3 tomatoes, cut into wedges
- 1 green pepper, cut into strips

For marinade, in Small Mix-N-Stor® pitcher, combine vinegar, oil, chopped onion, parsley, dry mustard, salt, and tarragon. Pour over beef in Season-Serve® container. Sprinkle with a little salt and pepper; pour marinade over. Apply Seal and marinate for several hours in refrigerator, turning container frequently.

To serve, drain beef, reserving marinade. Place salad greens in large Decorator Salad Bowl. Top with beef, pineapple, tomatoes, and green pepper; pour marinade over all. Toss lightly. Makes 4 servings.

TANGY STUFFED PEPPER SALAD

- ½ small head cabbage
- 1 medium carrot
- 1 1½-cup container STEW MEAT MIX, thawed
- ¼ cup sliced radish
- ¼ cup chopped unpeeled cucumber
- 1 8-ounce carton plain yogurt
- 2 teaspoons sugar
- 1 teaspoon lemon juice
- ½ teaspoon celery seed
- ¼ teaspoon garlic salt
- ¼ teaspoon onion salt
  Dash black pepper
- 2 large green peppers
  Hard-cooked egg (optional)

Coarsely shred cabbage and carrot into Grater Bowl; stir in the thawed Stew Meat Mix, sliced radish, and chopped cucumber. In Small Mix-N-Stor pitcher, combine yogurt, sugar, lemon juice, celery seed, garlic salt, onion salt, and pepper; mix well. Pour over meat-vegetable mixture, tossing to coat. Apply Seal to Grater Bowl and chill at least 1 hour.

Remove tops from green peppers. Cut peppers in half lengthwise and remove seeds. Parboil, following tip box on page 37. Chill peppers. Spoon vegetable mixture into prepared pepper cups. If desired, garnish with more sliced radish or chopped hard-cooked egg. Makes 4 servings.

PUFFY BEEF-BEAN CASSEROLE

- 2 tablespoons butter or margarine
- 2 tablespoons all-purpose flour
- 1 teaspoon prepared mustard
- ½ teaspoon salt
- ½ teaspoon prepared horseradish
- 1 cup milk
- 4 ounces shredded American cheese (1 cup)
- 1 1½-cup container STEW MEAT MIX
- 1 16-ounce can cut green beans, drained
- 3 egg whites
  Dash salt
- 3 egg yolks

In saucepan, melt butter or margarine. Blend in flour, mustard, ½ teaspoon salt, and horseradish. Add milk all at once; cook and stir till thickened and bubbly. Cook and stir 1 to 2 minutes more. Stir in ½ cup of the cheese; stir in Stew Meat Mix and green beans. Heat till cheese is melted and meat cubes break apart. Turn into a 1½-quart casserole.

In Large Mixing Bowl, beat egg whites and dash salt till stiff peaks form. In Small Mix-N-Stor pitcher, beat egg yolks till thick and lemon colored; stir in the remaining ½ cup cheese. Fold egg yolk mixture into beaten egg whites; spread atop hot beef mixture. Bake in 375° oven for 30 to 35 minutes or till golden. Makes 6 servings.

MARINATED BEEF CUBES TRAY

Serve this chilled meat platter for family meals or special occasions. The Dip-N-Serve® tray lets you take it to the living room or family room for casual entertaining—

1 large onion
15 large fresh mushrooms
4 cups water
¼ teaspoon lemon juice
⅛ teaspoon salt
1 1½-cup container STEW MEAT MIX
½ cup vinegar
2 teaspoons prepared mustard
1 teaspon salt
¼ teaspoon dried marjoram, crushed
¼ teaspoon pepper
¾ cup salad oil

Use Chop-N-Pour™ set to thinly slice onion; separate into rings. Thickly slice mushrooms. Place onion rings on strainer insert of Multi-Server™ container. For marinade, in a saucepan, combine water, lemon juice, and the ⅛ teaspoon salt; bring to boiling. Pour over the onion rings; immediately remove strainer insert and drain onion rings. Place the Stew Meat Mix, onion rings, and mushroom slices in Season-Serve container.

Combine vinegar, mustard, 1 teaspoon salt, marjoram, and pepper. Gradually blend in oil. Pour over beef and vegetables. Apply Seal and marinate several hours or overnight, turning occasionally.

Remove the meat, onion rings, and mushrooms from container, reserving marinade. Arrange on a lettuce-lined Dip-N-Serve tray. Garnish with chopped parsley, if desired. Serve additional marinade in Dip-N-Serve bowl. Makes 4 servings.

SPANISH BEEF-RICE SKILLET

Use the Handy Grater to shred the cheese. Save time and shred extra cheese and store for later use—

½ cup chopped green pepper
½ cup chopped onion
1⅓ cups quick cooking rice
¼ cup butter or margarine, melted
1 teaspoon instant beef bouillon granules
1¼ cups hot water
1 2-cup container ITALIAN SAUCE (see recipe, page 13) or one 15-ounce can meatless spaghetti sauce
1 teaspoon chili powder
1 1½-cup container STEW MEAT MIX
½ cup shredded cheddar or Monterey Jack cheese

In a skillet, cook green pepper, onion, and rice in butter or margarine, stirring constantly, until rice is lightly browned. In Small Mix-N-Stor pitcher, dissolve beef bouillon granules in hot water; pour into rice mixture in skillet along with the Italian Sauce or spaghetti sauce, chili powder, and Stew Meat Mix. Cover and cook, stirring frequently, till sauce and meat are thawed and heated and rice is tender, 10 to 12 minutes. Sprinkle each serving with some shredded cheese. Makes 4 to 6 servings.

TEXAS-STYLE CHILI

This chili is called a Tex-Mex recipe, indicating that it's one that originated in Texas but was inspired by Mexican cooking. Chili buffs insist that the meat must be cubed, never ground, and that the spicy mixture contain no beans. Instead, cooked beans, rice, or corn bread are often served alongside the chili —

1 1½-cup container STEW MEAT MIX
1 2-cup container MEAT BROTH
2 teaspoons sugar
2 teaspoons dried oregano, crushed
1 to 2 teaspoons cumin seed, crushed
½ teaspoon salt
⅛ teaspoon crushed red pepper (optional)
2 bay leaves
2 to 4 tablespoons chopped canned green chili peppers
2 tablespoons cornmeal Corn Bread (optional)

In a large skillet, combine Stew Meat Mix, Broth, sugar, oregano, cumin seed, salt, red pepper, and bay leaves. Cook, covered, over medium heat about 15 minutes or till meat and broth are thawed. Add chili peppers and cornmeal. Reduce heat and simmer, covered, for 20 minutes; stir occasionally. Remove bay leaves. Place a square of corn bread in each Stacking Bowl; ladle chili over top. Makes 4 servings.

START WITH GROUND MEAT MIX

GROUND MEAT MIX

3 **eggs**
2 **cups soft bread**
 crumbs
1 **cup chopped celery**
1 **cup chopped onion**
1 **cup shredded carrot**
3 **pounds ground beef**

In a Large Mixing Bowl, beat eggs slightly. Stir in bread crumbs, celery, onion, carrot, and 1 teaspoon *salt*. Add meat; mix well. Cook half the mixture at a time till meat is lightly browned. Drain off fat. Cool. Measure 2-cup portions into each of five 16-oz. Square Rounds® containers. Apply Seal. Label with contents, amount, and date. Freeze.

ONE-STEP SKILLET SUPPER

1 **2-cup container GROUND**
 MEAT MIX
1 **24-ounce can vegetable**
 juice cocktail
1 **cup elbow macaroni**
½ **cup chopped green**
 pepper
⅛ **teaspoon garlic powder**
1 **cup shredded cheddar**
 cheese

In a large skillet, combine Ground Meat Mix, vegetable juice, uncooked macaroni, green pepper, and garlic powder. Cover and cook over medium heat for 30 minutes, stirring occasionally. When macaroni is tender, remove lid from skillet and sprinkle with cheese. Cook, uncovered, over low heat for 5 minutes or till cheese is melted; serve immediately. Makes 4 servings.

STUFFED PEPPERS

The Multi-Server™ container is a natural for parboiling the green peppers—

4 **large green peppers**
 (about 1½ pounds)
10 **cups boiling water**
1 **2-cup container GROUND**
 MEAT MIX, thawed
1¼ **cups crushed potato**
 chips
¾ **cup buttermilk**
2 **eggs, beaten**
¼ **cup catsup**
¼ **teaspoon poultry**
 seasoning
 Paprika

Slice the tops off the large green peppers; remove seeds and rinse peppers. Place peppers on the strainer insert and place insert in Multi-Server container. Pour in enough boiling water to cover peppers. Cover the Multi-Server container and let peppers stand for 10 minutes. Lift strainer insert to drain peppers; sprinkle cavities with salt.

In Medium Mixing Bowl, combine the thawed Ground Meat Mix, 1 cup of the crushed potato chips, buttermilk, eggs, catsup, and poultry seasoning. Fill pepper cups with the meat mixture. Place filled peppers in 8x8x2-inch baking dish. Sprinkle with remaining potato chips and paprika.

Bake stuffed pepper cups in 375° oven for 30 minutes or till heated through. Makes 4 servings.

PARBOILING PEPPERS

The Multi-Server container is ideal for cooking green peppers "crisp-tender."

1. Wash, seed, and cut peppers as directed in the recipe. Arrange in the strainer insert. Place the strainer insert in the Multi-Server serving dish.

2. Pour in just enough boiling water to completely cover the vegetable. Cover the container and let it stand on the counter 10 minutes. No watching is required. Steam condensing on the inside of the cover will flow to the edge and drip into the serving dish below. Vegetable is easily drained by lifting the strainer insert from the serving dish.

To make savory Stuffed Peppers, parboil the fresh green peppers in the Multi-Server container and then stuff with the timesaving Ground Meat Mix.

START WITH GROUND MEAT MIX

SAUCY BEEF AND CABBAGE

- 1 2-cup container GROUND MEAT MIX
- ¼ cup water
- 1 medium head cabbage
- 2 tablespoons butter or margarine
- 2 tablespoons all-purpose flour
- 1 teaspoon instant beef bouillon granules
- ½ teaspoon celery seed
- ¼ teaspoon paprika
- ¼ teaspoon dried thyme, crushed
- ⅛ teaspoon pepper
- 1¼ cups milk
- 2 ounces shredded Monterey Jack cheese (½ cup)
- ¼ cup dairy sour cream

In saucepan, combine Ground Meat Mix and water. Cover and cook over low heat for 15 minutes; break up meat mixture with a fork. Cover and cook 5 minutes longer. Drain off liquid. Cut cabbage into 6 wedges. In a large covered skillet, cook cabbage in a small amount of boiling salted water 10 minutes or just till tender. Drain cabbage well.

To make sauce, in medium saucepan, melt butter or margarine. Stir in flour, beef bouillon granules, celery seed, paprika, thyme, and pepper. Add the milk all at once. Cook over medium heat, stirring constantly, till thickened and bubbly. Cook and stir 1 to 2 minutes more. Stir cheese and dairy sour cream into sauce. Heat through; do not boil. Stir in meat mixture. Arrange drained cabbage wedges on Dip-N-Serve® tray. Pour some of the sauce over the cabbage wedges. Serve remaining sauce in Dip-N-Serve bowl. Serves 6.

MEAL-IN-A-BOWL SOUP

- 1 2-cup container GROUND MEAT MIX
- 1 2-cup container MEAT BROTH* (see recipe, page 30)
- ⅔ cups water
- 1 cup frozen peas or one cup frozen cut green beans
- 1 large potato, peeled and cubed
- ½ cup sliced fresh mushrooms
- 1 medium carrot, chopped
- 1 small zucchini, sliced
- ¾ teaspoon dried basil, crushed
- ¼ teaspoon ground sage

In a large saucepan or Dutch oven, combine Ground Meat Mix, Meat Broth, water, frozen peas or green beans, potatoes, mushrooms, carrot, zucchini, basil, and sage. Cook over medium heat till meat and broth are thawed. Bring to boiling; reduce heat. Cover and simmer 15 minutes, stirring occasionally. Ladle into Stacking Bowls. Makes 6 servings.

*Note: Or, substitute 2 cups *beef broth* for the Meat Broth.

MEAT AND MAC SKILLET

- 1 cup elbow macaroni
- 1 2-cup container GROUND MEAT MIX
- ¼ cup water
- 1 8¾-ounce can whole kernel corn, drained
- 2 tablespoons snipped parsley
- 1 teaspoon chili powder
- ½ teaspoon salt
- ½ teaspoon garlic salt
- ¼ teaspoon ground cumin
- ¼ teaspoon pepper
- 1 8-ounce package cream cheese, softened
- ¾ cup milk
- 2 medium tomatoes
- 2 slices American cheese, halved diagonally

In saucepan, cook macaroni in a large amount of boiling salted water about 10 minutes or just till tender. Drain in 1-qt. Strainer and set aside. In a skillet, combine frozen Ground Meat Mix and ¼ cup water. Cover and cook over low heat for 15 minutes; break up meat with fork. Cover; cook 5 minutes more. Add drained corn, parsley, chili powder, salt, garlic salt, cumin, and pepper to meat mixture; mix well. Stir in cream cheese and milk. Stir in macaroni; heat through.

Cut tomatoes into wedges. Arrange tomato wedges and cheese triangles atop meat mixture. Cover skillet and heat over low heat for 8 to 10 minutes or just till cheese is melted and tomatoes are heated through. Makes 4 to 5 servings.

CORN-BURGER WHEELS

- 1⅓ cups HEARTY WHEAT MASTER MIX (see recipe, page 67)
- 1 cup milk
- 1 cup dairy sour cream
- 1 beaten egg
- 1 2-cup container GROUND MEAT MIX, thawed
- 1 tablespoon all-purpose flour
- 2 tablespoons catsup
- 1 7-ounce can whole kernel corn with sweet peppers, drained

In a Small Mix-N-Stor® pitcher, stir together Master Mix and ½ cup of the milk just till dough follows fork around bowl. On a lightly floured Pastry Sheet, knead dough 10 to 12 times. Use Rolling Pin to roll to 12x8-inch rectangle. Stir egg and ½ cup of the sour cream into thawed Ground Meat Mix mixture. Spread meat mixture evenly over dough. Roll up jelly-roll style, beginning at long side; seal. Cut into eight 1½-inch pinwheels. Arrange in 8x8-inch baking pan. Bake in 400° oven for 20 to 25 minutes or till browned. For sauce, in a small saucepan, combine remaining ½ cup sour cream and the flour. Add remaining ½ cup milk and the catsup. Cook and stir till thickened and bubbly. Cook and stir 1 to 2 minutes longer. Stir in corn; heat through. Serve poured over pinwheels. Makes 4 servings.

HAMBURGER PIE

A thrifty cook can save time, too, by substituting 2 cups leftover mashed potatoes for the cooked potatoes used in the casserole topping —

- 1 2-cup container GROUND MEAT MIX
- ¼ cup water
- 1 16-ounce can cut green beans, drained
- 1 10¾-ounce can condensed tomato soup
- ¼ cup water
- ¾ teaspoon salt
- ⅛ teaspoon pepper
- 3 medium potatoes, peeled and quartered (1 pound)
- 1 beaten egg
  Milk
- 2 ounces shredded American cheese (½ cup)

In 2-quart saucepan, combine frozen Ground Meat Mix and ¼ cup water. Cover and cook over low heat for 15 minutes; break up meat mixture with fork. Cook 5 minutes more. Drain off liquid. Stir in green beans, tomato soup, ¼ cup water, salt, and pepper. Turn meat mixture into a 1½-quart casserole.

In covered saucepan, cook potatoes in boiling salted water about 20 minutes or just till tender; drain in 1-qt. Strainer. Transfer hot potatoes to a Medium Mixing Bowl. Mash while hot; blend in egg. Add enough milk to make potatoes fluffy, yet stiff enough to hold their shape. Season with salt and pepper.

Drop potatoes in mounds atop meat mixture. Sprinkle with cheese. Bake, uncovered, in 350° oven for 25 to 30 minutes or till heated through. Makes 4 to 6 servings.

STIR-FRIED BEEF WITH VEGETABLES

- 1 2-cup container GROUND MEAT MIX
- ¼ cup water
- 2 tablespoons soy sauce
- 1 tablespoon cornstarch
- 1 teaspoon instant beef bouillon granules
- ¾ cup boiling water
- 2 tablespoons cooking oil
- 1 clove garlic, minced
- 1 teaspoon grated gingerroot
- 1 cup thinly sliced cauliflower
- 1 cup bias-sliced carrots
- 2 cups chopped spinach leaves
- 1 cup fresh pea pods
- 1 cup sliced fresh mushrooms
- 1 cup fresh bean sprouts
  Hot cooked rice

In saucepan, combine Ground Meat Mix and ¼ cup water. Cover and cook over low heat for 15 minutes; break up meat mixture with fork. Cover; cook 5 minutes longer. Set aside. In Small Mix-N-Stor pitcher, combine soy sauce and cornstarch; stir in bouillon granules. Add ¾ cup boiling water; stir to dissolve granules. Set aside.

Preheat large skillet or wok over high heat; add oil. Stir-fry garlic and gingerroot in hot oil for 30 seconds. Add cauliflower and carrots; stir-fry 3 minutes. Add vegetables; stir-fry 2 minutes. Remove vegetables to Medium Mixing Bowl. (Add more oil to skillet or wok, if necessary.) Add meat mixture to hot skillet or wok; stir-fry 2 to 3 minutes.

Stir bouillon mixture; add to skillet or wok. Cook and stir till bubbly. Return vegetables to wok; stir to combine. Cover; cook 1 minute. Makes 4 or 5 servings.

START WITH GROUND MEAT MIX

DOUBLE-DECKER TOSTADO LUNCH

Here's a special make-ahead lunch you can store and serve when minutes matter —

- 1 2-cup container GROUND MEAT MIX
- ¼ cup water
- 8 5-inch tostado shells
- 1 16-ounce can refried beans
- 4 ounces cheddar or Monterey Jack cheese
- 2 tablespoons taco seasoning mix
- ¼ cup pitted ripe olives, sliced
  Shredded lettuce

Place Ground Meat Mix and water in a saucepan. Cover and cook over low heat for 15 minutes, stirring occasionally; break up meat with a fork. Cover and cook 5 minutes longer. Drain off liquid.

Meanwhile, spread one side of each tostado shell with refried beans; set aside. Shred cheese on Handy Grater; remove grater and add taco seasoning mix. Apply storage Seal and shake vigorously to coat cheese. Add sliced olives. To assemble tostado, place 1 shell, bean side up, in the bottom of a Small Seal-N-Serve® bowl. Layer about ¼ cup meat mixture, a little shredded lettuce, and about 2 tablespoons of the cheese mixture over bean layer of each. Place second tostado atop; repeat meat, lettuce, and cheese layers. Makes 4 servings.

QUICK CHEESE-BURGER CHOWDER

The Chop-N-Pour™ set is ideal for chopping small amounts of vegetables —

- 1 2-cup container GROUND MEAT MIX
- ¼ cup water
- 2 cups cubed, peeled potatoes
- ½ cup chopped celery
- ¼ cup chopped onion
- 2 tablespoons chopped green pepper
- 1 tablespoon instant beef bouillon granules
- 1¼ cups water
- ½ teaspoon salt
- 2½ cups milk
- 3 tablespoons all-purpose flour
- 4 ounces cheddar cheese

In large saucepan, combine frozen meat mixture and ¼ cup water. Cover and cook over low heat for 15 minutes; break up meat mixture with fork. Cover; cook 5 minutes longer. Stir in potatoes, celery, onion, green pepper, bouillon granules, 1¼ cups water, and salt. Cover; cook 15 to 20 minutes or till vegetables are tender.

In Small Mix-N-Stor® pitcher, combine ½ cup of the milk and the flour; stir into meat mixture. Add remaining milk. Cook and stir till thickened and bubbly. Use Handy Grater or Grater Bowl to shred cheese. Add cheese to saucepan; heat and stir just till cheese melts. Garnish individual servings with additional shredded cheese, if desired. Makes 6 to 8 servings.

HOT MEXICAN BEEF BAKE

Pictured on page 11—

- 1 16-ounce can tomatoes, cut up
- 1 10-ounce can enchilada sauce
- ¼ cup sliced pitted ripe olives
- ¼ teaspoon salt
- 1 2-cup container GROUND MEAT MIX
- 6 ounces American cheese
- 1 cup cream-style cottage cheese
- 1 egg, slightly beaten
- 1 8-ounce package tortilla chips, slightly crushed

In medium saucepan, combine undrained tomatoes, enchilada sauce, sliced olives, and salt. Add Ground Meat Mix; simmer, covered, for 20 minutes, stirring occasionally. Shred cheese on Grater Bowl; remove grater and set aside ½ cup of the cheese for topping. Stir cottage cheese and egg into remaining shredded cheese.

Spread half of the meat mixture in 12x7½x2-inch baking dish. Top with half the cheese mixture and half of the tortilla chips. Repeat layers, ending with tortilla chips. Bake in 350° oven for 25 minutes. Sprinkle the reserved ½ cup shredded American cheese over top and return to oven about 5 minutes till cheese melts. Let stand 5 minutes before serving. Makes 6 servings.

Prepare and store Double-Decker Tostado Lunch in the Small Seal-N-Serve container early in the day, then pull from the refrigerator when you're ready to serve.

START WITH GROUND MEAT MIX

ORIENTAL SKILLET

- 1 2-cup container **GROUND MEAT MIX**
- 1 16-ounce can chop suey vegetables, drained
- 1 10-ounce package frozen peas
- 1 cup water
- 2 tablespoons cornstarch
- 1 teaspoon sugar
- ¼ teaspoon ground ginger
- 3 tablespoons soy sauce
- 2 tablespoons water
  Chow mein noodles

In large saucepan or skillet, combine Ground Meat Mix, chop suey vegetables, frozen peas, and 1 cup water. Simmer, covered, for 20 minutes, stirring occasionally. In Small Mix-N-Stor® pitcher, blend together cornstarch, sugar, and ginger; gradually stir in soy sauce and 2 tablespoons water. Add to beef mixture; cook and stir till thickened. Serve over chow mein noodles. Serves 4.

QUICK SPANISH HAMBURGER SOUP

- 1 2-cup container **GROUND MEAT MIX**
- 1 2-cup container **ITALIAN SAUCE (see recipe, page 13)**
- 1 4-ounce can mushroom stems and pieces, drained
- ¼ cup pimiento-stuffed olives, sliced
- 1½ cups water

In saucepan, combine Ground Meat Mix, Italian Sauce, mushrooms, olives, and water. Cover and simmer 30 to 35 minutes. Ladle into Stacking Bowls. Makes 4 servings.

TEXAS BEEF SKILLET

Use your Rolling Pin and Pastry Sheet to crush the corn chips; crush extra and store them to use as a crunchy salad topper—

- 1 2-cup container **GROUND MEAT MIX**
- ½ cup water
- 1 16-ounce can tomatoes, cut up
- 1 15½-ounce can red kidney beans
- ½ cup quick cooking rice
- 3 tablespoons chopped green pepper
- 1½ teaspoons chili powder
- ½ teaspoon salt
- ½ teaspoon garlic salt
- 3 ounces American, cheddar, or Monterey Jack cheese
  Corn chips or tortilla chips, crushed

In a skillet, combine frozen Ground Meat Mix and water. Cover and cook over low heat for 15 minutes; break up meat mixture with a fork.

Stir in undrained tomatoes, undrained kidney beans, rice, chopped green pepper, chili powder, salt, and garlic salt. Bring mixture to boiling; reduce heat. Cover and simmer for 20 minutes, stirring occasionally.

Meanwhile, shred cheese; sprinkle over meat mixture. Cover and heat about 3 minutes more or till cheese melts. Sprinkle crushed corn or tortilla chips around edge. Serve immediately. Pass additional chips, if desired. Makes 6 servings.

SOUTH-OF-THE BORDER SALAD

- 1 2-cup container **GROUND MEAT MIX**
- ¼ cup water
- 1 clove garlic, minced
- 1 8-ounce can tomato sauce
- 1 7½-ounce can tomatoes, cut up
- 1 4-ounce can green chili peppers, rinsed, seeded, and finely chopped
- 1 tablespoon all-purpose flour
- 2 teapoons chili powder
- 6 cups torn lettuce
- 1 15-ounce can garbanzo beans, drained
- ½ cup sliced pitted ripe olives
- 4 ounces shredded Monterey Jack or cheddar cheese (1 cup)
- 1 cup cherry tomatoes, halved
- 1 green pepper, cut into strips
- 1 avocado, peeled and sliced

In skillet, combine frozen Ground Meat Mix, water, and garlic. Cover and cook over low heat for 15 minutes; break up meat mixture with a fork. Cover and cook for 5 minutes longer. Drain off liquid. Stir in tomato sauce, undrained tomatoes, chili peppers, flour, and chili powder. Cook and stir till thickened and bubbly.

Meanwhile, in large Decorator Salad Bowl, combine lettuce, garbanzo beans, and olives; toss. Top with meat mixture; sprinkle with shredded cheese. Arrange cherry tomato halves, green pepper strips, and avocado slices atop salad. Makes 6 servings.

CHEESY BEEF-RICE BAKE

- 1 2-cup container GROUND MEAT MIX
- ¼ cup water
- 1 clove garlic, minced
- 1 cup long grain rice
- 2 tablespoons butter or margarine
- 3 cups water
- 1 cup shredded carrot
- 2 teaspoons instant beef bouillon granules
- 1 teaspoon dried parsley flakes
- ½ teaspoon minced dried onion
- ½ teaspoon salt
- ½ teaspoon dried basil, crushed
- 2 ounces American cheese

In saucepan, combine frozen Ground Meat Mix, ¼ cup water, and garlic. Cover and cook over low heat for 15 minutes; break up meat mixture with a fork. Cover and cook 5 minutes longer. Drain off liquid. Remove from pan and set aside. In same saucepan, cook uncooked rice in butter or margarine till golden brown, stirring frequently. Stir in water, carrot, bouillon granules, parsley flakes, dried onion, salt, and basil. Bring to boiling. Reduce heat; cover and simmer for 5 minutes. Stir in meat mixture.

Turn into a 1½-quart casserole. Cover; bake in 325° oven for 45 minutes, stirring twice. Use Handy Grater or Grater Bowl to shred cheese; sprinkle over casserole. Bake, uncovered, about 5 minutes longer or till cheese melts. Makes 6 servings.

PARMESAN BEEF AND PASTA BAKE

- 6 ounces elbow macaroni
- 1 beaten egg
- ⅓ cup grated Parmesan cheese
- ¼ cup milk
- 1 2-cup container GROUND MEAT MIX
- 1 8-ounce can tomato sauce
- ½ teaspoon ground cinnamon
- ⅛ teaspoon ground nutmeg
- 3 tablespoons butter
- 3 tablespoons all-purpose flour
- 1½ cups milk
- 1 beaten egg
- ¼ cup grated Parmesan cheese

Cook macaroni in a large amount of boiling salted water about 10 minutes or just till tender; drain in 1-qt. Strainer. Combine cooked macaroni, 1 beaten egg, the ⅓ cup Parmesan cheese, and the ¼ cup milk; set aside. In skillet, cook Ground Meat Mix and tomato sauce, covered, over low heat for 15 minutes. Break up meat with a fork. Stir in cinnamon, nutmeg, ½ teaspoon *salt*, and ⅛ teaspoon *pepper*; set aside.

For sauce, in saucepan, melt butter; stir in flour and ¼ teaspoon *salt*. Add the 1½ cups milk all at once; cook and stir till thickened and bubbly. Cook and stir 1 to 2 minutes more. Remove from heat. Stir about half of the hot mixture into 1 beaten egg; return to remaining hot mixture in saucepan. Stir in the ¼ cup grated Parmesan.

Place half of the macaroni mixture in an 8x8x2-inch baking dish. Spoon the meat mixture atop; add the remaining macaroni mixture. Spread the sauce over all. Bake, uncovered, in 350° oven for 40 to 45 minutes. Let stand 10 minutes before serving. Serves 6.

HERBED BEEF CASSEROLES

- ½ cup elbow or corkscrew macaroni
- ¼ cup milk
- 1 teaspoon all-purpose flour
- 1 2-cup container GROUND MEAT MIX, thawed
- 1 10¾-ounce can condensed cream of mushroom soup
- 1 cup frozen peas
- ¼ teaspoon ground sage
- 1 cup HERB STUFFING MIX (see recipe, page 45) or one cup herb-seasoned croutons
- 1 tablespoon butter or margarine, melted

Cook macaroni according to package directions; drain in 1-qt. Strainer. In Medium Mixing Bowl, stir milk into flour. Add thawed Ground Meat Mix, mushroom soup, peas, and sage. Stir in the drained macaroni. Turn meat-vegetable mixture into four 10-ounce individual casseroles or one 1-quart casserole.

In Medium Mixing Bowl toss together Herbed Stuffing Mix with the melted butter or margarine. Sprinkle ¼ cup Stuffing Mix mixture atop each casserole or 1 cup atop larger casserole. Bake casseroles in 350° oven about 30 minutes or till heated through (or, 45 minutes for 1-quart casserole). Makes 4 servings.

START WITH HERB STUFFING MIX

HERB STUFFING MIX

The Herb Stuffing Mix also doubles as crispy seasoned croutons. Use them to sprinkle atop your favorite salad or to float in a hearty soup or stew—

- 15 slices day-old white or whole wheat bread
- 2 tablespoons minced dried onion
- 2 tablespoons dried parsley flakes
- 1 teaspoon garlic salt
- ½ teaspoon ground sage
- ¼ teaspoon pepper
- 3 tablespoons cooking oil

Slice bread into ½-inch cubes. Spread the bread cubes evenly in a large shallow baking pan. Toast bread cubes in a 300° oven for 40 to 45 minutes or till golden, stirring once. Remove from oven; cool slightly.

In a Large Mixing Bowl, combine the bread cubes, onion, parsley flakes, garlic salt, sage, and pepper. Drizzle oil evenly over all. Apply Seal.

Turn the bowl several times to coat bread cubes. Store in an Ultra Clear Counterparts™ IV container. Makes 10 cups.

HERB STUFFING TIP

When a recipe calls for Herb Stuffing Mix, crushed, the cubes should be measured before crushing.

SPICY HAM PATTIES WITH APPLE RINGS

- 2 beaten eggs
- ½ cup applesauce
- 1½ cups HERB STUFFING MIX, finely crushed
- ⅓ cup nonfat dry milk powder
- ¼ cup chopped onion
- ½ teaspoon dry mustard
- ¾ pound ground fully cooked ham
- ½ pound ground pork
- 1 tablespoon brown sugar
- 2 teaspoons cornstarch
- ¼ teaspoon dry mustard
  Dash ground cloves
- ¾ cup applesauce
- 2 tablespoons water
- 1 tablespoon vinegar
- 1 medium apple

In Large Mixing Bowl, combine eggs, the ½ cup applesauce, and the crushed Herb Stuffing Mix; stir in milk powder, onion, and the ½ teaspoon mustard. Add ground ham and pork; mix well. Using Hamburger Press, shape mixture into 6 patties, oiling press, if necessary. Place in 13x9x2-inch baking pan. Bake in 350° oven for 40 to 45 minutes.

Meanwhile, in saucepan, combine brown sugar, cornstarch, ¼ teaspoon mustard, and cloves. Blend in the ¾ cup applesauce, water, and vinegar. Cook and stir till thickened. Core apple; slice into six rings. Add apple rings to saucepan; cover and simmer 15 minutes or till just tender. To serve, arrange an apple ring atop each patty. Spoon sauce over. Serves 6.

GARDEN ROW SALAD

- 2 medium carrots
- 1 small cucumber, halved and seeded
- 2 cups halved cherry tomatoes
- 3 stalks celery, finely minced
- 6 ounces cheddar cheese
- 3 hard-cooked eggs, sliced
- 8 slices crisp-cooked bacon, crumbled
- ½ cup mayonnaise or salad dressing
- 3 tablespoons catsup
- 1 tablespoon salad oil
- 1 teaspoon lemon juice
- ½ teaspoon Worcestershire sauce
- ⅛ teaspoon paprika
- ½ cup HERB STUFFING MIX
- 1 hard-cooked egg

In Grater Bowl, coarsely grate carrots; spread evenly on the bottom of a 7-cup Classic Sheer Canister. Coarsely grate cucumber; sprinkle atop carrot layer. Arrange cherry tomato halves over. Layer celery atop tomatoes.

In clean, dry Grater Bowl, grate cheese; sprinkle over celery layer. Arrange egg slices and crumbled bacon over cheese.

Stir together mayonnaise or salad dressing, catsup, salad oil, lemon juice, Worcestershire sauce, and paprika; mix well. Spread evenly over bacon layer. Apply Seal and refrigerate several hours or overnight. Before serving, sprinkle with Herb Stuffing Mix. Slice remaining hard-cooked egg. Garnish individual servings with the egg slices. Makes 4 servings.

Layer crunchy Garden Row Salad in a Tupperware 7-cup Classic Sheer™ Jr. Canister and store to allow the flavors to mellow. Add the croutons just before serving so they'll stay crisp and garnish with the sliced hard-cooked egg.

START WITH HERB STUFFING MIX

SAUCY MUSHROOM-BEEF PATTIES

- 1 3-ounce can chopped mushrooms
- 1 cup HERB STUFFING MIX
- 1 cup dairy sour cream
- ¼ cup finely chopped onion
- 2 teaspoons Worcestershire sauce
- ¼ teaspoon ground nutmeg
- 1 pound ground beef or ground pork
- 4 1-inch-thick slices French bread
- 2 tablespoons dijon-style mustard

Preheat broiler. Meanwhile, place 1-qt. Strainer over Small Mix-N-Stor® pitcher and drain mushrooms, reserving ¼ cup liquid.

In Medium Mixing Bowl, mix ⅓ cup of the mushrooms, the Herb Stuffing Mix, ⅓ cup of the sour cream, onion, Worcestershire sauce, and nutmeg. Add ground beef or pork; mix well. Shape in Hamburger Press into four patties. Broil 3 to 4 inches from heat 5 to 6 minutes. Turn; broil 5 to 6 minutes more.

Toast bread slices in broiler pan during last few minutes of broiling the meat patties. Meanwhile, in saucepan, mix the reserved mushroom liquid, remaining mushrooms, remaining sour cream, and mustard. Heat through; do not boil. Serve broiled patties on the toasted bread. Pass sauce to serve atop patties. Makes 4 servings.

TOSSED BEEF AND SPINACH SALAD

- 1 egg
- ⅔ cup salad oil
- 1 3-ounce package cream cheese, softened
- ¼ cup dairy sour cream
- 2 tablespoons crumbled blue cheese
- 1 tablespoon lemon juice
- ¼ teapoon garlic salt
- 8 ounces cooked roast beef
- 1 cup cherry tomatoes
- 3 cups torn romaine
- 3 cups torn fresh spinach
- 1 cup HERB STUFFING MIX
  Crumbled blue cheese (optional)

To make dressing, in Small Mix-N-Stor pitcher, beat egg slightly. Gradually add salad oil, beating on medium speed of portable electric mixer. Add softened cream cheese, sour cream, crumbled blue cheese, lemon juice, and garlic salt; beat till smooth. Cover and refrigerate till ready to serve.

Cut cooked beef into thin strips; season with a little salt. Halve cherry tomatoes.

In Decorator Salad Bowl, combine torn romaine, spinach, Herb Stuffing Mix, tomatoes, and the beef strips; spoon about ½ cup dressing atop. Top with additional crumbled blue cheese, if desired. Toss to coat vegetables. Pass remaining dressing. Makes 6 servings.

FISH AND SPUD BAKE

- 1 pound fresh or frozen perch or other fish fillets
- 1 10-ounce package frozen chopped spinach
- 3 medium potatoes, peeled and quartered
- 1 beaten egg
- ½ cup dairy sour cream
  Milk
- ¼ cup milk
- ¾ cup HERB STUFFING MIX, crushed
- 2 tablespoons butter or margarine, melted
  Lemon slices (optional)

Thaw fish, if frozen. Skin fish fillets; set aside. In medium saucepan, cook spinach according to package directions. Drain well in 1-qt. Strainer, pressing out excess liquid. In same saucepan, cook potatoes in boiling water about 20 minutes or just till tender; drain.

In Medium Mixing Bowl, mash hot cooked potatoes; blend in beaten egg and sour cream. If necessary, add enough milk to make potatoes fluffy, yet stiff enough to hold their shape. Season with salt and pepper, if desired. Stir in well-drained spinach. Turn into 10x6x2-inch baking dish. Dip fish fillets in the ¼ cup milk, then in crushed Herb Stuffing Mix. Place atop potato mixture; drizzle with the melted butter or margarine.

Bake, uncovered, in 350° oven for 30 to 40 minutes or till fish flakes easily when tested with a fork. Serve with lemon slices, if desired. Makes 4 to 5 servings.

CORNED BEEF BALLS WITH CHEESE SAUCE

1 beaten egg
2 tablespoons milk
⅔ cup HERB STUFFING MIX, finely crushed
1 12-ounce can corned beef, flaked
2 cups quick cooking rice
5 cups boiling water
1 10-ounce package frozen mixed vegetables
¼ teaspoon salt
1 recipe Cheese Sauce (see recipe, page 50)

In Large Mixing Bowl, combine egg, milk, crushed Herb Stuffing Mix, and canned corned beef. Form into 24 balls. Place on greased 15x10x1-inch pan. Bake in 350° oven for 20 minutes.

For rice ring, place Multi-Server™ strainer insert in dish. Place rice in strainer insert. In a saucepan, combine the 5 cups water, mixed vegetables, and salt. Bring to a boil and pour over uncooked rice; cover immediately. Let stand for 5 minutes. Stir rice mixture, then press into an ungreased Jel-Ring® mold. Unmold onto a Dip-N-Serve® tray. Fill center with the baked corned beef balls. Drizzle some of the Cheese Sauce over beef balls and rice ring; pass remaining Cheese Sauce. Makes 6 servings.

VEGETABLE AND CHEESE PIE

2 cups HERB STUFFING MIX, crushed
¼ cup butter or margarine, melted
1 cup chopped onion
1 clove garlic, minced
2 tablespoons butter or margarine
½ teaspoon dried savory, crushed
½ teaspoon dried oregano, crushed
¼ teaspoon salt
⅛ teaspoon pepper
4 cups cauliflower flowerets, (1 medium head)
½ cup sliced carrot
6 ounces cheddar cheese
2 eggs
¼ cup milk

Combine crushed Herb Stuffing Mix and the ¼ cup melted butter or margarine. Press mixture into a 9-inch pie plate. Bake in 375° oven for 8 to 10 minutes till golden. Set aside. In a saucepan, cook onion and garlic in 2 tablespoons butter or margarine till onion is tender but not brown. Add dried savory, dried oregano, salt, and pepper. Stir in cauliflower flowerets and carrot. Cook, covered, over low heat for 10 to 15 minutes or till vegetables are crisp-tender. Shred cheese on Handy Grater or Grater Bowl; sprinkle half over the bottom of prebaked pie shell; spoon vegetable mixture atop. In Small Mix-N-Stor pitcher, slightly beat eggs; blend in milk. Pour over vegetables in pie shell. Bake, uncovered, in 375° oven 15 minutes. Top with remaining cheddar cheese; bake 5 to 10 minutes or till set. Makes 4 to 6 servings.

SWISS-TUNA BURGERS

1 beaten egg
¼ cup nonfat dry milk powder
¼ cup water
1 tablespoon catsup
1 tablespoon prepared mustard
¼ teaspoon salt
1½ cups HERB STUFFING MIX, finely crushed
¼ cup chopped celery
2 tablespoons finely chopped onion
1 9¼-ounce can tuna, drained and flaked
6 slices process Swiss cheese
6 hamburger buns, split, toasted, and buttered

In Medium Mixing Bowl, combine beaten egg, nonfat dry milk powder, water, catsup, prepared mustard, and salt. Stir in the crushed Herb Stuffing Mix, chopped celery, and chopped onion. Add flaked tuna; mix well.

Using oiled Hamburger Press, shape tuna mixture into 6 patties. Place tuna patties on greased unheated broiler pan. Broil patties 5 inches from heat for 6 to 7 minutes or till heated through. Top with Swiss cheese slices; broil 1 to 2 minutes more or till cheese begins to melt. Place a broiled tuna patty on bottom half of each toasted hamburger bun; replace tops. Makes 6 servings.

START WITH HERB STUFFING MIX

DRESSED-UP ORANGE PORK STEAKS

- 4 pork shoulder steaks, cut ½ inch thick
- 1 medium orange
- 1 beaten egg
- 2½ cups HERB STUFFING MIX
- 1 stalk celery, finely chopped
- 1 small onion, finely chopped
- ¼ teaspoon salt
- Paprika

Trim excess fat from pork steaks; cook trimmings in skillet till 1 tablespoon fat accumulates. Discard trimmings. Brown the steaks in hot fat. Sprinkle with salt and pepper. Remove from heat; arrange pork steaks in 13x9x2-inch baking pan. Set aside.

On Handy Grater, grate enough orange peel to make 2 teaspoons; set aside. Squeeze juice from orange; add enough water to make ⅓ cup liquid. In Small Mix-N-Stor® pitcher, combine egg, orange peel, and juice mixture; add Herb Stuffing Mix, chopped celery, onion, and salt. Shape Herb Stuffing mixture into mounds by pressing into a ½-cup Measuring Cup. Place a mound of herb dressing on each pork steak. Cover tightly with foil. Bake in a 350° oven for 1 hour or till meat is tender. Sprinkle Herb Stuffing mounds with a little paprika. Makes 4 servings.

PORK SCHNITZEL

- 6 pork loin cutlets, cut ½ inch thick (about 1 pound)
- ¼ cup all-purpose flour
- ½ teaspoon seasoned salt
- 1 beaten egg
- 2 tablespoons milk
- 2 cups HERB STUFFING MIX, finely crushed
- ¼ cup cooking oil or shortening
- Hot cooked noodles
- 1 2-cup container CHICKEN BROTH (see recipe, page 25)
- ½ cup dairy sour cream
- 3 tablespoons cornstarch
- ¼ teaspoon dried dillweed

Pound pork cutlets to ¼- to ⅛-inch thickness. Cut small slits around edges. Coat meat with mixture of all-purpose flour and seasoned salt. In Stacking Bowl, combine egg and milk; seal and shake vigorously to blend. Dip cutlets in egg mixture, then in crushed Herb Stuffing Mix. In large skillet, cook cutlets, 3 at a time, in 2 tablespoons of the hot oil 2 to 3 minutes on each side or till done. Remove to platter; keep warm. Serve with hot cooked noodles. Spoon some dill sauce over; pass remaining sauce. Makes 6 servings.

For Dill Sauce, in medium saucepan, heat Chicken Broth, covered, over medium heat 10 to 12 minutes or till thawed. In Small Mix-N-Stor pitcher, combine sour cream, cornstarch, and dillweed; gradually stir in about ½ cup of the broth. Return all to saucepan. Cook and stir till thickened and bubbly. Cook and stir 1 to 2 minutes more. Makes 2¼ cups sauce.

HERBED CHICKEN CROQUETTES

Use the Cheese Sauce on page 50 to spoon over the croquettes—

- 1 1½-cup container COOKED CHICKEN, thawed (see recipe, page 25)
- 1 small onion
- 3 tablespoons butter
- ¼ cup all-purpose flour
- ½ cup chicken broth
- ⅓ cup milk
- 1 tablespoon snipped parsley
- 1 teaspoon lemon juice
- 1½ cups HERB STUFFING MIX, finely crushed
- 1 beaten egg
- 2 tablespoons water
- Cooking oil for deep-fat frying

Put the thawed Cooked Chicken and onion through coarse blade of a food grinder; set aside. In saucepan, melt butter; blend in flour. Add chicken broth and milk all at once; cook and stir till thickened and bubbly. Cook and stir 1 to 2 minutes more. Remove from heat. Stir in snipped parsley and the lemon juice. Add the ground chicken mixture; mix well. Turn into a Medium Mixing Bowl; seal and chill thoroughly. With wet hands, shape a scant ⅓ cup of the chilled mixture into a ball. Repeat with remaining mixture to form 8 balls. Roll each chicken ball in crushed Herb Stuffing Mix. Carefully shape each into a cone.

In Small Seal-N-Serve® dish, combine egg and water; seal and shake vigorously to blend. Dip each cone into egg mixture; roll again in crushed Herb Stuffing Mix. Fry 2 or 3 at a time in deep hot fat (365°) or till golden. Drain on paper toweling. Makes 4 servings.

BEEF AND CHEESE STRATA

To make your meal complete, serve hot cooked broccoli spears with the cheese-rich casserole—

    6 ounces sharp American
      or Swiss cheese
2½ cups HERB STUFFING
      MIX
    1 2.5-ounce package sliced
      smoked beef, snipped
    3 eggs
1¾ cups milk
    2 tablespoons finely
      chopped onion
    ½ teaspoon prepared
      mustard
    ⅛ teaspoon pepper
      Paprika

Shred cheese on Grater Bowl or Handy Grater. Layer half the Herb Stuffing Mix, all the cheese, and the snipped smoked beef in the bottom of a 10x6x2-inch baking pan. Top with remaining Herb Stuffing Mix.

In a Small Mix-N-Stor pitcher, beat eggs; blend in milk, chopped onion, mustard, and pepper. Pour mixture in baking pan. Sprinkle with paprika. Cover and let stand 1 hour at room temperature or several hours in the refrigerator.

Bake, uncovered, in a 325° oven about 1 hour or until knife inserted near center comes out clean. Let stand 5 minutes before serving. Makes 4 servings.

ZUCCHINI-CHICKEN CASSEROLE

    4 medium zucchini, halved
      lengthwise and cut
      into ½-inch-thick slices
    1 medium onion, chopped
    1 large carrot, shredded
    ¼ cup butter or margarine
2½ cups HERB STUFFING
      MIX
    1 1½-cup container
      COOKED CHICKEN,
      thawed (see recipe,
      page 25)
    1 10¾-ounce can condensed
      cream of chicken soup
    ½ cup dairy sour cream
    2 tablespoons butter

Cook zucchini in a little boiling, salted water till tender; drain. In saucepan, cook onion and carrot in the ¼ cup butter or margarine till tender but not brown. Remove from heat; stir in 1½ cups of the Herb Stuffing Mix, the thawed Cooked Chicken, soup, and sour cream. Gently stir in zucchini. Turn into 2-quart casserole. Melt the remaining 2 tablespoons butter; add remaining Herb Stuffing cubes. Toss gently; sprinkle over top of casserole. Bake, uncovered, in 350° oven for 30 to 40 minutes. Serves 6.

CRISPY BAKED CHICKEN

    1 2½- to 3-pound broiler-
      fryer chicken, cut up
    ½ cup milk
1½ cups HERB STUFFING
      MIX, finely crushed

Brush chicken pieces with milk. Pat crushed Herb Stuffing Mix onto each piece; shake off excess crumbs. Place chicken pieces, skin side up, in a lightly greased 15½x10x1-inch baking pan. Bake in 375° oven about 1 hour or till chicken tests done. Makes 4 servings.

ROAST HERB CHICKEN

    ½ cup chopped onion
    ¼ cup butter or margarine
    ½ teaspoon poultry
      seasoning
    4 cups HERB STUFFING
      MIX
    ½ cup chicken broth or water
    1 4- to 5-pound roasting
      chicken
      Cooking oil

Cook onion in butter till tender. In Large Mixing Bowl, add cooked onion and poultry seasoning to Stuffing Mix; drizzle with broth and toss. Rinse chicken; pat dry. Pull neck skin to back; secure. Spoon stuffing into body cavity; do not pack. Tie legs to tail. Twist wing tips under back.

Place bird, breast side up, on rack in shallow roasting pan. Brush with oil. Roast in 375° oven for 2 to 2½ hours. Baste occasionally with pan drippings. Makes 4 servings.

ZIPPY STUFFED FRANKS

Pictured on page 10—

    ¼ cup chopped onion
    1 tablespoon butter
    3 cups HERB STUFFING
      MIX, coarsely crushed
    ¼ cup catsup
    1 tablespoon pickle relish
    ¾ cup water
    1 pound (4) large frankfurters
    3 slices American cheese,
      cut into strips

Cook onion in butter till tender. In Medium Mixing Bowl, combine crushed Herb Stuffing Mix, onion, catsup, pickle relish, and water. Cut franks lengthwise almost to opposite side. Mound stuffing mixture in franks. Place on baking sheet. Bake in 400° oven for 10 to 12 minutes. Place cheese strips atop. Return to oven; bake 3 minutes or till cheese melts. Makes 4 servings.

START WITH CREAMY SAUCE MIX

CREAMY SAUCE MIX

- 1⅓ cups nonfat dry milk powder
- ¾ cup all-purpose flour
- 1 teaspoon salt
- ½ cup butter

In Medium Mixing Bowl, combine milk powder, flour, and 1 teaspoon *salt*. Cut in butter till crumbly. Transfer to Midi-Canister or Shelf Saver® container; apply Seal. Refrigerate till needed. Makes 3 cups.

For Medium White Sauce, in saucepan, combine ½ cup *Creamy Sauce Mix* and 1 cup *cold water*. Cook and stir till bubbly. Cook and stir 2 minutes more. Makes 1 cup.

For Cheese Sauce, in saucepan, combine ½ cup *Creamy Sauce Mix* and 1 cup *cold water*. Cook and stir till bubbly. Add 1 cup shredded *American cheese* and stir till melted. Makes 1¼ cups.

SPUNKY CREAM SAUCE

- ½ cup CREAMY SAUCE MIX
- 1 teaspoon instant chicken bouillon granules
- 1 cup cold water
- 2 teaspoons snipped chives
- 1 teaspoon prepared mustard
- 1 teaspoon prepared horseradish
- 1 teaspoon lemon juice

In a small saucepan, stir together Creamy Sauce Mix and bouillon granules. Stir in cold water. Cook and stir over medium heat till thickened. Add chives, mustard, horseradish, and lemon juice. Cook and stir 2 minutes more. Makes 1⅓ cups.

FISH ROLL-UPS WITH CHEESE SAUCE

- 1 pound fresh or frozen perch or other fish fillets
  Boiling water
  Spunky Cream Sauce (see recipe at left)
- 2 ounces Swiss cheese or Monterey Jack cheese
- 2 tablespoons fresh snipped parsley
- ¼ teaspoon paprika
  Cooked green beans (optional)

Thaw fish, if frozen. Roll up fish fillets; secure with a wooden pick. Place on strainer insert of Multi-Server™ container; put insert in serving dish. Slowly pour in enough boiling water to cover fish. Cover the container and let stand on the counter for 10 minutes.

Meanwhile, prepare Spunky Cream Sauce and cheese topping. For cheese topping, grate cheese on Handy Grater. Remove grater; add parsley and paprika. Apply storage Seal and shake to blend.

When fish flakes with a fork, remove strainer from Multi-Server container and drain fish. Place fillets on a heat-proof platter. Pour Spunky Cream Sauce and sprinkle cheese topping over. Place under broiler for 2 to 3 minutes or until cheese is melted and bubbly. Serve with cooked green beans, if desired. Makes 4 servings.

ELEGANT CREAMED CHICKEN

For a more elegant dinner, serve this over hot cooked noodles and pass fresh grated Parmesan cheese—

- 1 1½-cup container COOKED CHICKEN (see recipe, page 25)
- ¼ cup chopped onion
- ¼ cup water
- 1 cup CREAMY SAUCE MIX
- 1½ cups cold water
- 2 teaspoons instant chicken bouillon granules
- ½ cup thinly sliced celery
- ¼ cup sliced pimiento-stuffed olives
- 3 English muffins, split and toasted or toast points
  Snipped parsley

In saucepan, heat frozen Cooked Chicken, onion, and the ¼ cup water over medium-low heat for 10 to 12 minutes or till chicken is thawed. Stir occasionally to break up chicken. In Small Mix-N-Stor® pitcher, combine Sauce Mix and the 1½ cups cold water; add to saucepan mixture along with chicken bouillon granules. Cook and stir till thickened and bubbly; cook and stir 1 to 2 minutes more. Add sliced celery and pimiento-stuffed olives; heat through. Season to taste with pepper. Spoon over toasted English muffin halves or toast points. Sprinkle with parsley. Makes 6 servings.

Poach rolled fish fillets in a Tupperware Multi-Server container in only 10 minutes. The topping for Fish Roll-Ups With Cheese Sauce starts with our no-fail Creamy Sauce Mix.

START WITH CREAMY SAUCE MIX

HAM AND CHEESE CASSEROLE

- 1½ cups elbow macaroni
- 2 cups water
- 1⅓ cups CREAMY SAUCE MIX
- 2 ounces American cheese, shredded (½ cup)
- 1 teaspoon prepared mustard
- 2 beaten egg yolks
- 8 ounces fully cooked ham, diced
- 1 cup cream-style cottage cheese
- 1 medium dill pickle, finely chopped
- 1½ cups soft bread crumbs
- 2 tablespoons butter or margarine, melted

Cook macaroni in a large amount of boiling, salted water till tender, about 10 minutes. Drain in 1-qt. Strainer.

In saucepan, slowly blend 2 cups cold water into Creamy Sauce Mix. Cook and stir till thickened and bubbly. Cook and stir 1 to 2 minutes more. Add shredded cheese and mustard; cook and stir till cheese melts. Stir a moderate amount of hot mixture into beaten egg yolks; return to remaining hot mixture. Cook and stir till bubbly. Remove from heat. Stir in macaroni, ham, cottage cheese, and pickle. Turn into 2-quart casserole. Combine crumbs and melted butter or margarine in a Small Wonderlier® bowl; apply Seal. Shake till crumbs are coated. Sprinkle crumbs atop casserole. Bake in 350° oven for 40 to 50 minutes. Makes 8 servings.

EGGS BENEDICT-STYLE

- Mock Hollandaise Sauce (see recipe below)
- 1 7-ounce can luncheon meat
- 2 tablespoons butter
- 4 eggs
- 2 teaspoons water
- 2 English muffins, split and toasted

Prepare Mock Hollandaise Sauce and keep warm over low heat. Slice luncheon meat into 8 thin slices. Warm in an 8-inch skillet over low heat.

Meanwhile, in 10-inch skillet that has a tight fitting lid, melt butter. Carefully add eggs; season with some salt and pepper. When egg whites are set and edges are cooked, add water. Cover skillet and continue cooking until yolks are almost set.

To serve, place 1 toasted muffin half on serving plate. Arrange 2 slices luncheon meat and 1 cooked egg atop. Pour about ¼ cup sauce over. Repeat for remaining. Makes 4 servings.

MOCK HOLLANDAISE SAUCE

- ¼ cup CREAMY SAUCE MIX
- ¾ cup cold water
- 2 egg yolks
- 1 tablespoon lemon juice
  Dash paprika

In small saucepan, stir together Creamy Sauce Mix and cold water. Cook and stir over low heat until thickened and bubbly. Slightly beat the egg yolks; stir about half the cooked mixture into egg yolks. Return egg yolk mixture to saucepan. Bring to boiling. Cook and stir 1 to 2 minutes more. Remove from heat; stir in lemon juice and paprika. Makes ¾ cup.

SWISS BEEF BAKE

- 2 medium onions, cut into wedges
- 1 pound ground beef
- ⅔ cup CREAMY SAUCE MIX
- 1 teaspoon instant beef bouillon granules
- 1¼ cups cold water
- 1½ cups HERB STUFFING MIX (see recipe, page 45)
- ½ cup HERB STUFFING MIX, crushed
- 1 tablespoon butter or margarine, melted
- 2 ounces Swiss cheese

In skillet, cook onions and beef till meat is browned and onions are tender. Drain off fat. To skillet add Creamy Sauce Mix and bouillon granules. Blend water slowly into meat mixture. Cook and stir till thickened and bubbly; cook and stir 1 to 2 minutes more. Remove from heat. Stir in 1½ cups of the Herb Stuffing Mix. Turn into a 1½-quart casserole. In a Small Wonderlier Bowl, combine crushed Herb Stuffing Mix and melted butter or margarine. Apply Seal and shake till mixed. Sprinkle atop casserole. Bake, uncovered, in 350° oven for 20 minutes. Shred cheese on Grater Bowl or Handy-Grater; sprinkle atop casserole and bake 2 to 3 minutes more or till cheese melts. Makes 4 servings.

TURKEY BISCUIT RING

- 1 small onion, chopped
- 1 small stalk celery, chopped
- 1 tablespoon butter
- ⅓ cup CREAMY SAUCE MIX
- 2 cups cold water
- 2 cups finely chopped cooked turkey
- 2 cups HEARTY WHEAT MASTER MIX (see recipe, page 67)
- 2 tablespoons snipped parsley
- ½ cup CREAMY SAUCE MIX
- 1 teaspoon instant chicken bouillon granules
- 2 tablespoons diced pimiento

In saucepan, cook onion and celery in butter till tender. Combine the ⅓ cup Creamy Sauce Mix and ½ cup of the water; add to saucepan. Cook and stir till thickened and bubbly; cook and stir 1 to 2 minutes more. Remove from heat. Stir in turkey; set aside. In Medium Mixing Bowl, combine Hearty Wheat Master Mix and parsley; add ½ cup water. Stir till dough follows fork around bowl. On floured pastry sheet, knead dough 10 to 12 times; roll or pat to a 12x8-inch rectangle. Spread turkey mixture over dough. Roll jelly-roll style, starting at long end. Form into a ring on a greased baking sheet; pinch to seal. Make cuts at 2-inch intervals to, but not through, bottom of ring. Bake in 400° oven for 20 to 25 minutes. In small saucepan, combine the remaining ½ cup Sauce Mix, remaining 1 cup water, and the bouillon granules. Cook and stir till thickened and bubbly; cook and stir 1 to 2 minutes more. Add pimiento. Pass sauce. Serves 6.

CURRIED TURKEY OPEN-FACED SANDWICHES

Pictured on page 11—

- 1 medium apple
  Lemon juice
- 8 slices cooked turkey or chicken
- ⅓ cup CREAMY SAUCE MIX
- 1 to 1½ teaspoons curry powder
- ½ teaspoon instant chicken bouillon granules
- ⅔ cup water
- ¼ cup dairy sour cream
- 4 slices French bread, or other sliced bread, toasted
  Toasted coconut (optional)

Core and cut apple into 12 wedges; brush with lemon juice. In skillet, heat turkey slices in a small amount of water, covered, about 5 minutes, turning once.

Meanwhile, in small saucepan, combine Creamy Sauce Mix, curry powder, and chicken bouillon granules; stir in water. Cook and stir till thickened and bubbly; cook and stir 1 to 2 minutes more. Place sour cream in Refrigerator Bowl; gradually stir about half of the hot mixture into sour cream. Return all to saucepan. Heat through over low heat. Do not boil. To serve, place two turkey slices and three apple wedges atop each bread slice. Spoon sauce over. Sprinkle with toasted coconut, if desired. Makes 4 sandwiches.

CHICKEN DIVAN

- 2 10-ounce packages frozen cut broccoli
- ¾ cup CREAMY SAUCE MIX
- 1 teaspoon instant chicken bouillon granules
  Dash ground nutmeg
- 1 cup water
- 1 tablespoon lemon juice
- 1 teaspoon Worcestershire sauce
- 2 cups cooked chicken cut into julienne strips
- ½ cup grated Parmesan cheese
- ½ cup whipping cream
- ½ cup mayonnaise or salad dressing
  Paprika

Cook broccoli according to package directions; drain well. Arrange broccoli in a 12x7½x2-inch baking dish. In saucepan, combine Sauce Mix, bouillon granules, and nutmeg; stir in water. Cook and stir till thickened and bubbly; cook and stir 1 to 2 minutes more. Remove from heat; stir in lemon juice and Worcestershire sauce. Pour half of the sauce over broccoli. Sprinkle with about ⅓ of the cheese. Top with chicken and remaining sauce mixture. Sprinkle with another ⅓ of the cheese. Bake, uncovered, at 350° till heated through, about 20 minutes. Place cream in a Small Mix-N-Stor® pitcher; whip with rotary beater just till soft peaks form; fold in mayonnaise. Spread over all. Top with remaining cheese; sprinkle with paprika. Broil 4 inches from heat till golden, about 2 minutes. Makes 6 servings.

START WITH CREAMY SAUCE MIX

CAULIFLOWER-HAM CHOWDER

- 1 2-cup container CHICKEN BROTH (see recipe, page 25)
- 1 10-ounce package frozen cauliflower
- ½ of a small green pepper, chopped
- 1 10½-ounce can condensed cream of potato soup
- ¾ cup CREAMY SAUCE MIX
- 1 cup water
- 8 ounces fully cooked ham, diced
  HERB STUFFING MIX (see recipe, page 45), optional

In a saucepan, heat frozen Chicken Broth over medium-low heat about 15 minutes, stirring occasionally till thawed; bring to boiling. Pour over frozen cauliflower in Multi-Server™; lift insert to drain, reserving Broth. Cut up any large pieces of the cauliflower. Add cauliflower and chopped green pepper to hot Chicken Broth.

In Small Mix-N-Stor® pitcher, combine canned potato soup and the Creamy Sauce Mix; blend in the water. Add to vegetable mixture in saucepan. Cook and stir till thickened and bubbly. Stir in ham; heat through. Serve in four Small Seal-N-Serve® bowls or in Stacking Bowls. Sprinkle each serving with some of the Herb Stuffing Mix bread cubes, if desired. Makes 4 servings.

SWEET-SOUR CHICKEN MOLD

To quick-set gelatin mixture, place the Medium Mixing Bowl in the Large Mixing Bowl filled with ice water; stir mixture frequently—

- ¼ cup CREAMY SAUCE MIX
- ½ cup cold water
- ½ cup dairy sour cream
- 1 3-ounce package lemon-flavored gelatin
- 1¼ cups water
- 1 tablespoon lemon juice
- ½ teaspoon dried dillweed
- 1 small carrot, finely chopped
- 1 1½-cup container COOKED CHICKEN, thawed and finely chopped (see recipe, page 25)

In saucepan, combine Creamy Sauce Mix and the ½ cup cold water. Cook and stir till thickened and bubbly; cook and stir 1 to 2 minutes more. Remove from heat; stir in sour cream. Turn mixture into Medium Mixing Bowl; set aside. In same saucepan, combine gelatin and remaining water; heat and stir till gelatin dissolves. Blend gelatin mixture into sour cream mixture; add lemon juice and dillweed. Chill till partially set. Stir carrot and the chicken into partially set gelatin mixture. Turn into the Jel-N-Serve® mold. Chill till firm. Unmold onto Jel-N-Serve tray. Makes 4 servings.

CREAMY HAM SLAW

Ham and cheese turn this homemade cabbage slaw into a main dish salad—

- ¼ cup CREAMY SAUCE MIX
- ½ teaspoon dry mustard
- 1 cup milk
- 2 tablespoons vinegar
- 1 tablespoon lemon juice
- ½ of a small head green cabbage
- ¼ of a small head red cabbage
- 2 cups cubed fully cooked ham or one 6½-ounce can tuna, drained and flaked
- 6 ounces cheddar or Swiss cheese, cut into ½-inch cubes.

For dressing, in a saucepan, combine the Creamy Sauce Mix and dry mustard. Add milk; cook and stir till thickened and bubbly. Remove from heat. Stir in vinegar and lemon juice; chill in Refrigerator Bowl.

Shred cabbage on slicer blade of Grater Bowl. Remove grater. Add cubed ham or tuna and cheese to cabbage mixture in Grater Bowl. Pour the chilled dressing over. Apply storage Seal and turn several times to coat all ingredients. Place in refrigerator and chill several hours or overnight. Makes 4 servings.

The Tupperware Grater Bowl lets you shred, mix, and store Creamy Ham Slaw all in one bowl. The dressing begins with Creamy Sauce Mix.

START WITH EASY EGG PASTRY

EASY EGG PASTRY

- 3 cups flour
- 1 cup lard or shortening
- 1 egg
- ⅓ cup water
- 1 teaspoon vinegar

Place flour and ½ teaspoon *salt* in a Medium Mixing Bowl. Apply Seal; shake to blend.

Cut lard into flour mixture till it resembles small peas. Combine egg, water, and vinegar till blended. Make a well in dry ingredients; pour in egg mixture. Apply Seal to Mixing Bowl and shake vigorously till mixture forms a ball. Divide dough into thirds.

To make Pastry Crusts: Use Pastry Sheet and Rolling Pin to roll one portion of dough to fit a 9-inch metal pie plate. Crimp edges. Prick bottom and sides. Bake in 450° oven 12 minutes.

To make and use Frozen Pastry Crusts: Roll out dough and fit into a 9-inch pie plate as above. To store, place in 12″ Pie Taker; apply Seal and freeze. After removing from freezer, prick bottom and sides. Bake in 450° oven 12 to 15 minutes.

To make unrolled Frozen Pastry: Place one portion of dough in a Refrigerator Bowl. Label with date and contents; freeze. Use one Refrigerator Bowl portion when a recipe specifies Easy Egg Pastry for Single-Crust Pie. Use two portions when a recipe specifies Easy Egg Pastry for Double-Crust Pie.

COTTAGE CHEESE AND TUNA TURNOVERS

- 1 beaten egg
- 1 cup dry cottage cheese
- ½ cup chopped celery
- ¼ cup chopped carrot
- ¼ teaspoon salt
- ¼ teaspoon dried dillweed
- 1 9¼-ounce can tuna, drained and flaked
  EASY EGG PASTRY for a Double-Crust Pie
- ⅓ cup CREAMY SAUCE MIX (see recipe, page 50)
- ⅔ cup cold water
- ½ teaspoon dried dillweed

In a small bowl, combine the egg, cottage cheese, celery, carrot, salt, ¼ teaspoon dillweed, and dash *pepper*. Mix well. Fold in tuna and set aside. On lightly floured Pastry Sheet with Rolling Pin, roll one portion of the Easy Egg Pastry to an 8-inch square. Trim edges. Spoon half the filling over half the dough to within ½ inch of edge. Brush edges with a little milk; fold other half of pastry over filling. Press edges together and flute. Repeat with remaining dough and filling. Transfer rectangles to 15x10x1-inch baking pan. Brush tops with a little milk. Prick or slit tops. Bake in 300° oven for 30 minutes. Meanwhile, prepare sauce. In saucepan, thoroughly combine the Creamy Sauce Mix, cold water, and ½ teaspoon dillweed; cook and stir over medium heat till mixture is thickened and bubbly. Cook and stir 1 to 2 minutes more. Pass sauce with pies. Makes 6 servings.

REUBEN TRIANGLES

- 4 ounces Monterey Jack cheese
- 1 7-ounce can corned beef
- 1 8-ounce can sauerkraut, drained
- ¼ teaspoon caraway seed
  EASY EGG PASTRY for Double-Crust Pie
  Thousand Island Sauce

Shred cheese on Grater Bowl. Remove grater. Stir in flaked corned beef, sauerkraut, and caraway. Set aside. Use Pastry Sheet and Rolling Pin to roll one portion of pastry to a 13½x9-inch rectangle. Cut dough into six 4½-inch squares. Place ¼ cup meat mixture in center of each square. Fold half of pastry over filling to form a triangle. Seal. Repeat with remaining pastry and filling. Place on a greased 15x10x1-inch baking pan. Bake in 375° oven 40 minutes. Pass Thousand Island Sauce. Serves 6.

THOUSAND ISLAND SAUCE

- ½ cup CREAMY SAUCE MIX (see recipe, page 50)
- ½ teaspoon dry mustard
- 1 hard-cooked egg, chopped
- 2 tablespoons chopped pimiento-stuffed olives
- 1 tablespoon vinegar
- 1 tablespoon catsup
- 1 tablespoon finely chopped onion
- 1 teaspoon horseradish

In saucepan, combine Creamy Sauce Mix and mustard. Add 1 cup *water*; cook and stir till bubbly. Stir in remaining ingredients. Heat through. Makes 1⅓ cups.

The Tupperware Rolling Pin and Pastry Sheet help you roll out the Easy Egg Pastry to just the right dimensions. Cut decorative slits in the top of Cottage Cheese and Tuna Turnover before baking.

START WITH EASY EGG PASTRY

PINEAPPLE PORK PIE

  EASY EGG PASTRY for
  Double-Crust Pie
1½ pounds ground pork
1 small onion, chopped
1 10¾-ounce can
  condensed cream of
  mushroom soup
1 4-ounce can sliced
  mushrooms, drained
1 teaspoon salt
½ teaspoon dried thyme,
  crushed
¼ teaspoon pepper
1 20-ounce can pineapple
  slices
3 tablespoons brown sugar

Divide pastry into six portions. On floured Pastry Sheet with Rolling Pin, roll each portion of pastry to a 7-inch circle. Fit pastry into six 5-inch tart pans; press out bubbles. Do not prick. Flute edges.

In skillet, cook ground pork and onion till meat is brown and onion is tender. Drain off excess fat. Add soup, drained mushrooms, salt, dried thyme, and pepper to meat mixture in skillet; mix well. Spoon mixture into tart shells; top each tart shell with a pineapple slice. (Chill and save remaining fruit and juice in a Refrigerator Bowl for another use.) Sprinkle brown sugar atop each tart. Bake in 375° oven about 25 minutes or till pastry is golden brown. Makes 6 servings.

CORNISH BEEF PASTRIES

1 medium potato, peeled
  and chopped
⅔ cup chopped turnip,
  carrot, or rutabaga
½ cup chopped onion
1 pound beef round steak,
  cut into ¼-inch cubes
1 teaspoon salt
¼ teaspoon pepper
  EASY EGG PASTRY for
  Double-Crust Pie
  Milk
1 tablespoon sesame or
  poppy seed
  Catsup

Place potato, turnip, and onion in Medium Mixing Bowl with beef cubes. Add salt and pepper to beef mixture; mix well. Set aside.

Divide dough into five portions. Using Pastry Sheet and Rolling Pin, roll out each portion to a 7-inch circle. Place about ⅔ cup of the beef-vegetable filling in the center of each circle; bring sides of pastry over filling. Pinch edges to seal. Cut slits in pastry for escape of steam. Brush pastry lightly with milk and sprinkle with sesame or poppy seed. Carefully transfer pastries to an ungreased baking sheet. Bake in 375° oven for 35 to 40 minutes or till golden brown. Serve with catsup, if desired. Makes 5 servings.

MEAT LOAF-IN-A BLANKET

Pictured on page 10—

1 beaten egg
2 cups soft bread crumbs
2 tablespoons finely
  chopped onion
¼ teaspoon dried basil or
  thyme, crushed
1½ pounds lean ground
  beef
  EASY EGG PASTRY for
  Double-Crust Pie
1 beaten egg
⅓ cup CREAMY SAUCE MIX
  (see recipe, page 50)
1 teaspoon instant
  chicken bouillon
  granules
½ teaspoon dried dillweed
½ cup dairy sour cream

Combine one egg, bread crumbs, onion, basil, 1 teaspoon *salt*, and ½ cup *water*. Add beef; mix well. Pat into 8½x4½x2½-inch loaf pan. Bake in 350° oven 40 minutes. Drain. Turn oven temperature to 400°. Use Pastry Sheet and Rolling Pin to roll Easy Egg Pastry to a 16x12 inch rectangle. Trim to 12x11 inches. Turn meat loaf top side down in middle of pastry. Bring sides and ends up; seal, brushing edges with some of remaining beaten egg. Place in shallow greased baking pan. Decorate with cutouts of dough. Brush remaining beaten egg over all. Bake in 400° oven for 30 to 35 minutes. Meanwhile, combine Sauce Mix, bouillon, and dillweed. Stir in ⅔ cup cold *water*. Cook and stir till thickened. Cook and stir 2 minutes more. Gradually stir about half the sauce into sour cream; return all to saucepan. Heat through. Serve with meat. Serves 6.

GOULASH PIE

- 2 cups cubed cooked beef, lamb, or pork
- 2 cups peeled and chopped rutabaga
- 3 large carrots, chopped
- 1 large onion, chopped
- 1 tablespoon chopped parsley
- 1½ cups water
- ½ cup apple juice
- 1 teaspoon salt
- ¼ teaspoon dried marjoram, crushed
- ¼ teaspoon dried thyme, crushed
- ½ cup cold water
- ¼ cup all-purpose flour
- 1 teaspoon Kitchen Bouquet (optional)
  EASY EGG PASTRY for Single-Crust Pie

In large saucepan, combine meat cubes, rutabaga, carrots, onion, parsley, the 1½ cups water, the apple juice, salt, marjoram, and thyme; blend well. Cover and simmer about 15 minutes. Blend the ½ cup cold water into flour; stir into meat mixture. Cook, stirring constantly, till thickened and bubbly. Stir in Kitchen Bouquet, if desired. Keep hot. Using Pastry Sheet and Rolling Pin, roll out pastry to a 9-inch circle. Pour meat mixture into a 2-quart casserole. Place pastry atop hot mixture, crimping edges to sides of the casserole. Cut slits for the escape of steam. Bake in a 375° oven for 35 to 40 minutes or till pastry is golden. Let stand 10 minutes. Sprinkle with additional snipped parsley, if desired. Makes 6 servings.

CHILI-BEEF CUPS

- EASY EGG PASTRY for Double-Crust Pie
- 1 pound ground beef or ground pork
- 1 8-ounce can kidney beans
- 1 15¼-ounce can Mexican-style sandwich sauce
- ¼ cup water
- 4 ounces cheddar, Monterey Jack, or American cheese, shredded (1 cup)
  Shredded lettuce
  Chopped tomato

Using Pastry Sheet and Rolling Pin, roll out pastry, half at a time, to ⅛-inch thickness. Cut each half into five 4½-inch circles (reroll scraps, if needed.) Fit the dough circles over inverted muffin cups, pinching pleats at intervals to fit around the cups. Prick pastry with a fork.

Bake in a 450° oven for 7 to 10 minutes or till golden brown. Cool on a wire rack.

In a skillet, brown meat; drain off excess fat. Stir in kidney beans, Mexican-style sandwich sauce, and water; heat to boiling. With metal spatula, remove tarts from pans. Fill tarts with the hot meat-bean sauce. Sprinkle shredded cheese, lettuce, and chopped tomato atop each beef cup. Makes 5 servings.

TUNA CHEESE TARTS

- EASY EGG PASTRY for Double-Crust Pie
- 1 cup CREAMY SAUCE MIX (see recipe, page 50)
- 1⅓ cups cold water
- ½ teaspoon Worcestershire sauce
- ⅓ cup grated Parmesan cheese
- 1 6½-ounce can tuna, drained
- ¼ cup finely chopped celery
- 2 tablespoons chopped pimiento
  Paprika (optional)

Divide each half of Easy Egg Pastry into thirds. Use Pastry Sheet and Rolling Pin to roll each portion to tart size. Fit each circle to a 4¼-inch pie plate. Prick tarts well. Bake in a 450° oven for 7 to 10 minutes or till golden brown; cool tarts on a wire rack.

Meanwhile, in a saucepan, combine the Creamy Sauce Mix, water, and Worcestershire sauce; cook and stir over medium heat till mixture is thickened and bubbly. Cook and stir 1 to 2 minutes more. Stir in grated Parmesan cheese. Cook over low heat 1 minute more or till cheese melts. Add tuna, celery, and pimiento to cheese mixture. Heat through. Spoon tuna mixture into baked pastry shells. Sprinkle with paprika, if desired. Makes 6 servings.

START WITH EASY EGG PASTRY

SWISS AND FRANK QUICHE

EASY EGG PASTRY for Single-Crust Pie
- ¼ cup chopped onion
- 1 tablespoon butter or margarine
- 5 or 6 frankfurters, thinly sliced
- 4 ounces Swiss, Monterey Jack, or American cheese, shredded (1 cup)
- 3 slightly beaten eggs
- 1½ cups milk
- 1 teaspoon dry mustard
- ½ teaspoon salt
- ¼ teaspoon ground nutmeg
  Dash pepper

Using Pastry Sheet and Rolling Pin, roll pastry to a 12-inch circle. Place in a 9-inch pie plate; flute edge. Line pastry with foil; fill with dry beans. Bake in 450° oven for 7 minutes. Remove pastry shell from oven; reduce oven temperature to 325°.

Meanwhile, in a small skillet, cook the chopped onion in butter or margarine till tender but not brown. Place sliced frankfurters, shredded cheese, and cooked onion in baked pastry shell. In a Small Mix-N-Stor® pitcher, combine the eggs, milk, dry mustard, salt, ground nutmeg, and pepper. Pour mixture into pie shell. Bake pie in 325° oven for 35 to 40 minutes or till knife inserted near center comes out clean. Let stand 10 minutes before serving. Cut into wedges. Makes 6 servings.

HAM 'N APPLE TRIANGLES

Pack any leftover triangles in Square Rounds® containers. They're ideal "sandwiches" for kids' lunches—

EASY EGG PASTRY for Double-Crust Pie
- 10 ounces fully cooked ham or turkey, cut into ¼-inch cubes (2 cups)
- 1 8½-ounce can applesauce
- ¼ cup catsup
  Milk
- 1 tablespoon catsup

On lightly floured Pastry Sheet, use Rolling Pin to roll both portions of pastry together to make a 15x10-inch rectangle.

Cut rectangle into six 5x5-inch squares. Place ⅓ cup of the ham or turkey in the center of each pastry square. In a small bowl, combine 2 tablespoons of the applesauce and the ¼ cup catsup. Spoon applesauce mixture over meat on each square.

For each turnover, carefully bring corners of pastry together to form a triangle; pinch edges together to seal, moistening edges with a little water, if necessary. Place triangles on an ungreased baking sheet. Brush lightly with some milk. Bake in a 400° oven for 12 to 15 minutes or till golden.

Meanwhile, in saucepan, combine the remaining applesauce and remaining catsup; heat through. Pass hot applesauce mixture to serve atop turnovers. Makes 6 servings.

ITALIAN QUICHE

EASY EGG PASTRY for Double-Crust Pie
- 4 ounces bulk Italian sausage
- 3 eggs
- 1 cup ricotta or cream-style cottage cheese
- 4 ounces mozzarella cheese, shredded (1 cup)
- ½ cup sliced pepperoni, halved
- ½ cup cubed prosciutto or fully cooked ham
- ¼ cup grated Parmesan cheese
- 1 beaten egg
- 2 tablespoons milk

On floured Pastry Sheet with Rolling Pin, roll one portion of the pastry to a 12-inch circle. Fit the pastry circle into a 9-inch pie plate. Trim to ½ inch beyond edge of pie plate. Fold under and flute edge; do not prick crust. Bake in 450° oven for 5 minutes. Remove from oven; reduce oven temperature to 350°. Cook the Italian sausage till browned; drain off excess fat. Place the 3 eggs and the ricotta cheese in the Large Mix-N-Stor pitcher; beat together. Fold in the shredded mozzarella, sliced pepperoni, cubed ham, grated Parmesan, and the drained Italian sausage. Turn into pastry shell.

On lightly floured Pastry Sheet, roll remaining pastry dough to an 8-inch circle; cut into 6 wedges. Arrange wedges atop filling. Bake in 350° oven for 20 minutes. Combine the 1 beaten egg and milk; brush over wedges. Bake about 20 minutes more or till golden. Let stand 10 minutes. Makes 6 serving.

BEEF STEAK PIE

Brush the pastry topping with milk before baking to give it a golden brown color —

- 1½ pounds beef round steak, cut into 1-inch cubes
- ¼ cup all-purpose flour
- 1 large onion, chopped
- 2 tablespoons shortening
- 2 cups water
- 1 teaspoon salt
- ¼ teaspoon dried thyme, crushed
- ⅛ teaspoon pepper
- 2 cups diced raw potato
  EASY EGG PASTRY for Single-Crust Pie
  Milk

Place beef cubes and flour in the Medium Mixing Bowl; apply Seal. Shake well to coat meat. In large skillet, cook beef and onion in shortening till beef is browned and onion is tender. Add water, salt, thyme, and pepper to skillet. Cover; simmer 1½ hours. Add diced raw potato; cover and simmer 20 minutes. Turn meat into a 1½-quart casserole; season to taste with salt and pepper. Roll out Easy Egg Pastry on lightly floured Pastry Sheet with Rolling Pin to a circle that is ½ to 1 inch larger than casserole. Place pastry over hot mixture; seal to edge of casserole. Cut slits in pastry for escape of steam. Brush pastry with milk. Bake in 450° oven till golden, about 15 minutes. Makes 6 servings.

CHICKEN POT PIE

- 1 10-ounce package frozen mixed vegetables or one 16-ounce can mixed vegetables, drained
- ¼ cup chopped onion
- ¼ cup butter
- ¼ cup all-purpose flour
- 2 teaspoons instant chicken bouillon granules
- ½ teaspoon salt
- ¼ teaspoon dried thyme, crushed
- ¼ teaspoon ground sage
  Dash pepper
- 1⅓ cups milk
- 2 cups cubed cooked chicken or turkey
- 2 tablespoons snipped parsley
  EASY EGG PASTRY for Single-Crust Pie

Cook frozen vegetables according to package directions. Drain cooked or canned vegetables, reserving liquid. Add enough water to liquid to make 1 cup; set aside.

In skillet, cook onion in butter till onion is tender but not brown. Blend in flour, chicken bouillon granules, salt, thyme, sage, and pepper. Add the milk and reserved vegetable liquid. Cook and stir till thickened and bubbly. Cook and stir 1 to 2 minutes more. Stir in cubed chicken or turkey, mixed vegetables, and parsley; keep warm.

Use Rolling Pin and Pastry Sheet to roll Easy Egg Pastry to a 9-inch circle. Pour the hot chicken mixture into a 2-quart casserole. Place pastry atop hot filling, crimping edges to sides of casserole. Cut slits in top for escape of steam.

Bake in 375° oven for 35 to 40 minutes or till crust is golden. Let stand 10 minutes before serving. Serves 6.

CORN RAREBIT OVER PASTRY SQUARES

- EASY EGG PASTRY for Single-Crust Pie
- ½ cup chopped green pepper
- ¼ cup chopped onion
- 2 tablespoons butter or margarine
- 1 tablespoon all-purpose flour
- ¼ teaspoon chili powder
- 1 cup tomato juice
- 1 8-ounce can whole kernel corn, drained
- 4 ounces American, cheddar, Monterey Jack, or process Swiss cheese, shredded (1 cup)
- ½ cup sliced pitted ripe olives

For Pastry Squares, using lightly floured Pastry Sheet and Rolling Pin, roll out Pastry to ⅛-inch thickness. Using a straight edge ruler, cut with a pastry wheel or table knife into 2-inch squares. Place on a baking sheet. Bake in a 450° oven for 6 to 8 minutes or till golden.

Meanwhile, in saucepan, cook green pepper and onion in butter or margarine till tender but not brown. Add flour and chili powder; stir to blend. Stir in tomato juice and drained corn. Cook, stirring constantly, till thickened and bubbly. Stir in shredded cheese by handfuls; cook and stir over low heat till cheese is melted. Stir in olives. Place about one quarter of the pastry squares on each of 4 plates. Spoon rarebit over pastry. Makes 4 servings.

Skip-a-Step BAKING

Now you can serve your family home-baked breads, cookies and cakes, and pies and cobblers any day of the week. You'll discover how to short-cut the time-consuming "scratch" method with the time-saving techniques and step-saving recipes included in this chapter. The recipes couldn't be simpler, or the results more delicious!

Pictured clockwise from bottom left are: Spicy Marble Coffee Cake, Whole Wheat Butterhorns, Easy Lemon-Blueberry Muffins, Pizza Roll-Up, Boston Cream Pie, and Banana Split Pie. (See Index for recipe pages.)

QUICK AND EASY BREADS

WHOLE WHEAT YEAST BUN MIX

     8   cups all-purpose flour
     6   cups whole wheat flour
     2   cups nonfat dry milk powder
     1   cup packed brown sugar
     2   tablespoons salt
     1   cup shortening that does not require refrigeration

In a Fix-N-Mix® bowl, stir together flours, dry milk powder, brown sugar, and salt. Cut in shortening till mixture resembles coarse meal. Transfer to a Maxi-Canister or Econo Canister.® Apply Seal. Store up to 6 weeks at room temperature. For longer storage, place in freezer. To measure, spoon lightly into Measuring Cup; level with spatula. Makes 17 cups mix.

WHOLE WHEAT POTATO PANCAKES

     2   large potatoes, peeled
     ½   cup WHOLE WHEAT YEAST BUN MIX
     ½   teaspoon salt
     2   beaten eggs
     2   tablespoons cooking oil

Grate potatoes on medium grater of Grater Bowl. Remove grater; sprinkle Bun Mix and salt over potatoes. Apply storage Seal and shake gently till potato shreds are evenly coated. Stir in eggs. Measure ⅓ cup mixture for each pancake. In a large skillet, cook pancakes in hot oil over medium heat about 3 minutes per side or till pancakes are golden. Makes 6 pancakes.

WHOLE WHEAT PECAN PIZZA

     1   package active dry yeast
     ½   cup warm water (110° to 115°)
     2   cups WHOLE WHEAT YEAST BUN MIX
     1   medium orange
     ½   cup packed brown sugar
     ¼   cup honey
     1   cup broken pecans
         Pecan halves (optional)

In Large Mixing Bowl, dissolve yeast in warm water. Stir in Bun Mix. Turn out onto lightly floured Pastry Sheet. Knead till smooth and elastic (12 to 15 strokes). Shape into a ball. Return to Mixing Bowl that has been washed and greased. Turn dough once to grease surface. Apply Seal; let rise in warm place till double (about 1½ hours). Punch dough down. With floured hands, press into a greased 11-inch quiche pan or press an 11-inch circle into a 12-inch pizza pan, building up sides and crimping edge. Prick slightly with fork. Using Handy Grater, grate enough orange peel to make 1 teaspoon; set aside. Squeeze 2 tablespoons juice. In small saucepan, combine brown sugar, honey, orange juice, and orange peel; heat till sugar is dissolved. Stir in broken pecans. Spread over dough to 1 inch of the edge. Garnish with additional pecan halves, if desired. Bake in 400° oven about 20 minutes or till crust is lightly browned. Cool on wire rack. Remove cooled coffee cake from dish. Store in 12″ Pie Taker. Makes 1 coffee cake.

WHOLE WHEAT JAM TWISTS

     1   package active dry yeast
     ⅓   cup warm water (110° to 115°)
     1   slightly beaten egg
     2   cups WHOLE WHEAT YEAST BUN MIX
     ¼   cup peanut butter
     3   tablespoons strawberry or red raspberry preserves
     1   tablespoon butter or margarine, melted

In Large Mixing Bowl, dissolve yeast in warm water. Stir in egg. Add Bun Mix and beat well. Turn out onto a well floured Pastry Sheet. Cover and let rest for 30 minutes.

Use Rolling Pin to roll to a 14x10-inch rectangle. Carefully spread the peanut butter lengthwise over half of the rectangle. Carefully spread jam or preserves over the peanut butter, cutting up large pieces of fruit, if necessary. Fold dough lengthwise making a 14x5 rectangle; seal edges. Cut dough crosswise into fourteen 5x1-inch strips. Loosely twist each strip and arrange about 2 inches apart on a greased baking sheet. Brush strips with the butter or margarine. Cover and let rise in a warm place till double (30 to 40 minutes). Bake in 375° oven for 12 to 15 minutes or till golden. Cool on wire rack. Store in Bacon Keeper. Makes 14 twists.

Kids will love peanut-butter-and-jam-filled Whole Wheat Jam Twists and apple juice for a nutritious after-school snack. Keep a batch handy in a Bacon Keeper.

QUICK AND EASY BREADS

WHOLE WHEAT BUTTERHORNS

Pictured on page 62—

- 2 packages active dry yeast
- 1¾ cups warm water (110° to 115°)
- 6 cups WHOLE WHEAT YEAST BUN MIX
- 6 tablespoons butter, softened
- ½ cup finely chopped nuts
  Melted butter

In Large Mixing Bowl, dissolve yeast in warm water. Add Bun Mix. Mix well. Turn out on a lightly floured Pastry Sheet, kneading to make moderately stiff dough that is smooth and elastic (6 to 8 minutes total). Shape into a ball. Return to Mixing Bowl that has been washed and greased, turning once to grease surface. Apply Seal and let rise in warm place till double (about 1½ hours).

Punch down; turn out onto lightly floured Pastry Sheet. Divide dough into 3 equal portions; shape each into a ball. Cover and let rest 10 minutes.

On lightly floured Pastry Sheet, use Rolling Pin to roll one ball of dough into a 12-inch circle; spread with 2 tablespoons of the softened butter and sprinkle with ⅓ of the nuts. Cut circle into 12 wedges. To shape rolls, begin at wide end of wedge and roll toward point. Place, point down, 2 to 3 inches apart on greased baking sheet. Repeat with remaining dough. Cover rolls; let rise in warm place till nearly double (20 to 30 minutes). Brush with melted butter. Bake in 400° oven for 10 to 12 minutes or till done. Remove from baking sheet; cool. Brush again with melted butter, if desired. Makes 36.

CINNAMON TWIST

- ¾ cups milk
- 1 package active dry yeast
- 4 cups WHOLE WHEAT YEAST BUN MIX
- 2 slightly beaten eggs
- ½ cup sugar
- 2 teaspoons ground cinnamon
- 3 tablespoons butter or margarine, melted

In saucepan, heat milk to lukewarm (115° to 120°). In Large Mixing Bowl, dissolve yeast in milk; add Bun Mix. Mix well. Add eggs; mix well. Turn out onto lightly floured Pastry Sheet; knead till smooth and elastic (12 to 15 strokes). Return to Mixing Bowl that has been washed and greased. Turn dough once to grease surface. Apply Seal and let rise in warm place till doubled (about 1½ hours). Punch down; let rest 10 minutes. Meanwhile, combine sugar and cinnamon. On lightly floured Pastry Sheet, roll one half of the dough to a 20x9-inch rectangle. Brush with half the melted butter. Sprinkle with half the sugar mixture. Roll up jelly-roll fashion, beginning with long side. Seal edges. With sharp knife, cut roll in half lengthwise. Place side by side, cut sides up. Seal ends. Twist several times by lifting one portion of dough over the other. Moisten and seal ends. Shape into a ring, sealing ends together. Place in a greased 8-inch or 9-inch round baking pan. Repeat with remaining. Cover; let rise till nearly double (about 45 minutes). Bake in 350° oven for 25 minutes. Drizzle with Powdered Sugar Icing, if desired. Makes 2.

SUPER SANDWICH BRAID

- 1 package active dry yeast
- ¾ cup warm water (110° to 115°)
- 4 cups WHOLE WHEAT YEAST BUN MIX
- 1 beaten egg
- 2 tablespoons butter or margarine, melted
- ½ teaspoon caraway seed or dill seed
- 1 3-ounce package (¾ cup) dried or smoked beef, finely snipped
- 2 ounces shredded Swiss or cheddar cheese (½ cup)
  Melted butter

In Large Mixing Bowl, dissolve yeast in warm water. Add Bun Mix; mix well. Add egg; mix well. Turn out onto a lightly floured Pastry Sheet. Knead until smooth. Cover dough; let rest 10 minutes.

On lightly floured Pastry Sheet, use Rolling Pin to roll dough to a 14x9-inch rectangle. Cut dough lengthwise into three 14x3-inch strips. Brush strips with some of the 2 tablespoons melted butter; sprinkle with the caraway seed or dill seed. Sprinkle a third of the beef and cheese lengthwise down center of one strip of dough. Bring lengthwise edges of strip together enclosing filling; pinch edges together to seal. Repeat with remaining dough strips and filling. Place strips side by side on a large greased baking sheet, seam side down; braid together and secure ends. Cover; let dough rise till nearly double (about 30 minutes). Bake in 375° oven for 25 to 30 minutes or till done. Transfer to wire rack; brush loaf with melted butter. Serve warm. Makes 1 loaf.

POWDERED SUGAR ICING

Use this icing to drizzle over your favorite fresh-from-the-oven sweet rolls and coffee breads—

- 1 cup sifted powdered sugar
- ¼ teaspoon vanilla
  Milk

In Small Mix-N-Stor® pitcher, combine the powdered sugar, vanilla, and enough milk to make of drizzling consistency (about 1½ tablespoons).

HEARTY WHEAT MASTER MIX

This nutty all-purpose mix can be used for biscuits, muffins, and even pancakes—

- 8 cups all-purpose flour
- 2 cups whole wheat flour
- ½ cup wheat germ
- ⅓ cup baking powder
- ¼ cup packed brown sugar
- 1 tablespoon salt
- 2 cups shortening that does not require refrigeration

In a Fix-N-Mix® bowl, combine flours, wheat germ, baking powder, brown sugar, and salt. Cut in shortening till mixture resembles coarse crumbs. Store in sealed Large Decorator Canister at room temperature for up to 6 weeks. Makes 12 to 14 cups.

WHOLE WHEAT PANCAKES

- 2 cups HEARTY WHEAT MASTER MIX
- 2 eggs
- 1 cup milk

Place Hearty Wheat Master Mix in a Large Mix-N-Stor pitcher. In Small Mix-N-Stor pitcher, slightly beat eggs; stir milk into eggs. Add egg and milk all at once to Mix, stirring till blended but still slightly lumpy. Pour about ¼ cup batter onto hot, lightly greased griddle. Cook till golden, turning to cook other side. Makes 8 pancakes.

WHOLE WHEAT BISCUIT CRACKERS

- 2½ cups HEARTY WHEAT MASTER MIX
- ½ teaspoon cream of tartar
- ¾ cup buttermilk

In Medium Mixing Bowl, stir together Hearty Wheat Master Mix and cream of tartar. Add buttermilk. Stir with fork just till dough follows fork around bowl. Turn out onto lightly floured Pastry Sheet; knead about 6 strokes. Use Rolling Pin to roll to a ¼-inch thickness. Cut with a floured 2½-inch biscuit cutter. Place on ungreased baking sheet and bake in 350° oven for about 20 minutes or till lightly browned. Split hot biscuits with sharp knife; place, cut side up, on baking sheet. Dry in 300° oven for 15 to 20 minutes. Makes about 3½ dozen biscuit crackers (halves).

WHOLE WHEAT BISCUITS

- 2 cups HEARTY WHEAT MASTER MIX
- ½ cup milk

Place Hearty Wheat Master Mix in a Medium Mixing Bowl; make a well in center. Add milk. Stir with a fork just till dough follows fork around bowl. On lightly floured Pastry Sheet, knead 10 to 12 strokes. Use Rolling Pin to roll to ½-inch thickness. Cut dough with floured 2½-inch biscuit cutter. Bake on baking sheet in 450° oven for 10 to 12 minutes. Makes 10 biscuits.

WHOLE WHEAT MUFFINS

- 3 cups HEARTY WHEAT MASTER MIX
- 3 tablespoons granulated sugar
- 1 egg
- 1 cup milk

In Large Mix-N-Stor pitcher, combine Hearty Wheat Master Mix and sugar. In a Small Mix-N-Stor pitcher, slightly beat the egg; stir milk into egg. Add egg and milk all at once to dry mixture. Stir till moistened. Fill greased or paper bake cup-lined muffin cups ⅔ full. Bake in 400° oven for 20 to 25 minutes or till golden. Makes 12 muffins.

QUICK AND EASY BREADS

QUICK BREAD MIX

    10 cups all-purpose flour
    ⅓   cup baking powder
    ¼   cup sugar
    4   teaspoons salt
    2   cups shortening that
        does not require
        refrigeration

In Fix-N-Mix® bowl; thoroughly stir together flour, baking powder, sugar, and salt; mix well. Cut shortening into dry ingredients till mixture resembles coarse cornmeal. Store in Medium Decorator Canister or Ultra-Clear Counterparts™ VI container for up to 6 weeks at room temperature. Freeze for longer storage.

To measure, spoon mix into measuring cup; level with spatula. Makes 12 cups.

QUICK BANANA NUT BREAD

    1   8-ounce package cream
        cheese, softened
    1   cup sugar
    1   cup mashed ripe banana
    2   eggs
    2   cups QUICK BREAD MIX
    ½   cup chopped pecans
        or walnuts

In Medium Mixing Bowl, cream together softened cream cheese and sugar till light and fluffy; beat in banana and eggs. Stir in Quick Bread Mix and nuts just till moistened. Turn into greased 9x5x3-inch loaf pan. Bake in 350° oven for 60 to 65 minutes. Cover with foil last 15 minutes if bread browns too quickly. Cool in pan 10 minutes; remove from pan. Cool thoroughly on wire rack before slicing. Makes 1 loaf.

SPICY MARBLE COFFEE CAKE

Pictured on page 62—

    2   cups QUICK BREAD MIX
    ¼   cup granulated sugar
    1   beaten egg
    ⅔   cup milk
    2   tablespoons shortening
    2   tablespoons light
        molasses
    ½   teaspoon ground
        cinnamon
    ¼   teaspoon ground nutmeg
    ¼   teaspoon ground cloves
    ¼   cup packed brown sugar
    2   tablespoons QUICK
        BREAD MIX
    1   tablespoon butter or
        margarine, melted
    ¼   teaspoon ground
        cinnamon

In Large Mix-N-Stor® pitcher, combine the 2 cups Quick Bread Mix and granulated sugar. Add egg, milk, and shortening. Beat with portable electric mixer till smooth. Divide batter in half. To one half of the batter, stir in molasses, the ½ teaspoon cinnamon, nutmeg, and cloves. In a greased 8x8x2-inch baking pan, drop plain batter by teaspoons checkerboard fashion over bottom of pan. Fill empty spaces with the spiced batter. Swirl batters to marble. Combine the brown sugar, 2 tablespoons Quick Bread Mix, melted butter or margarine, and ¼ teaspoon cinnamon; mix well. Sprinkle atop batter. Bake in 375° oven for 25 to 30 minutes. Serve warm. Makes 9 servings.

SUNSHINE MUFFINS

These fresh-tasting pineapple-and orange-flavored muffins are great served warm for breakfast or as a pleasant accompaniment to a salad luncheon—

    1   8¼-ounce can crushed
        pineapple
        Milk
    1½ cups QUICK BREAD MIX
    3   tablespoons sugar
    1   beaten egg
    1   tablespoon sugar
    1   tablespoon grated
        orange peel

In 1-qt. Strainer over Small Mix-N-Stor pitcher, drain pineapple, reserving pineapple syrup. Add milk to reserved syrup to make ¾ cup liquid.

In Medium Mixing Bowl, combine Quick Bread Mix and 3 tablespoons sugar. Combine beaten egg, pineapple syrup mixture, and ¼ cup of the drained crushed pineapple; add all at once to dry ingredients, stirring just till moistened.

Fill greased or paper bake cup-lined muffin pans ⅔ full. Stir together remaining drained crushed pineapple, 1 tablespoon sugar, and grated orange peel. Spoon about 1 tablespoon of the pineapple mixture atop batter in each muffin pan.

Bake in 400° oven for 20 to 25 minutes or till golden. Serve warm. Makes 8 muffins.

DOUBLE ORANGE COFFEE CAKE

2½ cups QUICK BREAD MIX
3 tablespoons granulated sugar
1 beaten egg
½ cup milk
⅓ cup packed brown sugar
⅓ cup chopped walnuts
2 tablespoons all-purpose flour
2 tablespoons butter or margarine, melted
Orange juice
¾ cup sifted powdered sugar

In Medium Mixing Bowl, stir Quick Bread Mix and granulated sugar together. Add egg and milk; stir till blended. Knead on lightly floured Pastry Sheet (8 to 10 strokes). Divide dough in 2 almost-equal parts. Use Rolling Pin to roll larger part to 8-inch circle; place in greased 9-inch pie plate, patting dough ½ inch up sides. For filling, mix brown sugar, walnuts, flour, and melted butter or margarine. Sprinkle over dough in pie plate. Roll remaining dough to 7-inch circle; place atop filling. With kitchen scissors, snip 1-inch slashes around edge of top layer. Bake in 375° oven for 25 to 30 minutes. Remove from pie plate. Drizzle with orange glaze. Garnish with shredded orange peel, if desired. Serve warm. Makes 10 to 12 servings.

For orange glaze, add enough orange juice (1 to 1½ tablespoons) to sifted powdered sugar to make of drizzling consistency.

EASY LEMON-BLUEBERRY MUFFINS

Make these lemon-sparked muffins filled with plump, fresh blueberries when berries are in season. Pictured on page 62—

1 cup fresh or frozen blueberries
1 beaten egg
⅓ cup sugar
2 tablespoons butter or margarine, softened
1 lemon
Milk
2 cups QUICK BREAD MIX
Melted butter or margarine
2 tablespoons sugar

Thaw blueberries, if frozen; drain. In Medium Mixing Bowl, combine egg, ⅓ cup sugar, and 2 tablespoons softened butter or margarine. Use Handy Grater to finely shred enough peel from lemon to make 1 tablespoon; set aside. Squeeze lemon; add enough milk to lemon juice to make ⅔ cup liquid. Add to mixture in Mixing Bowl. Stir in Quick Bread Mix; mix well. Gently fold in blueberries. Spoon batter into greased or paper bake cup-lined muffin cups ⅔ full.

Bake in 400° oven about 25 minutes or till golden. While warm, dip muffin tops in some melted butter or margarine, then in a mixture of 2 tablespoons sugar and the reserved lemon peel. Makes 12 muffins.

MOCHA-RAISIN BREAD

1 tablespoon instant coffee crystals
½ cup milk
3 cups QUICK BREAD MIX
¾ cup packed brown sugar
¼ cup all-purpose flour
1 beaten egg
1 cup mashed ripe banana
1 cup raisins
½ cup chopped walnuts

Dissolve coffee crystals in milk; set aside. In Large Mix-N-Stor pitcher, stir together Quick Bread Mix, brown sugar, and flour. In Small Mix-N-Stor pitcher. Combine egg, banana, and coffee mixture. Add to dry ingredients, stirring just till moistened. Fold in raisins and nuts. Grease bottoms only of two 1-pound coffee cans. Divide batter between two cans. Bake in 350° oven about 50 minutes. (Or, bake in one greased 9x5x3-inch loaf pan in 350° oven for 55 to 60 minutes.) Cool in pans for 10 minutes; remove from pans. Cool thoroughly. Makes 1 large or 2 small loaves.

QUICK MIX WAFFLES

2 beaten egg yolks
1⅓ cups milk
2 tablespoons cooking oil
2 cups QUICK BREAD MIX
2 stiff-beaten egg whites

In Small Mix-N-Stor pitcher, combine egg yolks, milk, and cooking oil. In Large Mix-N-Stor pitcher, place Quick Bread Mix. Add egg mixture, beating just till blended. Carefully fold in stiff-beaten egg whites, leaving a few fluffs of egg white; do not overmix. Bake in preheated waffle baker according to manufacturer's directions. Makes three 9-inch waffles.

QUICK AND EASY BREADS

FREEZER BREAD DOUGH

- 5¾ to 6¼ cups all-purpose flour
- 2 packages active dry yeast
- 2 cups milk
- 6 tablespoons butter or margarine
- ⅓ cup sugar
- 2 teaspoons salt
- 2 eggs

In Large Mixing Bowl, combine 2½ cups of the flour and the yeast. In saucepan, heat together the milk, butter or margarine, sugar, and salt just till warm (115° to 120°), stirring constantly till butter or margarine almost melts. Add liquid to dry ingredients in Mixing Bowl along with eggs. Beat at low speed of electric mixer for ½ minute, scraping sides of bowl constantly. Beat 3 minutes at high speed. Stir in as much of the remaining flour as you can mix in with a spoon. Turn out onto a lightly floured Pastry Sheet. Knead in enough of the remaining flour to make a stiff dough that is smooth and elastic (6 to 8 minutes total). Divide dough into thirds. Shape each of two portions into loaves. Store in Freez-N-Save® container with a double thickness of waxed paper between. Divide remaining dough into 16 portions. Shape each into a smooth ball. Arrange the 16 balls 1 inch apart in a Cold Cut Keeper. Apply Seal; freeze firm. To conserve on freezer space, transfer frozen balls to a smaller container such as the Deli-Keeper. Makes 2 loaves and 16 balls.

When you start with Freezer Bread Dough, home-baked breads are a snap. From one recipe you can bake two loaves of Busy-Day White Bread (see recipe, page 72), one pan of Honey-Walnut Pull-Aparts, and eight Short-Cut Cloverleaf Rolls (see recipe, page 72).

HONEY-WALNUT PULL-APARTS

- 3 tablespoons butter or margarine
- ⅓ cup packed brown sugar
- ¼ cup honey
- ½ teaspoon maple flavoring
- ½ cup chopped walnuts
- 8 balls FREEZER BREAD DOUGH

In a medium saucepan, melt butter or margarine; blend in brown sugar and honey. Stir in maple flavoring and nuts. Pour into 8x1½-inch round baking pan. Arrange the frozen Freezer Bread Dough balls evenly atop. Cover and let rise in a warm place till double, about 3 to 3½ hours. (Or, let rise overnight in refrigerator.) Bake in a 350° oven for 20 to 25 minutes or till golden. Let stand in pan for 2 minutes; invert onto serving plate. Serve or store in a 9″ Pie Taker. Makes 8 rolls.

REHEATING ROLLS

It's easy to reheat rolls when you use the Multi-Server™ container. Pour 2 cups of boiling water into the Multi-Server serving dish. Place up to 10 rolls in the strainer insert and place over hot water in the serving dish. Cover Multi-Server container and let stand for 15 minutes or till rolls are warmed. Remove strainer insert from serving dish and pour off water before serving.

ALMOND-LEMON STICKY BUNS

To tote these homemade rolls to the office or a friend's house, allow them to cool; then place on a Fresh-N-Fancy® base and apply Seal —

- 1 loaf FREEZER BREAD DOUGH
- ½ cup sugar
- ⅓ cup dark corn syrup
- ¼ cup butter or margarine
- 1 teaspoon finely shredded lemon peel
- 2 tablespoons lemon juice
- ¾ cup toasted sliced almonds
- 2 tablespoons butter or margarine, melted
- ¼ cup sugar
- ¼ teaspoon ground nutmeg

Let dough thaw at room temperature about 1½ hours. In small saucepan, combine ½ cup sugar, dark corn syrup, ¼ cup butter or margarine, lemon peel, and lemon juice. Cook and stir just till sugar dissolves and mixture boils. Pour in bottom of ungreased 13x9x2-inch baking pan. Sprinkle almonds over.

On lightly floured Pastry Sheet, use Rolling Pin to roll dough to 16x8-inch rectangle. Brush with 2 tablespoons melted butter. Combine ¼ cup sugar and nutmeg; sprinkle over dough. Beginning with long side, roll up jelly-roll fashion; seal edge. Cut into sixteen 1-inch slices. Place, cut side down, atop sugar mixture in pan. Cover and let rise in warm place till nearly double (30 to 45 minutes). Bake in 375° oven for 20 to 25 minutes. Immediately loosen sides and turn out onto wire rack placed atop waxed paper to catch drippings. Makes 16 rolls.

QUICK AND EASY BREADS

CHERRY-CHEESE COFFEE CAKE

- 1 loaf FREEZER BREAD DOUGH
- 1 12-ounce can cherry cake and pastry filling
- ½ cup raisins
- 2 3-ounce packages cream cheese, softened
- ⅓ cup granulated sugar
- ¼ cup milk
- 2 tablespoons all-purpose flour
- ¼ teaspoon almond extract
- ½ cup all-purpose flour
- ¼ cup packed brown sugar
- 3 tablespoons butter or margarine

Thaw frozen bread dough in refrigerator overnight. On lightly floured Pastry Sheet, use Rolling Pin to roll dough to a 13x9-inch rectangle. Place in greased 13x9x2-inch baking pan. Cover and let rise in warm place till almost double (1 to 1½ hours). Stir raisins into cherry filling; spread evenly over dough. In Small Mix-N-Stor® pitcher, combine cream cheese, the granulated sugar, milk, the 2 tablespoons flour, and the almond extract; beat smooth. Pour mixture over filling. Combine the remaining flour and the brown sugar; cut in butter till mixture resembles coarse crumbs. Sprinkle mixture over cheese layer. Bake in 350° oven for 40 minutes. Cool; cut into squares. Makes 16 servings.

CINNAMON SWIRL LOAF

- 1 loaf FREEZER BREAD DOUGH
- ¼ cup sugar
- 1 teaspoon ground cinnamon
  Powdered Sugar Icing (see recipe, page 67)

Thaw Freezer Bread Dough for 1½ to 2 hours. On lightly floured Pastry Sheet, use Rolling Pin to roll dough to a 15x7-inch rectangle. Brush entire surface lightly with some water. Combine sugar and cinnamon. Sprinkle mixture over the dough. Beginning with narrow end, roll up jelly-roll style; seal edge and ends. Place, sealed edge down, in greased 9x5x3-inch loaf pan. Let rise till almost double (about 1 hour). Bake in 375° oven for 35 to 40 minutes or till done, covering with foil the last 15 minutes to prevent overbrowning. Remove from pans; cool on wire rack. Drizzle warm loaf with Powdered Sugar Icing, if desired. Makes 1 loaf.

BUSY-DAY WHITE BREAD

- 1 loaf FREEZER BREAD DOUGH

Place frozen Freezer Bread Dough in a greased 8x4x2-inch loaf pan. Cover; let rise in a warm place till nearly double (about 6 hours). Bake in a 375° oven for 35 to 40 minutes or till done. Test by tapping on the top with your finger. A hollow sound means the loaf is properly baked. If top browns too fast, cover loosely with foil the last 15 minutes of baking. Remove from pan; cool on a wire rack. Makes 1 loaf.

PIZZA ROLL-UP

Pictured on page 63—

- 1 loaf FREEZER BREAD DOUGH
- ¼ cup tomato paste
- 1 teaspoon dried oregano, crushed
- ¼ teaspoon garlic powder
- 4 ounces pepperoni, chopped (1 cup)
- 4 ounces shredded mozzarella cheese (1 cup)

Thaw Bread Dough for 1½ to 2 hours. Use Pastry Sheet and Rolling Pin filled with warm water to roll out to 12x9-inch rectangle. Spread with tomato paste. Sprinkle with remaining ingredients. Roll up jelly-roll fashion from long side; seal. Place on greased baking sheet, seam side down. Brush with water; sprinkle with a little salt. Let rise till almost double (about 1 hour). Make shallow slashes across top at 2-inch intervals. Bake in 375° oven for 30 minutes or till done. Serve warm. Makes 4 to 6 servings.

SHORT-CUT CLOVERLEAF ROLLS

Here's a short-cut trick that lets you serve fancy rolls anytime. Pictured on pages 70 and 127—

- 8 balls FREEZER BREAD dough

Lightly grease 8 muffin cups. Place frozen Freezer Bread Dough balls in lightly greased muffin cups. Cover and let thaw for 1½ to 2 hours. Using scissors dipped in flour, snip top in half, then snip again to make 4 points. Let rise about 1 hour. Bake in 375° oven for 12 to 15 minutes. Makes 8.

RAISIN BREAKFAST WHEELS

- 1 4-ounce container whipped cream cheese
- 3 tablespoons butter or margarine, softened
- 2 tablespoons orange marmalade

• • •

- 16 slices raisin bread
- 2 tablespoons sugar
- ½ teaspoon ground cinnamon

In Small Mix-N-Stor pitcher, combine whipped cream cheese, 2 tablespoons of the softened butter or margarine, and orange marmalade. Make four 4-layer sandwiches spreading cream cheese mixture between slices of raisin bread. Cut sandwiches into 3 strips. Coil each strip, cut side up, in muffin pan, curving slightly to fit. Spread remaining softened butter or margarine over tops. Combine sugar and cinnamon; sprinkle over tops. Bake in 375° oven for 10 to 12 minutes. Serve warm. Makes 12.

BLUE CHEESE STRIPS

- 2 frankfurter buns
- 3 tablespoons crumbled blue cheese
- 3 tablespoons butter or margarine
- 1 teaspoon poppy seed

Cut frankfurter buns into fourths lengthwise to make strips. In small skillet, melt blue cheese with butter or margarine. Brush blue cheese mixture on cut sides of buns with pastry brush. Sprinkle with poppy seed. Place on baking sheet. Bake in 375° oven 10 minutes. Serve hot. Makes 8.

LEMON-PEPPER SANDWICH LOAF

- 1 1-pound loaf unsliced white or whole wheat sandwich bread
- ½ cup butter or margarine, softened
- 1 tablespoon snipped chives
- ½ teaspoon finely shredded lemon peel
- 1½ teaspoons lemon juice
- ⅛ teaspoon pepper
- 1 tablespoon prepared mustard
- 2 teaspoons poppy seed
- 8 slices Swiss cheese (8 ounces)
- 8 slices bacon, crisp-cooked, drained, and crumbled

Cut bread into 9 slices, cutting to, but not through, bottom crust. In Small Mix-N-Stor pitcher, cream butter or margarine until light and fluffy. Add snipped chives, lemon peel, lemon juice, mustard, and poppy seed; set aside 3 table-spoons of the lemon-butter mixture. Spread remainder on all cut surfaces of bread. Place 1 slice cheese in each cut; sprinkle bacon over cheese. Spread the reserved lemon-butter mixture on top and sides of loaf. Bake on ungreased baking sheet in 350° oven for 15 to 20 minutes. Makes 9 servings.

BUTTER MOLD TIP

An easy accompaniment for homemade breads is a butter mold, like the one pictured on page 62. Press ¾ cup softened butter or margarine into a Dessert Set dish. Run a thin metal spatula around the edge of dish to release. Invert butter mold onto Dessert Set base. Smooth edges. Use tip of spatula to make vertical swirls on sides and top. Refrigerate in a Classic Sheer™ 5-cup Jr. Canister till firm.

CHOOSE-A-BREAD PICK-A-SPREAD

Choose from French bread, dinner or hard rolls, or rye or whole wheat bread to carry any of these tasty spreads. Prepare in the 10- or 20-oz. Servalier® bowls. Store in the refrigerator till the next time you want to make bread time special—

Mustard-Parsley Spread: Combine 6 tablespoons *butter or margarine*, softened; 2 tablespoons finely snipped *parsley*; 2 teaspoons prepared *mustard*; and ½ teaspoon dried *oregano*, crushed.

Garlic Spread: Stir together 6 tablespoons *butter or margarine*, softened, and ½ teaspoon *garlic powder*.

Parmesan Spread: Stir together 6 tablespoons *butter or margarine*, softened; ¼ cup grated *Parmesan cheese*; and 1 tablespoon snipped *chives*.

Caraway-Cheese Spread: Stir together one 4-ounce container *whipped cream cheese with pimiento*, 1 tablespoon thinly sliced *green onion*, and 1 teaspoon *caraway seed*.

Peppy Cheese Butter Spread: Combine 1½ cups shredded *Swiss, cheddar, Monterey Jack, or American cheese*; ¼ cup *butter or margarine*, softened; 2 tablespoons finely snipped *parsley*; and 2 teaspoons prepared *horseradish*.

Herb Butter Spread: Cream together 6 tablespoons *butter or margarine*, softened; ½ teaspoon dried *marjoram*, crushed; ½ teaspoon dried *thyme*, crushed; and ¼ teaspoon *garlic powder*.

Mince-Oatmeal Bars
2 cups Basic Cookie Mix
3/4 cup Quick-cooking oats
1 beaten egg
1 tablespoon water
1 cup prepared mince meat
1 cup sifted powdered sugar
1/4 teaspoon ground ginger
Milk

SHORT-CUT COOKIES AND CAKES

BASIC COOKIE MIX

- 5 cups all-purpose flour
- 2½ cups sugar
- 2½ teaspoons baking powder
- 1½ teaspoons salt
- 1⅔ cups shortening that does not require refrigeration

In Large Mixing Bowl, thoroughly stir together flour, sugar, baking powder, and salt. Cut in shortening till mixture resembles coarse meal. Store in 14-cup Large Canister. Store up to 6 weeks at room temperature. For longer storage, place in freezer. To measure, lightly spoon mix into Measuring Cup; level. Makes about 11 cups.

GRANOLA RAISIN BARS

- 2 cups BASIC COOKIE MIX
- 1 egg
- ½ cup milk
- ¼ cup packed brown sugar
- ½ teaspoon vanilla
- 1 cup granola
- ½ cup raisins
- 2 tablespoons butter or margarine, melted

In Large Mix-N-Stor® pitcher, combine Basic Cookie Mix, egg, milk, brown sugar, and vanilla; stir till combined. Stir in half of the granola and all of the raisins. Pour batter in greased 9x9x2-inch baking pan. Stir together remaining granola and melted butter or margarine; sprinkle over top. Bake in 350° oven for 25 minutes or till done. Cool on wire rack. Cut into bars. Makes 24.

MINCE-OATMEAL BARS

- 2 cups BASIC COOKIE MIX
- ¾ cup quick-cooking rolled oats
- 1 beaten egg
- 1 tablespoon water
- 1 cup prepared mincemeat
- 1 cup sifted powdered sugar
- ¼ teaspoon ground ginger
  Milk

In Medium Mixing Bowl, combine Basic Cookie Mix, rolled oats, egg, and water; mix well. Pat half the mixture in greased 9x9x2-inch baking pan; spoon mincemeat atop. Finely crumble remaining oat mixture over mincemeat. Bake in 350° oven for 30 to 35 minutes. In Small Mix-N-Stor pitcher, combine powdered sugar, ginger, and enough milk (2 to 3 tablespoons) to make drizzling consistency. Drizzle over warm cookies. Cool; cut into bars. Makes 24.

PEANUT MOLASSES COOKIES

- 1¾ cups BASIC COOKIE MIX
- 1 egg
- ¼ cup molasses
- ½ cup chopped peanuts

In Medium Mixing Bowl, beat together Basic Cookie Mix, egg, and molasses; stir in peanuts. Drop from teaspoon onto ungreased cookie sheet. Bake in 375° oven for 8 to 10 minutes. Cool 1 minute; remove to rack. Cool completely. Makes about 30 cookies.

ORANGE-COCONUT DROPS

- 2½ cups BASIC COOKIE MIX
- ¼ cup orange marmalade
- 1 egg
- 3 tablespoons orange juice
- 1 cup flaked coconut

In Medium Mixing Bowl, combine Basic Cookie Mix, marmalade, egg, and orange juice; beat well. Stir in coconut. Drop from teaspoon 2 inches apart on a greased cookie sheet. Bake in 375° oven for 8 to 10 minutes. Frost with Orange Butter Frosting (see page 83), if desired. Makes 30 cookies.

DOUBLE CHOCOLATE DROPS

- 2¼ cups BASIC COOKIE MIX
- 1 egg
- ¼ cup milk
- 2 squares (2 ounces) unsweetened chocolate, melted
- ½ cup semisweet chocolate pieces
- ½ cup chopped nuts

In Medium Mixing Bowl, beat together Basic Cookie Mix, egg, and milk. Blend in melted chocolate. Stir in chocolate pieces and nuts. Drop from teaspoon 2 inches apart on greased cookie sheet. Bake in 375° oven for 10 to 12 minutes. Frost with Chocolate Butter Frosting (see page 76), if desired. Makes 30.

Keep the Basic Cookie Mix on hand when busy baking days hit. Use this mix to bake Orange-Coconut Drops, Mince-Oatmeal Bars, and Double Chocolate Drops; they make extra special lunch-box fillers too.

SHORT-CUT COOKIES AND CAKES

HOMEMADE BROWNIE MIX

- 5 cups sugar
- 3 cups all-purpose flour
- 2 cups unsweetened cocoa powder
- 1 tablespoon baking powder
- 1 tablespoon salt
- 3½ cups shortening that does not require refrigeration

In Large Mixing Bowl, stir together dry ingredients. Lightly cut in shortening till mixture resembles evenly distributed, coarse crumbs. Do not overblend. Store in canister up to 6 weeks at room temperature. For longer storage, place in freezer. To measure, pack mix into Measuring Cup; level with spatula. Makes about 7½ cups packed mix (enough for 5 single recipes of Brownies).

To make Brownies: In Medium Mixing Bowl, beat 2 eggs and 1 teaspoon vanilla. Add 1½ cups packed Homemade Brownie Mix; stir till nearly smooth. If desired, stir in ½ cup chopped nuts or semisweet chocolate pieces or butterscotch pieces. Spread in greased 8x8x2-inch baking pan. Bake in 350° oven for 25 to 30 minutes. Cool on wire rack. Cut into bars. Makes 16. (Or, double recipe; bake in a greased 15x10x1-inch baking pan in 350° oven for 20 to 25 minutes.) Frost with Chocolate Butter Frosting (see recipe at right), if desired. Store in the Snack-Stor® container.

CHOCOLATE BUTTER FROSTING

- 6 tablespoons butter
- 4½ to 4¾ cups sifted powdered sugar
- ¼ cup milk
- 2 squares (2 ounces) unsweetened chocolate, melted and cooled
- 1½ teaspoons vanilla

In a Small Mix-N-Stor® pitcher, beat butter till light and fluffy. Gradually beat in half of the powdered sugar. Beat in milk, chocolate, and vanilla; beat in remaining powdered sugar. Beat in additional milk, if necessary, for spreading consistency. Frosts tops and sides of two 8- or 9-inch layers, top of one 15x10-inch pan bar cookies, about 24 cupcakes, or 48 cookies.

CHOCOLATE WAFFLE DROPS

- 1 cup packed HOMEMADE BROWNIE MIX
- ½ cup all-purpose flour
- ½ teaspoon ground cinnamon
- 2 eggs
- ½ cup chopped nuts

In Large Mix-N-Stor pitcher, stir together packed Homemade Brownie Mix, flour, and cinnamon. Beat eggs and add to dry ingredients. Blend in nuts. (Mixture will be stiff like cookie dough.)

Drop from teaspoon 2 inches apart on preheated waffle baker; bake till done, about 1 minute. Remove to rack to cool. Sift powdered sugar over cookies. Store in the Medium Canister. Makes 48 cookies.

PEANUT BUTTER BROWNIE BARS

- 1 cup peanut butter
- ½ cup sugar
- 3 eggs
- 1 teaspoon vanilla
- 1½ cups packed HOMEMADE BROWNIE MIX
- ¼ cup chopped peanuts

In Medium Mixing Bowl, beat peanut butter, sugar, and 1 egg till well blended. Spread in ungreased 9x9x2-inch baking pan. Beat 2 eggs and vanilla. Stir in Homemade Brownie Mix and peanuts; spread over peanut butter mixture. Sprinkle with additional peanuts. Bake in 350° oven about 35 minutes. Cool; cut into bars. Store in the Cold Cut Keeper. Makes 20 bar cookies.

SURPRISE MERINGUE KISSES

- 3 egg whites
- 1 teaspoon vanilla
- ¼ teaspoon cream of tartar
- ¼ teaspoon peppermint extract (optional)
  Dash salt
- 1 cup sugar
- 44 milk chocolate kisses

In Medium Mixing Bowl, beat egg whites, vanilla, cream of tartar, extract, and salt till soft peaks form. Gradually add sugar; beat till very stiff peaks form. Drop by tablespoon 1½ inches apart on lightly greased cookie sheet. Press a chocolate kiss into each cookie. With table knife, bring meringue up over candy. Bake in 275° oven for 30 minutes. Immediately remove to rack; cool. Store in the Medium Canister. Makes 44 cookies.

PEANUT CRISP BARS

½ cup granulated sugar
½ cup light corn syrup
1 cup peanut butter
2 cups crisp rice cereal
¼ cup butter or
margarine
¼ cup packed brown sugar
1 tablespoon milk
½ teaspoon vanilla
1¼ cups sifted powdered
sugar

In saucepan, combine granulated sugar, corn syrup, and dash *salt*. Cook and stir till sugar is dissolved. Blend in peanut butter; stir in cereal. Pat evenly into a Bacon Keeper. Melt butter and brown sugar; remove from heat. Add milk and vanilla. Stir in powdered sugar; beat smooth. Spread over cereal mixture; chill. Cut into bars. Makes 24 cookies.

NO-BAKE DROP COOKIES

2 cups sugar
¼ cup unsweetened cocoa
powder
½ cup milk
½ cup butter or margarine
1 tablespoon light corn
syrup
¼ cup peanut butter
2 cups quick-cooking
rolled oats

In heavy saucepan, stir together sugar and cocoa powder; stir in milk. Add butter and corn syrup; bring to boiling, stirring occasionally. Boil vigorously for 3 minutes. Stir in peanut butter, then rolled oats.

Return mixture to boiling. Remove from heat; beat till slightly thickened. Immediately drop from a teaspoon onto waxed paper. (If mixture spreads too much, beat a little longer.) Cool. Store in Stacking Canister . Makes 36 cookies.

PUMPKIN-FILLED OATMEAL COOKIES

At Halloween time, cut slits for a jack-o-lantern face—

¾ cup shortening
½ cup packed brown sugar
1 egg
¼ cup light molasses
1 cup quick-cooking rolled
oats
2 cups all-purpose flour
1 teaspoon salt
½ teaspoon baking soda
½ cup canned pumpkin
½ cup granulated sugar
½ teaspoon ground
cinnamon
½ teaspoon ground ginger
¼ teaspoon ground nutmeg

In a Large Mixing Bowl, cream the shortening and brown sugar; beat in egg and molasses. Place rolled oats in blender container; cover. Blend till finely chopped. In a Small Mix-N-Stor pitcher, stir together oats, flour, salt, and soda. Stir into creamed mixture. Apply Seal to Mixing Bowl and chill.

Meanwhile, in a small saucepan, combine pumpkin, granulated sugar, cinnamon, ginger, and nutmeg. Cook and stir till bubbly; cool.

On a floured Pastry Sheet, use Rolling Pin to roll dough to a ⅛-inch thickness. Cut into thirty-six 3-inch circles. Place 1 teaspoon of the pumpkin mixture atop half of the circles. Place on an ungreased cookie sheet. Cut decorative slits in remaining circles, if desired; place atop filling. Seal edges with a fork. Bake in a 375° oven for 12 minutes. Store in the Cold Cut Keeper. Makes 18 cookies.

CAROB CANDY SQUARES

½ cup honey
½ cup peanut butter
½ cup unsweetened carob
powder or 1 square
(1 ounce) unsweetened
chocolate
1 cup roasted soybeans or
dry-roasted peanuts
1 cup raisins, cut-up pitted
dates, or cut-up pitted
figs
1 cup flaked coconut

In medium saucepan, stir together honey and peanut butter over low heat just till melted. Remove from heat; blend in carob powder. (Or, melt chocolate with honey and peanut butter.) Stir in soybeans, raisins, and ¾ cup of the coconut till well coated. Press mixture into a Deli-Keeper. Press remaining coconut lightly atop. Apply Seal and chill till firm. Cut into squares with table knife. Store sealed in refrigerator. Makes 24 squares.

POPCORN-GRANOLA BARS

6 cups popped popcorn
2 cups plain granola
3 cups tiny marshmallows
½ cup butterscotch
pieces (3 ounces)
⅓ cup peanut butter
2 tablespoons butter or
margarine
¼ teaspoon salt

In a Fix-N-Mix® bowl, combine popcorn and granola; set aside. In a heavy saucepan, combine marshmallows, butterscotch pieces, peanut butter, butter, and salt. Stir over low heat till the mixture is smooth. Pour over popcorn mixture; stir quickly to coat evenly. Press mixture into a buttered Cold Cut Keeper. Let cool; cut into bars. Makes 48 bars.

SHORT-CUT COOKIES AND CAKES

BALLOON CAKE

1½ cups sugar
½ cup butter, softened
⅓ cup chunk-style peanut
butter
3 squares (3 ounces)
unsweetened chocolate,
melted and cooled
2 eggs
1½ teaspoons vanilla
2½ cups all-purpose flour
2½ teaspoons baking
powder
1 teaspoon salt
1⅔ cups milk
Butter Frosting (see
recipe, page 83)
Red rope licorice
Assorted candies

In Large Mix-N-Stor® pitcher,
cream sugar, butter, and peanut
butter till light and fluffy. Add
chocolate, eggs, and vanilla; beat
at low speed of an electric mixer till
blended; beat 2 minutes at
medium speed. Stir together dry
ingredients. Add to creamed
mixture alternately with milk,
beating after each addition. Pour
into a greased and lightly floured
13x9x2-inch baking pan. Bake in
350° oven for 30 to 35 minutes or
till done. Cool 10 minutes on wire
rack; remove from pan. Cool
thoroughly. Place on a
Fresh-N-Fancy® base and frost
with Butter Frosting. Press licorice
around top and bottom edges of
cake. Form balloons by tying
licorice rope with slip knots and
arrange atop frosted cake. Fill
centers of balloons with candies.
To store, apply Fresh-N-Fancy
Seal. Makes 12 to 15 servings.

PUMPKIN CAKE ROLL

¾ cup all-purpose flour
1 teaspoon baking powder
½ teaspoon salt
2 teaspoons ground
cinnamon
1 teaspoon ground ginger
½ teaspoon ground nutmeg
3 eggs
1 cup sugar
⅔ cup canned pumpkin
1 teaspoon lemon juice
1 cup chopped walnuts
Sifted powdered sugar
Cream Cheese Filling
(see recipe below)

In Small Mix-N-Stor pitcher, stir
together flour, baking powder, salt,
and spices. In a small mixing bowl,
beat eggs at high speed of electric
mixer till thick and lemon colored.
Gradually beat in sugar till
dissolved. Stir in pumpkin and
lemon juice. Fold dry ingredients
into pumpkin mixture. Spread in
lightly greased and floured
15x10x1-inch jelly roll pan.
Sprinkle with walnuts. Bake in a
375° oven 12 to 15 minutes.
Immediately loosen edges of
cake and turn onto a towel
sprinkled with powdered sugar.
Starting with narrow end, roll cake
and the towel together, nuts on
outside. Cool.
For Cream Cheese Filling, in a
Small Mix-N-Pour pitcher, beat 2
3-ounce packages *cream cheese*,
¼ cup *butter or margarine*, and ½
teaspoon *vanilla* till smooth. Beat
in 1 cup *powdered sugar*. Unroll
cake; spread with filling. Reroll;
chill in inverted Jumbo Bread
Server or Kracker Keeper. Makes
10 servings.

CHOCO-BUTTERMILK CAKE

2 cups all-purpose flour
2 cups sugar
1 teaspoon baking soda
½ teaspoon salt
1 cup butter or margarine
1 cup water
⅓ cup unsweetened cocoa
powder
2 eggs
½ cup buttermilk or sour
milk
1½ teaspoons vanilla
Buttermilk Chocolate
Frosting (see recipe
below)

In Large Mixing Bowl, stir together
flour, sugar, baking soda, and salt.
In medium saucepan, combine
butter or margarine, water, and
cocoa powder. Bring mixture just
to boiling, stirring constantly.
Remove from heat. Add cocoa
mixture to dry ingredients; beat at
low speed of electric mixer just till
combined. Add eggs, buttermilk,
and vanilla; beat 1 minute at low
speed. (Batter will be thin.) Turn
batter into greased and floured
13x9x2-inch baking pan. Bake in
350° oven 25 minutes. Turn out on
wire rack to cool slightly; transfer to
a Fresh-N-Fancy base. Frost.
*For Buttermilk Chocolate
Frosting,* in a saucepan, combine
¼ cup *butter or margarine*, 3
tablespoons *cocoa powder*, and 3
tablespoons *buttermilk*; bring to
boil. Remove from heat. Add 2¼
cups sifted *powdered sugar* and
½ teaspoon *vanilla*; beat till
smooth. Stir in ¾ cup coarsely
chopped *pecans*. Pour hot frosting
over the warm cake, spreading
evenly. Makes 12 to 15 servings.

*Delight kids at a party with festive Balloon Cake. And, you can bake and
decorate ahead when you use the Fresh-N-Fancy container.*

SHORT-CUT COOKIES AND CAKES

BOSTON CREAM PIE

The cake in this recipe is a Hot Milk Sponge Cake. If you like, bake the batter in a greased 9x9x2-inch baking pan as directed. Frost as desired. Pictured on page 63—

- 2 eggs
- 1 cup sugar
- 1 cup all-purpose flour
- 1 teaspoon baking powder
- ¼ teaspoon salt
- ½ cup milk
- 2 tablespoons butter
- Vanilla Cream Filling (see recipe at right)
- Chocolate Glaze (see recipe at right)

In Medium Mixing Bowl, beat eggs at high speed of electric mixer 4 minutes or till thick and lemon colored. Gradually add sugar, beating at medium speed 4 to 5 minutes or till sugar is nearly dissolved. Mix flour, baking powder, and salt. Add to egg mixture; stir just till blended.

In small saucepan, heat milk and butter till butter melts; stir into batter. Beat at low speed till well mixed. Turn into greased and floured 9x1½-inch round baking pan. Bake in a 350° oven for 25 to 30 minutes or till done. Cool 10 minutes on wire rack. Remove from pan; cool thoroughly. Split cake horizontally into 2 layers. Place 1 layer on 10″ Cake Taker Base; spread with Vanilla Cream Filling. Place second layer atop. Spread Chocolate Glaze over top of cake, drizzling down sides. Apply Seal to store. Makes 8 servings.

VANILLA CREAM FILLING

Next time, serve the vanilla cream filling as a pudding dessert with fresh fruit on top —

- ⅓ cup sugar
- 2 tablespoons all-purpose flour
- 1 tablespoon cornstarch
- ¼ teaspoon salt
- 1¼ cups milk
- 1 tablespoon butter or margarine
- 2 slightly beaten eggs
- 1 teaspoon vanilla

In a saucepan, combine sugar, flour, cornstarch, and salt. Stir in milk; add butter or margarine. Cook and stir over medium heat till thickened and bubbly. Reduce heat; cook and stir 2 minutes more. Gradually stir about half the hot mixture into eggs; return to remaining hot mixture. Cook and stir till nearly bubbly; reduce heat. Cook and stir 1 to 2 minutes more but do not boil. Remove from heat; stir in vanilla. Cover surface with waxed paper. Chill.

CHOCOLATE GLAZE

- ¼ cup sugar
- 2 teaspoons cornstarch
- ⅓ cup water
- ½ square (½ ounce) unsweetened chocolate, cut up
- ½ teaspoon vanilla

Combine sugar, cornstarch, and dash *salt*. Stir in water; add chocolate. Cook and stir till bubbly. Cook and stir 2 minutes more. Stir in vanilla.

BUSY-DAY CAKE

This one-bowl cake takes just minutes to mix—

- ⅓ cup shortening
- 1½ cups all-purpose flour
- ¾ cup sugar
- ¾ cup milk
- 1 egg
- 2½ teaspoons baking powder
- 1½ teaspoons vanilla

In Medium Mixing Bowl, beat shortening on medium speed of electric mixer 30 seconds. Add flour, sugar, milk, egg, baking powder, vanilla, and ½ teaspoon *salt;* beat till blended. Beat 2 minutes on medium speed. Turn batter into greased and floured 9x9x2-inch baking pan. Bake in 375° oven for 25 to 30 minutes. Cool. Store in the Fresh-N-Fancy® container. Frost with Butter Frosting or Orange Butter Frosting (see recipes, page 83) or Chocolate Butter Frosting (see recipe, page 76). Makes 9 servings.

CAKE PAN TIP

To be sure cakes slide out of the pan easily, prepare the pan before you begin mixing. Generously apply shortening, (about 1 tablespoon to the bottom of the pan). If you plan to frost the cake, spread the shortening up the sides of the pan. Add 2 to 3 teaspoons of flour to the greased pan. Tilt and tap the pan to distribute the flour evenly. When the greased area is flour-dusted, dump the excess flour.

APPLE UPSIDE-DOWN CAKE

1 large tart cooking apple
¼ cup butter or margarine
½ cup honey
½ cup broken walnuts
1 package 1-layer-size spice cake mix

Core unpeeled apple and slice into ⅛-inch-thick rings. In a 10-inch oven-proof skillet melt butter. Stir in honey; add apple rings. Cook for 3 minutes, turning apples once. Remove from heat. Sprinkle with nuts. In Medium Mixing Bowl, prepare cake mix according to package directions. Pour batter over apples. Bake in a 350° oven for 30 to 35 minutes. Cool for 5 minutes in pan. Invert onto serving plate; serve warm. Store leftover cake in 12″ Pie Taker. Makes 8 servings.

CRUNCHY APRICOT CAKE

1 21-ounce can apricot pie filling
1 package 1-layer-size yellow cake mix
½ cup coconut
½ cup chopped pecans
¼ cup butter or margarine, melted

Spread pie filling in the bottom of a 9x9x2-inch baking pan. In Medium Mixing Bowl, prepare cake mix according to package directions. Pour batter over pie filling; sprinkle with coconut and chopped pecans. Drizzle with melted butter. Bake in 350° oven about 40 minutes. Serve warm. Makes 9 servings.

NO-BAKE FRUITCAKE

1 cup tiny marshmallows
½ cup evaporated milk
1 teaspoon grated orange peel
½ cup orange juice
4 cups graham cracker crumbs
¼ teaspoon ground nutmeg
¼ teaspoon ground cinnamon
1½ cups pitted dates, snipped
1 cup mixed candied fruits and peels, chopped
¼ cup maraschino cherries, sliced

In a Small Mix-N-Stor® pitcher, mix together marshmallows, evaporated milk, orange peel, and juice. In Large Mixing Bowl, combine remaining ingredients. Add milk mixture; blend well. Press graham cracker mixture firmly into Jel-N-Serve® mold. Apply Seal. Store in refrigerator. Unmold.

GUMDROP CUPCAKES

1 14½-ounce package gingerbread mix
½ cup water
1 egg
½ cup applesauce
¾ cup tiny gumdrops
½ cup chopped walnuts
½ cup raisins

Reserve 2 tablespoons gingerbread mix. In Medium Mixing Bowl, combine remaining mix, water, and egg. Beat 1 minute on low speed of electric mixer. Stir in applesauce. Quarter gumdrops; toss with reserved mix to coat. Fold gumdrops, nuts, and raisins into batter. Spoon into 18 paper bake cup-lined muffin cups. Bake in 350° oven 20 to 25 minutes. Store in a 12″ Pie Taker. Makes 18.

LAST-MINUTE FRUITCAKE

2½ cups all-purpose flour
1 teaspoon baking soda
1 teaspoon salt
¼ teaspoon ground cinnamon
¼ teaspoon ground cloves
¼ teaspoon ground nutmeg
½ cup shortening
¾ cup sugar
1 egg
1 teaspoon instant coffee crystals
¼ cup water
1 cup applesauce
2 cups diced mixed candied fruits and peels
1 cup raisins
1 cup chopped nuts

Stir together flour, baking soda, salt, cinnamon, cloves, and nutmeg. In Large Mixing Bowl, beat shortening on medium speed of electric mixer about 30 seconds. Add sugar and beat till fluffy. Add egg; beat well. Dissolve coffee crystals in water; stir in applesauce. Add dry ingredients and applesauce mixture alternately to beaten mixture, beating on low speed after each addition just till combined. Fold in mixed fruits and peels, raisins, and nuts.

Turn batter into two greased and floured 8x4x2-inch loaf pans. Bake in 325° oven for 1 to 1¼ hours or till cakes test done. Place cakes on wire racks; cool for 10 minutes. Remove from pans; cool completely. Store in the Square-Keeper® container in refrigerator at least 24 hours before serving. Makes 2 loaves.

SHORT-CUT COOKIES AND CAKES

PEANUT BUTTER-FILLED FUDGE CUPCAKES

Kids will love the surprise inside—

- 1 cup all-purpose flour
- ⅓ cup unsweetened cocoa powder
- ¾ teaspoon baking soda
- ½ teaspoon salt
- ⅓ cup shortening
- 1 cup packed brown sugar
- 1 teaspoon vanilla
- 2 eggs
- ½ cup milk
- 1 3-ounce package cream cheese, softened
- ¼ cup chunky peanut butter
- 1 tablespoon honey
- 1 tablespoon milk

In Medium Mixing Bowl, stir together flour, cocoa powder, soda, and salt. In Large Mixing Bowl, beat shortening about 30 seconds. Add brown sugar and vanilla; beat well. Add eggs, one at a time, beating well after each. Add dry ingredients alternately with the ½ cup milk, beating well after each addition. In Medium Mixing Bowl, combine cream cheese, peanut butter, honey and 1 tablespoon milk; beat well. Place a scant 2 tablespoons batter in paper bake cup-lined muffin cups. Spoon about 1 rounded teaspoon cream cheese mixture into center of each; fill cups half full with remaining batter (about 1 tablespoon each). Bake in 375° oven 20 minutes or till done. Cool on wire rack. Store in 12″ Pie Taker. Makes 16 to 18 cupcakes.

CARROT CAKE

- 2 cups all-purpose flour
- 2 cups sugar
- 1 teaspoon baking powder
- 1 teaspoon baking soda
- 1 teaspoon salt
- 1 teaspoon ground cinnamon
- 3 cups finely shredded carrot
- 1 cup cooking oil
- 4 eggs
  Cream Cheese Frosting (see recipe below)
- ½ cup chopped nuts

In Large Mixing Bowl, stir together flour, sugar, baking powder, soda, salt, and cinnamon. Add shredded carrot, oil, and eggs; beat with electric mixer till well combined. Beat on medium speed for 2 minutes. Turn into greased and floured 13x9x2-inch baking pan or two 9x1½-inch round baking pans. Bake large pan in 325° oven for 50 to 60 minutes or till cake tests done. (Bake 9-inch layers in 325° oven about 40 minutes or till cake tests done.) Cool on wire rack. (Remove layers from pans after cooling 10 minutes). Cool thoroughly. Frost. Sprinkle with chopped nuts. Store in Fresh-N-Fancy® container or 10″ Cake Taker. Makes 12 servings.

For Cream Cheese Frosting, in Small Mix-N-Stor® pitcher, beat together one 3-ounce package *cream cheese*, ¼ cup *butter or margarine*, and 1 teaspoon *vanilla*. Gradually add 2 cups sifted *powdered sugar*, beating till smooth.

FUDGE PUDDING CAKE

- 1 package 1-layer-size chocolate cake mix
- 1 tablespoon instant coffee crystals
- 2½ cups water
- 1 package 4-serving-size regular chocolate pudding mix
  Whipped cream

In Medium Mixing Bowl, prepare cake mix according to package directions. Turn into greased and floured 9x9x2-inch baking pan. Dissolve coffee crystals in water; stir into pudding mix. Pour over cake batter. Bake in 350° oven for 40 to 45 minutes. Serve warm with whipped cream. Serves 9.

BUTTER FROSTING

Next time, try the Orange Butter Frosting variation—

- 6 tablespoons butter
- 4½ to 4¾ cups sifted powdered sugar
- ¼ cup milk
- 1½ teaspoons vanilla

In a Large Mix-N-Stor pitcher, beat butter till light and fluffy. Gradually add about half the powdered sugar; beat well. Beat in milk and vanilla, then remaining powdered sugar. Beat in additional milk, if necessary, to make of spreading consistency. Frosts tops and sides of two 8- or 9-inch layers, top of one 15x10-inch pan bar cookies, about 24 cupcakes, or 48 cookies.

Orange Butter Frosting: Prepare Butter Frosting, except use *orange juice* for milk and beat in 1 teaspoon finely shredded *orange peel* with the vanilla.

No-frost Peanut Butter-Filled Fudge Cupcakes make a nutritious after-school or lunch-box treat served along with mugs of cold milk.

PRIZE-WINNING PIES AND COBBLERS

SPICY BUTTERSCOTCH PIE

- Graham Cracker Crust (see recipe at right)
- ¼ cup finely chopped walnuts
- 1 4-serving-size package *instant* butterscotch pudding mix
- ½ teaspoon ground cinnamon
- ¼ teaspoon ground nutmeg
  Dash ground ginger
- 1¾ cups milk
- 1 4-ounce carton frozen whipped dessert topping, thawed

Prepare Graham Cracker Crust as directed, except stir walnuts into crumbs with sugar.

In a Small Mix-N-Stor ® pitcher, combine pudding mix, cinnamon, nutmeg, and ginger. Add milk and beat according to package directions. Turn *1 cup* of the pudding mixture into pie crust, spreading evenly in bottom. To remaining pudding mixture, stir in *half* the dessert topping; spread evenly over entire surface. Apply Seal and chill till set. Dollop remaining dessert topping over pie. Sprinkle with cinnamon, if desired. Cut pie with table knife to serve. Apply Seal. Chill to store. Serves 8.

TOPPING TIP

Save extra whipped cream to use later as a dessert garnish. Drop heaping spoonfuls of whipped cream onto the bottom of a chilled Cold Cut Keeper, swirling tops with the spoon. Apply Seal; store in the freezer for up to 3 months. Lift from Cold Cut Keeper with a spatula and thaw in the refrigerator about 45 minutes before using as a dessert garnish.

GRAHAM CRACKER CRUST

- 18 graham cracker squares
- ¼ cup sugar
- 6 tablespoons butter or margarine, melted

Place crackers on Pastry Sheet. Use Rolling Pin to crush into fine crumbs; measure 1¼ cups crumbs. Place crumbs in Medium Mixing Bowl; stir in sugar. Stir melted butter into crumb mixture; apply Seal and toss to thoroughly combine. Turn into a 9″ Pie Taker base; spread evenly. Press onto the bottom and sides to form a firm, even crust. Apply Seal; chill 1 hour or till firm.

CHEESECAKE FRUIT PIE

- Graham Cracker Crust (see recipe above)
- 2 cups tiny marshmallows or 20 large marshmallows
- 2 tablespoons milk
- 1 cup dairy sour cream
- 1 3-ounce package cream cheese, softened
- 1 teaspoon vanilla
- 1 17-ounce can fruit cocktail, drained

Prepare Graham Cracker Crust. In saucepan, heat marshmallows and milk over low heat till melted. Cool 10 minutes. In Large Mixing Bowl, beat sour cream, cream cheese, vanilla, and dash *salt* with electric mixer till smooth. Stir in marshmallow mixture and fruit. Turn into crust. Chill till set. Apply Seal; chill to store. Serves 8.

BLUEBERRY YOGURT CHIFFON PIE

- Graham Cracker Crust (see recipe at left)
- ¼ cup sugar
- 1 envelope unflavored gelatin
- ½ teaspoon salt
- ¼ cup water
- 2 slightly beaten egg yolks
- 1 cup cream-style cottage cheese
- 1 8-ounce carton (1 cup) blueberry yogurt
- 2 egg whites
- ¼ cup sugar
  Unsweetened whipped cream (optional)

Prepare Graham Cracker Crust. Chill. In saucepan, combine ¼ cup sugar, gelatin, and salt; stir in water and egg yolks. Cook and stir till the mixture is slightly thickened; cool.

Sieve cottage cheese; stir in gelatin mixture. Add yogurt; beat till blended. In a Small Mix-N-Stor pitcher, beat egg whites till soft peaks form. Gradually add ¼ cup sugar, beating till stiff peaks form. Fold stiff-beaten egg whites into the gelatin mixture. Chill till mixture mounds when spooned. Turn into chilled crumb crust. Apply Seal; chill several hours or overnight till set. Garnish with dollops of unsweetened whipped cream, if desired. Apply Seal and chill to store. Makes 8 servings.

Rich and creamy Spicy Butterscotch Pie makes the perfect totable party dessert. The Graham Cracker Crust is formed right in the 9″ Pie Taker base.

PRIZE-WINNING PIES AND COBBLERS

APPLE PIE

EASY EGG PASTRY for
for Double-Crust Pie
(see recipe, page 57)
6 to 8 (2 pounds) cooking
   apples, peeled,
   quartered, and cored
1 tablespoon lemon juice
   (optional)
1 cup sugar
2 tablespoons all-purpose
   flour
½ to 1 teaspoon ground
   cinnamon
   Dash ground nutmeg
1 tablespoon butter or
   margarine
   Sugar (optional)

Use Pastry Sheet and Rolling Pin to roll pastry to fit 9-inch pie plate. Line pie plate with half the pastry. Trim pastry to edge of pie plate. Use Grater Bowl slicing blade to slice 6 cups apples; remove grater. If apples lack tartness, sprinkle with the 1 tablespoon lemon juice. Add sugar, flour, cinnamon, and nutmeg to Grater Bowl; apply storage Seal and gently shake bowl to coat apples with sugar. Fill pastry lined pie plate with apple mixture; dot with butter. Cut slits in top crust for escape of steam; place pastry atop filling. Seal and flute edge. Sprinkle some sugar atop, if desired. To prevent over-browning, cover edge of pie with foil. Bake in 375° oven for 25 minutes. Remove foil; bake for 20 to 25 minutes more or till crust is golden. Cool on wire rack. Store in 9" Pie Taker. Makes 8 servings.

FRENCH CRUNCH PEACH PIE

1 EASY EGG PASTRY
   SHELL (see recipe,
   page 57)
2 eggs
1 tablespoon lemon juice
⅓ cup sugar
1 29-ounce can and one
   16-ounce can peach
   slices, drained
1 cup finely crushed
   vanilla wafers
   (22 wafers)
½ cup chopped toasted
   almonds
¼ cup butter or margarine,
   melted
   Vanilla ice cream or cheddar cheese triangles

Line Pastry Shell with foil and fill with beans (see Single-Crust Pastry at right). Do not prick pastry. Bake in 450° oven for 5 minutes.

In Medium Mixing Bowl, beat eggs and lemon juice till blended; stir in sugar. Fold in drained peaches; turn into the partially baked pastry shell. Stir together vanilla wafer crumbs, almonds, and butter or margarine; sprinkle over peach mixture. To prevent overbrowning, cover edge of pie with foil. Bake in 375° oven for 20 minutes. Remove foil; bake for 20 to 25 minutes more or till filling is set in center. Cool on rack before serving. Serve with scoops of ice cream or cheese triangles. Cover and store in 9" Pie Taker. Makes 8 servings.

PASTRY TIP

1. Roll out dough, on lightly floured Pastry Sheet, to a 12-inch circle. For easier rolling, fill Rolling Pin with ice water.

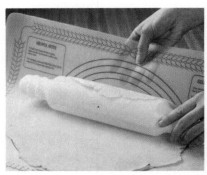

2. Wrap pastry around Rolling Pin by lifting Pastry Sheet with pastry.

3. Unroll pastry loosely into pie plate. Fit pastry by lifting edges gently into plate and pushing into plate. Trim pastry ½ inch beyond edge of plate; fold under and flute.

CHOCOLATE LAYER PIE

 EASY EGG PASTRY for
  Single-Crust Pie (see
  recipe, page 57)
1 6-serving-size package
  regular chocolate
  pudding mix
1 4-serving-size package
  instant vanilla
  pudding mix
1 cup milk
1 cup dairy sour cream
2 tablespoons milk
  Chocolate curls (optional)

Using Rolling Pin, roll out pastry on lightly floured Pastry Sheet. Line a 9-inch pie plate. Trim pastry to ½ inch beyond edge. Flute edge; prick pastry. Fill with dry beans, referring to tip below. Bake in 450° oven for 10 to 12 minutes or till golden. Cool thoroughly on wire rack.

In saucepan, prepare chocolate pudding according to package directions for pie filling. Cover surface; cool to room temperature. In Medium Mixing Bowl, prepare vanilla pudding according to package directions for pie except use 1 cup milk; stir in sour cream. Beat mixture with electric mixer or rotary beater at low speed for 1½ to 2 minutes or till creamy and well blended. Stir 1 cup of the prepared vanilla pudding into the cooled chocolate, mixing till smooth. Spread chocolate filling evenly in baked pastry shell. Add the 2 tablespoons milk to the remaining vanilla pudding, stirring till smooth. Immediately spread vanilla pudding over chocolate filling. Place in 9″ Pie Taker; apply Seal. Chill 3 to 4 hours or overnight. Garnish pie with chocolate curls, if desired. Cover and chill to store. Makes 8 servings.

QUICK APPLE CREAM PIE

1 21-ounce can French
  apple pie filling
1 EASY EGG PASTRY
  SHELL, baked and
  cooled (see recipe,
  page 57)
1 4-serving-size package
  instant vanilla pudding
  mix
1¾ cups buttermilk
2 tablespoons sliced
  toasted almonds

Pour pie filling into baked pastry shell. In Small Mix-N-Stor® pitcher, combine pudding mix and buttermilk. Beat about 30 seconds or till thickened. Pour pudding mixture over the pie filling. Place in 9″ Pie Taker; apply Seal and chill. Garnish with toasted almonds. Cover and chill to store. Makes 8 servings.

BANANA-NUT TURNOVERS

The glaze on these pastries can be achieved on two-crust pies, too. Simply brush the crust with milk and sprinkle with sugar as directed in this recipe—

 EASY EGG PASTRY for
  Double-Crust pie
  (see recipe, page 57)
4 medium bananas
2 tablespoons lemon juice
½ cup chopped pecans
⅓ cup packed brown sugar
¾ teaspoon ground
  cinnamon
  Milk
  Granulated sugar

Use Pastry Sheet and Rolling Pin to roll each package of pastry to a 12-inch square. With a pastry wheel or table knife, cut each square into four 6-inch squares. Slice half a banana onto each pastry square. Sprinkle each with a little lemon juice. Top each with 1 tablespoon pecans. In a 10-oz. Servalier® bowl, combine brown sugar and cinnamon; sprinkle about 1 tablespoon over each square. Fold each pastry square in half diagonally; moisten edges and seal. Place on baking sheet. Brush with milk; sprinkle with granulated sugar. Bake in 375° oven for 25 to 30 minutes. Makes 8.

SINGLE-CRUST PASTRY TIP

For a more uniformly shaped pastry shell, after pricking the shell with a fork, line it with foil and fill with dry beans to prevent puffing. The weight of the beans keeps the pastry in shape. Bake pastry in 450° oven for 5 minutes. Remove beans and foil; continue baking 5 to 7 minutes more or till pastry is golden.

If a recipe calls for partially baking an unpricked crust before adding filling (such as for custard pies or quiches), fill pastry shell with foil and beans to keep pastry in shape. Partially bake pastry in 450° oven 5 minutes. Add filling; continue baking according to recipe directions.

PRIZE-WINNING PIES AND COBBLERS

BANANA SPLIT PIE

Pictured on page 63 —

    1 EASY EGG PASTRY
         SHELL
         (see recipe, page 57)
    2 medium bananas
    1 tablespoon lemon juice
    1 quart strawberry ice
         cream
  ½ of a 4½-ounce container
         (1 cup) frozen
         whipped dessert
         topping, thawed
  ⅓ cup maraschino cherries
         (12), halved
    2 tablespoons chopped
         walnuts
  ½ cup tiny marshmallows
  ¼ cup semisweet chocolate
         pieces
    2 tablespoons milk

Prick bottom and sides of Pastry with a fork. Bake in 450° oven for 10 to 12 minutes or till golden. Cool on wire rack.

Thinly slice bananas and sprinkle with lemon juice; arrange on bottom of pastry shell. In Large Mixing Bowl, soften ice cream till just pliable; spread over bananas. Freeze firm in 9″ Pie Taker.

Spread dessert topping over ice cream. Top with cherries; sprinkle with nuts. Return pie to freezer; freeze firm.

In saucepan, combine marshmallows, chocolate pieces, and milk. Cook and stir over low heat till thoroughly combined.

To serve, let pie stand about 30 minutes at room temperature. Drizzle warm or cool chocolate sauce over pie; serve immediately. Makes 8 servings.

S'MORE PIE

         Graham Cracker Crust
         (see recipe, page 84)
    3 eggs
    2 cups milk
    1 6-serving size package
         regular vanilla pudding
         mix
    1 cup tiny marshmallows
  ½ cup milk chocolate
         pieces
  ½ teaspoon vanilla
  ¼ teaspoon cream of
         tartar
    6 tablespoons sugar

Prepare Graham Cracker Crust as directed except press crumb mixture firmly onto bottom and sides of 9-inch pie plate. Bake in 375° oven for 5 to 6 minutes or till browned. Cool.

Separate egg yolks from whites; set whites aside. In saucepan, beat egg yolks slightly. Stir in milk and vanilla pudding mix. Cook and stir till thickened and bubbly. Remove from heat. Cover surface; cool. Place marshmallows in baked crust. Sprinkle chocolate pieces evenly over marshmallows. Spoon filling atop.

In Medium Mixing Bowl, beat the egg whites, vanilla, and cream of tartar at medium speed of electric mixer till soft peaks form. Gradually add sugar, about 1 tablespoon at a time, beating at high speed about 4 minutes more or till stiff peaks form. Spread the meringue over filling; seal to edge. Bake in 350° oven for 12 to 15 minutes or till meringue is golden. Cool. Place in 9″ Pie Taker. Cover and chill to store. Makes 8 servings.

MIRACLE CUSTARD PIE

    2 cups milk
    4 eggs
  ½ cup sugar
  ½ cup all-purpose flour
  ¼ cup butter or margarine,
         cut up
    1 teaspoon vanilla
    1 cup flaked coconut
         Ground nutmeg

In blender container, combine milk, eggs, sugar, flour, cut-up butter or margarine, vanilla, and ¼ teaspoon *salt*. Cover; blend about 10 seconds or till well mixed (do not overblend). Stir in coconut. Pour egg mixture into greased 9-inch pie plate. Sprinkle a little nutmeg atop filling. Bake in 350° oven about 40 minutes or till knife inserted near center comes out clean. (As pie bakes, it forms its own soft crust.) Cool. Place in 9″ Pie Taker. Cover and chill to store. Makes 8 servings.

CUSTARD PIE TIP

Custard pies consist of an egg and milk mixture in which the egg cooks and thus thickens the pie during baking. Variations include pumpkin and pecan pies.

To check for doneness after baking for the recommended time, insert a knife near center; if it comes out clean with no custard filling clinging to it, the pie is done.

Or, gently shake the pie. If the area that appears to be liquid is less than the size of a quarter, the pie is done. Remember, it will continue to set after it is removed from the oven.

STRAWBERRY FUNNYCAKE

Here's an easy version of the Pennsylvania Dutch pie and cake all in one. Try the chocolate variation, too —

EASY EGG PASTRY for
Single-Crust Pie
(see recipe, page 57)
1   10-ounce package frozen
      strawberries, thawed
½   cup sugar
¼   cup butter or margarine
2   tablespoons light corn
      syrup
1   1-layer-size package
      white cake mix

Use Rolling Pin and Pastry Sheet to roll pastry to fit 9-inch pie plate. Flute edges high; set aside. For Strawberry Sauce, use a 1-qt. Strainer over a Small Mix-N-Stor® pitcher to drain strawberries; measure and reserve ½ cup syrup. In medium saucepan, combine sugar, butter, reserved strawberry syrup, and corn syrup. Cook and stir till thickened and bubbly; cook and stir 1 to 2 minutes more. Remove from heat; stir in strawberries. Cool to lukewarm.

In Medium Mixing Bowl, prepare cake mix according to package directions. Pour batter into unbaked pastry shell. Pour strawberry sauce evenly over batter. Bake in 350° oven 40 to 45 minutes. Cool at least 1 hour. Serve with ice cream, if desired. Place in 9" Pie Taker; cover and chill to store. Serves 8.

Chocolate Funnycake: For chocolate sauce, in Small Mix-N-Stor pitcher, stir together ½ cup *sugar* and ¼ cup *unsweetened cocoa powder*. Blend in ½ cup *hot water* and ½ teaspoon *vanilla*. Continue as directed for Strawberry Funnycake except use chocolate sauce in place of strawberry sauce.

HONEY-RHUBARB BETTY

1   pound fresh or frozen
      rhubarb
¾   cup sugar
1   teaspoon ground nutmeg
      Dash salt
2   tablespoons water
6   tablespoons butter
½   cup honey
5   slices bread

Thaw rhubarb, if frozen; cut into ½-inch slices. In Large Mix-N-Stor pitcher, combine rhubarb, sugar, nutmeg, salt, and water. Turn into a 10x6x2-inch baking dish. In medium saucepan, melt butter with honey. Cut bread slices into ½-inch cubes; stir into butter and honey. Spoon evenly over top of rhubarb. Bake in 375° oven 30 minutes or till topping is golden. Serves 4 to 6.

PEANUT BUTTER-BANANA CRUNCH

4   cups sliced bananas
1   tablespoon lemon juice
½   teaspoon ground
      cinnamon
½   cup all-purpose flour
½   cup packed brown sugar
⅓   cup chunk-style peanut
      butter
3   tablespoons butter or
      margarine
      Whipped cream
      (optional)

Place bananas in 8x1½-inch round baking dish. Add lemon juice and cinnamon, stirring lightly to coat fruit. In Medium Mixing Bowl, combine flour and brown sugar; cut in peanut butter and butter till mixture is crumbly. Sprinkle over bananas. Bake in 375° oven for 25 minutes. Top with whipped cream, if desired. Serves 6.

FRESH FRUIT CRISP

For 4 servings, double the recipe and bake in a 1-quart casserole or in four individual dishes —

2   tablespoons quick-
      cooking rolled oats
2   tablespoons brown
      sugar
1   tablespoon all-purpose
      flour
1   tablespoon chopped
      pecans (optional)
⅛   teaspoon ground
      cinnamon
      Dash salt
      Dash ground nutmeg
1   tablespoon butter or
      margarine
2   cups sliced peeled
      peaches, apples, or
      pears
2   teaspoons granulated
      sugar
      Vanilla ice cream or
      light cream

In Small Mix-N-Stor pitcher, stir together rolled oats, brown sugar, flour, pecans, cinnamon, salt, and nutmeg. Cut in butter or margarine till mixture is crumbly; set aside.

Divide fresh peaches, apples, or pears between two 1-cup casseroles. Sprinkle granulated sugar over fruit. Cover fruit with rolled oat mixture. Bake in 325° oven 45 to 50 minutes or till fruit is tender when tested with a fork. Serve warm with vanilla ice cream or light cream. Makes 2 servings.

PRIZE-WINNING PIES AND COBBLERS

ORANGE WHOLE WHEAT COBBLER

For 4 servings, double the recipe and bake in an 8x1½-inch round baking pan—

- 2 tablespoons sugar
- 1 tablespoon cornstarch
- ½ cup water
- ¼ cup orange marmalade
- 2 tablespoons frozen orange juice concentrate
- 2 tablespoons butter or margarine
- ½ cup HEARTY WHEAT MASTER MIX (see recipe, page 67) or packaged biscuit mix
  Dash ground nutmeg
- 3 tablespoons milk
- ½ pint (1 cup) vanilla ice cream (optional)

In small saucepan, thoroughly stir together sugar and cornstarch. Blend in water, orange marmalade, and orange juice concentrate. Cook and stir till thickened and bubbly. Cook and stir 1 to 2 minutes longer. Stir in butter or margarine. Keep hot.

In Small Mix-N-Stor® pitcher, stir together Hearty Wheat Master Mix and nutmeg. Add milk, stirring just till moistened. Pour hot orange sauce into a 5x5x1½-inch baking dish. Immediately drop dough in 2 portions atop orange sauce. Bake in 350° oven about 25 minutes or till topping is done.

Spoon warm cobbler and orange sauce into 2 Dessert Set dishes. Place vanilla ice cream atop each serving, if desired. Spoon some of the orange sauce over ice cream. Makes 2 servings.

PEANUT-PEACH COBBLER

If you prefer, substitute half a roll of purchased refrigerated sugar cookie dough, cut into 9 slices, for the Basic Cookie Mix biscuits—

- 2 cups BASIC COOKIE MIX (see recipe, page 75)
- 1 egg
- 1 tablespoon milk
- 1 teaspoon vanilla
- ⅓ cup peanut butter
- ¼ cup packed brown sugar
- ¼ cup butter or margarine
- 1 tablespoon lemon juice
- 1 29-ounce can peach slices
  Vanilla ice cream

In Medium Mixing Bowl, combine Basic Cookie Mix, egg, milk, and vanilla; mix well to make a very stiff dough and set aside. In a saucepan, combine peanut butter, brown sugar, butter or margarine, and lemon juice. Cook and stir till peanut butter and butter have melted and mixture is smooth. Add undrained peach slices; cut up any large pieces. Cook over medium heat till bubbly, stirring frequently. Meanwhile, divide cookie dough into 9 portions. Shape each into a ball; flatten slightly into biscuit shape. Turn hot peach mixture into an 8x8x2-inch baking dish. Immediately top with cookie dough pieces. Bake in 400° oven for 25 minutes or till golden. Serve warm with ice cream. Makes 9 servings.

BLUEBERRY SLUMP

This quick and easy dessert is not new at all. In colonial New England, sweetened biscuit dough cooked atop steaming fruit and sugar mixtures were called "slumps"—

- 1 cup all-purpose flour
- 2 tablespoons sugar
- 2 teaspoons baking powder
- ¼ teaspoon salt
- 1 tablespoon butter or margarine
- 4 cups fresh or frozen blueberries
- 1 cup water
- ⅓ cup sugar
  Dash salt
- 1 tablespoon lemon juice
- ½ cup milk
  Light cream

In Medium Mixing Bowl, stir together flour, 2 tablespoons sugar, baking powder, and ¼ teaspoon salt; cut in butter or margarine till mixture resembles coarse crumbs. Set aside.

In medium saucepan, combine blueberries, water, ⅓ cup sugar, and dash salt. Bring to boiling; reduce heat. Cover and simmer 5 minutes. Stir in lemon juice. Add milk to dry ingredients; stir till moistened. Drop dough in 6 spoonfuls into bubbling sauce (don't overlap). Cover tightly; cook over low heat 10 minutes without lifting cover. Serve hot with cream. Makes 6 servings.

Serve warm Orange Whole Wheat Cobbler spooned into the Tupperware Dessert Set. The dumplings start with the Hearty Wheat Master Mix.

Nutritious MENUS

It's easy to supply your family with appealing, wholesome meals when you're up on a few of the basics of good nutrition. This chapter provides a sampling of well-balanced menus for breakfasts, lunches, and dinners. And, there's an update on the old-fashioned Four (it's now Five) Food Groups and how to apply them to your daily menu planning.

Pictured clockwise from bottom left are: Barbecue Fried Chicken, Pick-A-Dillies, Creamy Potato Salad, and Party Deviled Eggs. (See Index for recipe pages.)

PLANNING TO EAT RIGHT

To make your meal planning easier, you need to consider good nutrition, your family's food preferences and budget, the family's mealtime schedule, and the meal preparation time. Also, consider what food storage space you have available. If you're watching your food budget, keep in mind current good food buys, taking advantage of seasonal foods and specials when you can.

Mealtime schedules are an important consideration. With busy workdays and even busier evening schedules for some family members, consider planning menus around make-ahead foods (both the refrigerated and frozen types), and quick-to-cook dishes. Or, consider enlisting family members to pitch in. And use work- and time-saving appliances, for food preparation, too.

One efficient way to plan menus is to plan for several days or a week at a time. Equipped with recipes, newspaper food ads, and a knowledge of good nutrition (review the basic food groups at right), write out your menus, thinking about the entire day's variety of foods. At the same time, write out a detailed shopping list — it saves looking up all the recipes again. One well-planned trip to the grocery store with a shopping list in hand should save you both time and money.

PLANNING NUTRITIOUS MEALS

To help you plan nutritious meals incorporating foods from the basic food groups, follow this seven-step guideline, keeping in mind all the day's menus:

1. Plan the protein main dish from the meat group.

2. Add a bread or cereal product to complement the main dish.

3. Choose a vegetable.

4. Pick a fruit or vegetable salad to complement the main dish.

5. Add a dessert that's appropriate to the rest of the meal. Fruits make a good dessert, as do milk-based desserts, such as pudding. Remember that a light dessert is best after a heavy meal and vice versa.

6. Choose a beverage. This is an excellent place for a serving from the milk group.

7. After the first four food group requirements are met, you can add extras from the fifth "fats-sweets" group to complement the meal and suit your family's tastes. Include these foods in moderation.

Perhaps not every meal will include all seven steps. Just make sure that all the day's menus include the proper amounts from the basic food groups, and that they include a wide variety of foods. To plan meals, simply plug in a specific food for each food group serving listed.

Combination foods — those that include foods from more than one food group — short-cut meal preparation. For example, a casserole may include a serving from the meat group, a serving from the vegetable group, and a bread/cereal serving, such as rice. Determine the foods in the dish, then determine what groups they come from to calculate the servings from the Basic Five Food Groups.

OTHER CONSIDERATIONS

Although nutrition is a top consideration when planning meals, it's not everything. If you want to be sure that well-planned

nutrients are eaten and are enjoyed, you may want to consider the aesthetic appeal of the food as well. It's important that foods have eye and taste appeal, and look and taste good together, too. Likewise, the table setting can provide a pleasing background for the food. Plan a variety of foods in the day's menus, as well as variety of color, form, flavor, texture, and temperature. Proper seasoning also is important. For example:

● Variety in color — Add a colorful garnish to a food that lacks color. A sprig of parsley, bright red radishes, cherry tomatoes, or a spiced crab apple can do wonders for plain meat and potatoes.

● Variety in the form of food — serving too many small pieces, too many similar shapes, or too many mixtures at one meal may not be visually appealing. Plan a contrast in sizes and shapes. Leave some foods whole and serve others sliced, cubed, mashed, or cut into matchstick-size strips.

● Variety in flavor — Complement a bland food with a tart or zippy food. Usually plan only one highly seasoned food per menu.

● Variety in texture — Serve some soft foods with some crisp ones. Breadsticks, croutons, and lettuce add "crunch."

● Variety in temperatures — Plan a balance of hot and cold foods. Then serve hot foods piping hot and cold foods well chilled.

● Season foods carefully so that their flavor isn't hidden by the seasoning.

● Try new foods and seasonings; experiment by serving only one new food at a meal, especially when serving youngsters.

THE BASIC FIVE FOOD GROUPS

Vegetables and Fruits	Breads and Cereals	Milk and Cheeses	Meats, Fish, Poultry, and Beans	Fats, Sweets, and Alcohol
Foods in this group include:				
All vegetables and fruits (fresh, canned, frozen, or dried) and their juices.	All foods based on whole grains or enriched flour or meal. Includes breads, biscuits, muffins, waffles, pancakes, pasta, rice, barley, bulgur, and cereals.	All types of milk, yogurt, cheese, ice milk, ice cream, and foods prepared with milk (milk shakes, puddings, and creamed soups).	Beef, veal, lamb, pork, poultry, fish, shellfish, variety meats, dry beans or peas, soybeans, lentils, eggs, peanuts and other nuts, peanut butter, and seeds.	Fats and oils; mayonnaise and salad dressings; concentrated sweets; sugared beverages; alcoholic beverages; unenriched, refined flour products.
Number of servings suggested daily:				
Everyone — 4 servings. (For vitamin C, use citrus fruits, melons, berries, tomatoes, or dark green vegetables daily. For vitamin A, use dark green or deep-yellow vegetables.)	Everyone — 4 servings. (For fiber, include some whole grain bread or cereal every day.)	Children, under 9 — 2 to 3 servings. Children, 9 to 12 — 3 servings. Teens — 4 servings. Adults — 2 servings. Pregnant women — 3 servings. Nursing mothers — 4 servings.	Everyone — 2 servings.	No serving number is recommended. In moderation, these foods can be used to round out meals, as long as requirements from the other categories are satisfied.
A serving consists of:				
½ cup or a typical portion such as 1 medium orange, ½ medium grapefruit, 1 medium potato, or 1 wedge of lettuce.	1 slice bread; 1 biscuit or muffin; 1 pancake or waffle; ½ to ¾ cup cooked pasta, rice, bulgur, or cereal; or 1 ounce ready-to-eat cereal.	1 cup milk or yogurt, 2 cups cottage cheese, 1⅓ ounces cheese, 2 ounces process cheese food or spread, or 1½ cups ice cream	2 to 3 ounces lean cooked meat, poultry, or fish; 1 to 1½ cups cooked dry beans, peas, or lentils; 2 eggs; or ¼ cup peanut butter	No specific serving size is recommended.
Major nutrients supplied:				
Carbohydrates, fiber, and vitamins A and C. Dark green vegetables are good sources of riboflavin, folacin, iron, and magnesium. Certain greens are valued for calcium.	Carbohydrates, protein, B vitamins, and iron. Whole grain products provide magnesium, folacin, and fiber.	Protein, calcium, riboflavin, and vitamins A, B_6, and B_{12}. When fortified, these products also provide vitamin D.	Protein, phosphorus, and vitamin B_6. Foods of animal origin provide vitamin B_{12}. Meats, dry beans, and dry peas provide iron. Liver and egg yolks provide vitamin A. Dry beans, peas, and nuts provide magnesium.	These foods provide very few nutrients in proportion to the number of calories they contain. Vegetable oils provide vitamin E and essential fatty acids.

BREAKFASTS IN A HURRY

ON-THE-RUN BREAKFAST

SLICED BANANAS IN ORANGE
JUICE
HOMEMADE GRANOLA WITH
MILK OR CREAM
COFFEE   CHOCOLATE MILK

HOMEMADE GRANOLA

*To store the granola more than
two weeks, store in the freezer—*

  5 cups regular rolled oats
  2 cups shredded coconut
  1 cup coarsely chopped
     almonds
  1 cup sesame seeds
  1 cup shelled sunflower
     seeds
  1 cup unsweetened wheat
     germ
  1 cup honey
  ½ cup cooking oil
  1 cup dried apricots,
     chopped
  1 cup raisins

In Fix-N-Mix® bowl, combine rolled
oats, shredded coconut, almonds,
sesame seeds, sunflower seeds,
and wheat germ. Combine honey
and oil. Stir into oat mixture.
Spread out in two 13x9x2-inch
baking pans or large shallow
roasting pan. Bake in 300° oven for
45 to 50 minutes or till light golden
brown, stirring every 15 minutes.
Remove from oven; stir in dried
apricots and raisins. Remove to
another pan to cool. Stir
occasionally during cooling to
prevent lumping. Store in Cereal
Storer. Makes 13 cups.

KID'S FAVORITE BREAKFAST

ORANGE JUICE
CINNAMON TOAST
PEANUT BUTTER AND
JELLY OATMEAL
MILK OR CREAM

MENU TIP

*School-age children can help
speed up breakfast preparation
by making the cinnamon toast.
Keep a Spice Tower shaker of
cinnamon-sugar on hand for
sprinkling over hot buttered
toast. Combine ¼ cup granulated sugar and 1 tablespoon
ground cinnamon. Stir to blend.*

PEANUT BUTTER AND JELLY OATMEAL

  2 cups milk
  1 cup quick-cooking rolled
     oats
  ½ cup packed brown sugar
  ¼ cup peanut butter
     Strawberry, grape, and
     apple, or other jelly
     Sliced banana (optional)
     Milk or cream (optional)

In saucepan, bring milk just to boiling; stir in rolled oats. Cook and stir
1 minute. Remove from heat; stir in
brown sugar and peanut butter.
Cover; let stand a few minutes.
Spoon into Stacking Bowls. Add
about 1 teaspoon of jelly to each
bowl. Arrange banana slices in
each. Serve warm with milk, if
desired. Serves 4.

BREAKFAST FOR TWO

GRAPEFRUIT HALVES WITH
BROWN SUGAR
BAKED EGGS AND HAM
COFFEE OR TEA

MENU TIP

*Make the most of your mornings.
Speed breakfast preparation by
tossing the Stuffing Mix and
melted butter the night before.
Store in a sealed Wonderlier®
bowl in the refrigerator. Shred
the cheese, then store in a sealed
Handy Grater. Tuck the chopped
ham in with the cheese.*

BAKED EGGS AND HAM

  ½ cup HERB STUFFING MIX
     (see recipe, page 45)
     or plain croutons
  2 tablespoons butter or
     margarine, melted
  4 eggs
     Pepper
  2 tablespoons shredded
     process Swiss cheese
  ½ cup chopped fully cooked
     ham

Place Stuffing Mix and melted
butter or margarine in a ½-qt. pink
Wonderlier bowl; apply Seal. Turn
gently till stuffing mix is coated.
Butter two shallow 6-inch baking
dishes; break 2 eggs into each.
Sprinkle with a little pepper. Divide
cheese and ham between casseroles. Place buttered Stuffing
Mix around edges. Bake in 350°
oven for 18 minutes or till eggs are
of desired doneness. Makes 2
servings.

*Start the day off right with energy-packed Peanut Butter And Jelly
Oatmeal. Let the kids choose their favorite topper.*

BREAKFASTS IN A HURRY

HEARTY BREAKFAST

ORANGE JUICE
SAUSAGE LINKS
DELUXE SCRAMBLED EGGS
HONEY-WALNUT PULL-APARTS
(see recipe, page 71)
COFFEE   MILK

MENU TIP

This traditional breakfast goes together much faster than it appears. Let the Honey-Walnut Pull-Aparts rise in the refrigerator overnight. Slip them into the oven to bake while you cook the sausage and eggs.

DELUXE SCRAMBLED EGGS

- 8   eggs
- ⅓   cup milk
- ½   teaspoon salt
      Dash pepper
- 2   tablespoons butter or margarine
- 1   large tomato, chopped
- 1   tablespoon snipped parlsey

In Large Mix-N-Stor® pitcher, beat together eggs, milk, salt, and pepper till blended. Melt butter in skillet till hot. Pour in egg mixture. Reduce heat. As mixture begins to set on bottom and sides of skillet, lift and fold with spoon or spatula. Cook till eggs are almost set; fold in tomato and parsley. Heat through. Serve immediately. Serves 4.

THE UN-BREAKFAST

ORANGE JUICE
BREAKFAST WHEELS
PEANUT-HONEY SIPPER

BREAKFAST WHEELS

Next time use cheddar or mozzarella cheese —

- 2   English muffins, split and toasted
      Butter or margarine
      Currant jelly
- 8   slices fully cooked ham (4 ounces)
- 1   apple, pared, cored, and sliced crosswise into 4 circles
- 4   1-ounce slices process Swiss cheese

Spread muffin halves with butter or margarine and currant jelly. Top with slices of ham, apple, and then cheese. Place on baking sheet. Broil 4 inches from heat for 3 to 4 minutes or till cheese is melted and lightly browned. Serve immediately. Makes 4 open-faced sandwiches.

PEANUT-HONEY SIPPER

- 2   cups milk
- ¼   cup creamy peanut butter
- 1   tablespoon honey
- 4   marshmallows

In a blender container, combine first 3 ingredients. Cover; blend smooth. Pour into saucepan; heat till almost boiling. Pour into Multi-Mugs® set. Top with marshmallows. Makes 4 servings.

PANCAKE BREAKFAST

OVEN PANCAKE
WARM SPICED APPLESAUCE
FRIED SAUSAGE PATTIES
HOT CHOCOLATE

MENU TIP

You can get a head start on this hearty breakfast by preparing the pancake batter the night before. Place the cover on the Mix-N-Stor® pitcher and refrigerate.

Spice homemade applesauce to your liking, or heat one 16-ounce can applesauce with ½ teaspoon ground cinnamon.

OVEN PANCAKE

To serve this giant pancake, cut it into wedges —

- 3   tablespoons butter
- 3   eggs
- ½   cup all-purpose flour
- ¼   teaspoon salt
- ½   cup milk
      Sifted powdered sugar
      Hot Maple Syrup (see recipe at far right)

Melt butter in 10-inch oven-going skillet over low heat. In Small Mix-N-Stor pitcher, beat eggs till well mixed. Add flour and salt; beat with rotary beater till smooth. By hand, stir in milk and the melted butter. Pour batter into skillet. Bake in 450° oven for 15 minutes. Reduce temperature to 350°. Bake 5 to 10 minutes more. Sprinkle powdered sugar over. Serve with syrup. Makes 4 servings.

WINTER MORNING BREAKFAST

TOMATO JUICE
PEACH RICE PUDDING
WHOLE WHEAT TOAST
UNCOOKED GRAPE JELLY
COFFEE   MILK

PEACH RICE PUDDING

- 1 cup quick cooking rice
- 1 cup milk
- 2 tablespoons butter
- 1 16-ounce can peach slices
- 2 eggs, beaten
  Dash ground nutmeg

In saucepan, combine rice and milk; bring to boiling. Cover; reduce heat and cook 5 minutes. Stir in butter and undrained peach slices. Stir eggs and nutmeg into rice mixture. Cook and stir 2 minutes more. Spoon into Cereal or Stacking Bowls. If desired, serve with milk. Serves 4.

UNCOOKED GRAPE JELLY

- 2 cups bottled or reconstituted frozen grape juice
- 4 cups sugar
- ½ of a 6-ounce bottle of liquid fruit pectin
- ½ cup lemon juice

In Large Mix-N-Stor pitcher, mix grape juice and sugar. In Small Mix-N-Stor pitcher, mix pectin and lemon juice. Add pectin to grape mixture; stir 3 minutes. Pour at once into six 8-oz. Tumblers, leaving 1-inch headspace. Apply Seals; let stand at room temperature 24 hours. Label; store up to 6 weeks in refrigerator or 1 year in freezer. Makes six 8-oz. Tumblers.

BREAKFAST-IN-A-TUMBLER

SUNSHINE ORANGE DRINK
OR
STRAWBERRY-ORANGE
WAKE-UP
BUTTERED, TOASTED
ENGLISH MUFFINS

SUNSHINE ORANGE DRINK

- ⅓ cup frozen orange juice concentrate, thawed
- ⅓ cup nonfat dry milk powder
- 1 egg
- 1 to 2 teaspoons honey
- 1 teaspoon vanilla
- 6 ice cubes (1½ cups)
  Orange slices (optional)

Combine orange juice concentrate, milk powder, egg, honey, and vanilla in blender container; cover and blend till well mixed. Add ice cubes, one at a time, blending thoroughly. Pour into two 12-oz. Tumblers. Garnish each tumbler with an orange slice, if desired. Serve at once. Serves 2.

STRAWBERRY-ORANGE WAKE-UP

- 1 cup orange juice
- 1 egg
- 1 10-ounce package frozen strawberries, partially thawed
- ½ cup nonfat dry milk powder
- ½ cup cold water

In a blender container, combine all ingredients. Cover; blend till mixture is smooth. Pour into two 12-oz. Tumblers. Makes 2 servings.

WEEKEND FAMILY BREAKFAST

FRUIT MELANGE
(see recipe, page 136)
CRISP-COOKED BACON
SLICES
DOUBLE CORN WAFFLES
HOT MAPLE SYRUP   BUTTER
COFFEE   MILK

DOUBLE CORN WAFFLES

- 1 cup all-purpose flour
- 2 teaspoons baking powder
- 1 teaspoon baking soda
- 1 teaspoon sugar
- 1 cup yellow cornmeal
- 2 beaten egg yolks
- 1½ cups buttermilk
- ¼ cup cooking oil
- 1 8¾-ounce can cream-style corn
- 2 egg whites

In Large Mixing Bowl, stir together flour, baking powder, soda, sugar, and ½ teaspoon *salt;* stir in cornmeal. In Small Mix-N-Stor pitcher, combine egg yolks, buttermilk, and cooking oil; add to dry ingredients. Stir in corn. In Medium Mixing Bowl, beat egg whites till stiff peaks form. Fold into batter. Bake in preheated waffle baker according to manufacturer's directions. Waffles may be frozen in Quartet™ Set containers. Reheat in a toaster. Makes twelve 4-inch square waffles.

HOT MAPLE SYRUP

- 1 cup light corn syrup
- ½ cup packed brown sugar
  Dash maple flavoring
- 1 tablespoon butter

In a saucepan, heat corn syrup, brown sugar, and ½ cup *water* till sugar dissolves. Add maple flavoring and butter. Makes 2 cups.

LUNCHES TO GO

PAK-N-CARRY™ LUNCH

CHICKEN BUNDLES
CELERY STICKS AND GRAPES
CHOCOLATE WAFFLE DROPS
(see recipe, page 76)
MILK

CHICKEN BUNDLES

2½ cups chopped, cooked
     chicken
6 slices bacon, crisp-
     cooked and crumbled
1 8-ounce carton sour
     cream dip with onion
¾ cup chopped celery
½ cup pecans, chopped
¼ cup mayonnaise
½ teaspoon salt
1 loaf FREEZER BREAD
     DOUGH, thawed (see
     recipe, page 71)

In Medium Mixing Bowl, combine
all ingredients except FREEZER
BREAD DOUGH. Divide bread
dough in 12 equal parts. For each
bundle, roll one portion dough on
lightly floured Pastry Sheet to
5-inch circle with Rolling Pin. Place
a generous ¼ cup chicken mixture
on half the circle; fold over other
half and seal with a fork. Place
bundles on greased baking
sheets; cover and let rest for 18 to
20 minutes. Prick top with fork. If
desired, brush with milk. Bake in
375° oven for 20 to 22 minutes.
Cool; transfer to Cold Cut Keeper.
Freeze. For each lunch, pack one
or two bundles in the Square-A-
Way® container of the Pak-N-
Carry kit or in a 16-oz. Square
Rounds® container. Makes 12
bundles.

MAKE-AHEAD LUNCH

ZESTY BEEF SANDWICHES
ON
WHOLE WHEAT BREAD
GRAPE-NECTARINE COMPOTE
GRANOLA RAISIN BARS
(see recipe, page 75)
MINT CHOCOLATE MALT DRINK

ZESTY BEEF SANDWICHES

*Butter bread all the way to the
edges to keep filling from
soaking through —*

3 tablespoons mayonnaise
     or salad dressing
2 tablespoons chili sauce
1 teaspoon prepared
     mustard
¼ teaspoon salt
⅛ teaspoon pepper
¼ of a small head of
     cabbage
1 cup chopped cooked beef

For dressing, in Small Mix-N-Stor®
pitcher, blend together
mayonnaise or salad dressing,
chili sauce, mustard, salt, and
pepper till smooth and creamy.
Shred cabbage on Handy Grater
or Grater Bowl. Stir cabbage and
meat into dressing till well coated.
Place cover on Mix-N-Stor pitcher
and refrigerate to blend flavors, if
desired. Spread mixture on your
favorite buttered bread or rolls for
sandwiches. Makes about 1¼
cups filling or enough for 4
sandwiches.

GRAPE-NECTARINE COMPOTE

3 small fresh nectarines
     or peaches
1 cup grapes
½ cup orange juice
1 tablespoon honey

Peel, pit, and slice nectarines into
a Small Mix-N-Stor pitcher. Halve
and seed grapes. Add to
nectarines or peaches along with
orange juice and honey; stir gently.
Divide among 4 Snack Set cups;
apply Seals and chill. Makes 4
servings.

MINT CHOCOLATE MALT MIX

½ cup white butter mints,
     chopped
3 cups nonfat dry milk
     powder
2 cups chocolate-flavored
     malted milk powder
½ cup sweetened cocoa mix

Place butter mints on Pastry
Sheet. Roll with water-filled Rolling
Pin till finely powdered. In a
Medium Mixing Bowl, combine
powdered mints, dry milk powder,
malted milk powder, and cocoa
mix. Apply Seal and shake till well
blended. Store in a canister. When
packing lunch, place 3
tablespoons mix in Pak-N-Carry
6-oz. Tumbler. At serving time, fill
Tumbler to within ½ inch of rim
with very hot *water*. Stir to mix well.
Makes 6 cups mix.

*Make a dozen Chicken Bundles at a time and freeze them in a Cold Cut
Keeper. Pack them for lunch in a Pak-N-Carry kit in the morning; they'll
defrost by lunch time.*

LUNCHES TO GO

HERO LUNCH

CORNED BEEF-TURKEY
HEROES
ZIPPY CARROTS AND
ZUCCHINI
FRESH FRUIT CRISP
(see recipe, page 89)
ORANGE JUPITER DRINK

CORNED BEEF-
TURKEY HEROES

- 4 **kaiser rolls or hamburger buns
  Tartar sauce
  Blue cheese, Russian,
  or Italian salad
  dressing**
- 1 **3- or 4-ounce package
  thinly sliced smoked
  corned beef**
- 4 **thin onion slices**
- 2 **slices Swiss cheese,
  cut in half**
- 1 **3- or 4-ounce package
  thinly sliced smoked
  turkey**

Use a sharp knife to cut kaiser rolls
or hamburger buns in half
horizontally. Lightly spread cut
surfaces of kaiser rolls or
hamburger buns with tartar sauce
and choice of salad dressings.
Layer slices of the corned beef,
onion, Swiss cheese, and turkey
on rolls. Replace top of rolls. Pack
each sandwich in a 16-ounce
Square Rounds® container.
Makes 4 sandwiches.

ZIPPY CARROTS
AND ZUCCHINI

- ½ **cup sugar**
- ½ **cup vinegar**
- ½ **cup water**
- 1 **tablespoon mustard seed**
- 2 **inches stick cinnamon**
- 3 **whole cloves**
- 3 **medium carrots, cut
  into 2½-inch strips**
- 1 **medium zucchini, cut
  into 2½-inch strips**

In a saucepan, combine sugar,
vinegar, water, mustard seed,
cinnamon, and cloves. Add
carrots; cover and simmer till
crisp-tender. Add zucchini sticks;
return to boiling. Remove from
heat; cool. Transfer to
Pick-A-Deli™ container; apply
Seal. Chill at least 8 hours. Makes
3 cups.

ORANGE JUPITER
MIX

- 1 **9-ounce jar orange-
  flavored breakfast
  drink powder**
- ½ **cup sugar**
- 1¾ **cups nonfat dry milk
  powder**
- 2 **teaspoons vanilla**

In a canister, stir together
breakfast drink powder, sugar, and
milk powder. Blend in vanilla till
thoroughly dispersed (small beads
will form). Apply Seal to store.
When packing lunch, place ¼ cup
mix in a Pak-N-Carry™ 6-ounce
Tumbler. At serving time, fill
Tumbler to within ½-inch of rim
with cold *water*. Stir to mix well.
Makes 4 cups mix.

FRUIT AND SPICE
LUNCH

PINEAPPLE-HAM
SANDWICHES
SPICY PEANUT SNACK MIX
CUBES OF SWISS CHEESE
FROZEN APPLE JUICE

PINEAPPLE-HAM
SANDWICHES

- 1 **8¼-ounce can crushed
  pineapple, well
  drained**
- ¼ **cup mayonnaise or salad
  dressing**
- 1 **tablespoon brown sugar**
- 2 **teaspoons prepared
  mustard**
- ½ **pound ground fully
  cooked ham (1¾ cups)**
- 12 **slices white or rye
  bread
  Butter or margarine,
  softened
  Lettuce leaves (optional)**

In Medium Mixing Bowl, combine
pineapple, mayonnaise or salad
dressing, brown sugar, and
mustard. Add ground ham; mix
well. Spread each slice of bread
with butter. Spread about ⅓ cup of
ham mixture on each of 6 slices of
bread. Top each with a slice of
bread, buttered side down. Pack
sandwiches in Snack-Stor®
container; freeze.

To pack lunch, place one
sandwich in the Square-A-Way®
container of the Pak-N-Carry kit. At
serving time, add lettuce to
sandwich, if desired. Makes 6
servings.

SPICY PEANUT SNACK MIX

Pack these instead of chips —

- 1 **egg white**
- 2 **teaspoons water**
- 3 **tablespoons sugar**
- ¾ **teaspoon ground cinnamon**
- ⅛ **teaspoon ground nutmeg**
- ⅛ **teaspoon ground ginger**
- 5 **cups bite-size shredded corn, wheat, or rice squares**
- 1 **8-ounce jar dry roasted peanuts**

In Small Mix-N-Stor® pitcher, blend egg white and water; stir in sugar and spices. Beat till frothy.

In 13x9x2-inch baking pan, mix cereal and nuts. Add egg white mixture; toss to coat. Bake in 350° oven for 15 minutes. Remove from oven and stir. Cool 5 minutes. Remove from pan; cool thoroughly. Store in canister. Makes 7 cups.

FREEZING SANDWICHES

Frozen sandwiches are a real time-saver when packing lunches. These ingredients freeze well: cream cheese, cooked egg yolk, sliced or ground cooked meat, tuna or salmon, and peanut butter. Seal the bread by spreading butter to the edges.

Instead of lettuce, pack bean sprouts or alfalfa sprouts to add to sandwiches at lunch time.

Save money by freezing single-serving portions of fruit juice in 6-oz. Tumblers. Remember to leave about ½-inch headspace when filling.

MEAL-IN-A-SANDWICH

BOLOGNA-CHEESE CLUB
SANDWICHES
PICK-A-DILLIES
CHOCOLATE MILK

BOLOGNA-CHEESE CLUB SANDWICHES

- 1½ **cups finely chopped bologna (6 ounces)**
- 2 **tablespoons finely chopped onion**
- 1 **5-ounce jar process cheese spread**
- ¼ **cup sweet pickle relish, drained**
- 2 **tablespoons mayonnaise or salad dressing**
- 2 **tablespoons chopped green pepper**
- 2 **teaspoons prepared mustard**
- 8 **slices white or rye bread**
  Butter or margarine, softened
  Lettuce
  Tomato slices

In Medium Mixing Bowl, stir together bologna, onion, cheese spread, pickle relish, mayonnaise or salad dressing, green pepper, and mustard. Spread all the bread slices with butter or margarine. Spread 4 of the bread slices with ½ cup filling. Top with remaining bread slices, buttered side down.

Pack sandwiches in a two Deli-Keeper containers; freeze. (To pack lunch, pack one sandwich in the Square-A-Way container of the Pak-N-Carry kit.) Place lettuce and tomato slices in the 16-oz. Square Rounds container. At serving time, add lettuce and tomato to sandwich. Makes 4 sandwiches.

PICK-A-DILLIES

- 1 **quart sliced dill pickles**
- ½ **cup cider vinegar**
- 2 **cups sugar**
- 2 **tablespoons mixed pickling spices**

Drain pickles in 1-qt. Strainer. In a Pick-A-Deli container, combine vinegar and sugar. Tie spices in a cheesecloth bag; add to Pick-A-Deli container along with pickles. Apply Seal and let stand at room temperature, gently shaking occasionally till sugar dissolves (about 4 hours). Refrigerate at least 4 days before serving. Remove spice bag after one week, if desired. Makes 1 quart.

LUNCH-BOX IDEAS

Planned-over meals save time and money when filling lunch boxes. Prepackage individual servings from these recipes for tomorrow's lunch. They'll stay fresh in a Tupperware® container on the refrigerator shelf:

Pasta-Filled Tomatoes (see recipe, page 33)
Barbecue Fried Chicken (see recipe, page 107)
Reuben Triangles, (see recipe, page 57)
Super Sandwich Braid (see recipe, page 66)
Pizza Roll-Up (see recipe, page 72)
Creamy Potato Salad (see recipe, page 107)
Fancy Family Meat Loaf (see recipe, page 104)
Marinated Bean Salad (see recipe, page 108)

THRIFTY FAMILY MEALS

DINING OUT AT HOME DINNER

ORANGE HAM RING
OR
FANCY FAMILY MEAT LOAF
BAKED POTATOES
BUTTERED BROCCOLI
HOT ROLLS   BUTTER
MILK   COFFEE

ORANGE HAM RING

3   beaten eggs
½   cup orange juice
½   cup finely crushed
      saltine crackers
      (14 crackers)
2   tablespoons prepared
      mustard
1   pound ground fully cooked
      ham
1   pound ground pork
½   cup orange marmalade
      Orange slices, halved

In a Large Mixing Bowl, combine eggs, orange juice, cracker crumbs, and 1 tablespoon of the mustard. Add ground meats; mix well. Spoon evenly into a Jel-Ring® mold. Firmly pack the meat mixture. Invert into a shallow pan with sides. Remove mold. Bake in 350° oven for 50 minutes or till done. Spoon off fat. In saucepan, heat together orange marmalade and remaining 1 tablespoon mustard. Brush loaf with half the marmalade mixture. Bake for 10 minutes longer. Arrange orange slices atop loaf. Brush with remaining marmalade mixture. Garnish with endive and spiced crab apples, if desired. Makes 8 servings.

FANCY FAMILY MEAT LOAF

2   beaten eggs
¾   cup milk
1   cup HERB STUFFING MIX,
      (see recipe, page 45)
      finely crushed
¼   cup finely chopped
      onion
½   teaspoon ground sage
1½ pounds ground beef
¼   cup catsup
2   tablespoons brown sugar
1   teaspoon dry mustard

In Large Mixing Bowl, combine eggs and milk. Stir in crushed Stuffing Mix, onion, sage, 1 teaspoon *salt,* and ⅛ teaspoon *pepper.* Add ground beef; mix well. Spoon evenly into Jel-N-Serve ® mold. Firmly pack meat mixture. Invert onto shallow baking pan with sides. Remove mold. Bake, uncovered, in 350° oven for 50 minutes. Spoon off excess fat. In Refrigerator Bowl, combine remaining ingredients; spread over meat loaf. Return to oven; bake 10 minutes longer. Serves 6.

DIVIDED SERVING DISH TIP

Use the Divided Serving Dish to serve hot cooked vegetables and fresh-from-the-oven dinner rolls or muffins. It makes table service easy because you only have to pass one dish.

MOLDED MEAT LOAF TIP

1. Assemble Jel-N-Serve or Jel-Ring mold with inner or design Seal. Spoon the meat mixture into mold. Using your hands or the back of a spoon, firmly pat the meat mixture into the mold so it will hold its shape when inverted.

2. To unmold, place a 12-inch pizza pan (or other shallow baking pan with sides) upside down atop the Jel-N-Serve or Jel-Ring mold. Holding the pan and mold firmly together, invert them. Release inner or design Seal. Lift off the Seal, then the mold. Bake as directed.

Use the Jel-Ring mold to form and unmold ground meat mixtures into extra-special dinner entrees such as Orange Ham Ring pictured here. Serve hot cooked vegetables and dinner rolls from the Divided Serving Dish for easy table service.

THRIFTY FAMILY MEALS

MAN-PLEASER SUPPER

BOLOGNA BUNWICHES
BUTTERMILK-CORN CHOWDER
RELISH TRAY
CHOCO-MINT FREEZE
(see recipe, page 140)
MILK   ICED TEA

MENU TIP

If necessary, these hot sand-
wiches can wait in the oven. But-
ter the buns before filling and
wrap in foil.
    Wait until the last minute to
add the buttermilk to the soup;
heat through and serve im-
mediately with the hot sand-
wiches.

BOLOGNA BUNWICHES

- ½ cup chopped green pepper
- ½ cup chopped onion
- 2 tablespoons cooking oil
- 1 8-ounce can kidney beans, drained
- 1 8-ounce can tomato sauce
- 6 ounces bologna, cut into strips
- 1 teaspoon chili powder
- ½ cup shredded cheddar cheese
- 6 frankfurter buns, split and toasted

In medium saucepan, cook green pepper and onion in oil till onion is tender but not brown. Add kidney beans, tomato sauce, bologna strips, and chili powder; heat through. Add shredded cheese. Cook and stir till cheese is melted. To serve, spoon into frankfurter buns. Makes 6.

BUTTERMILK-CORN CHOWDER

You'll need about 4 ears of fresh
corn to make 2 cups. Use a sharp
knife to cut just the kernel tips,
then scrape the cob with dull
edge of knife—

- 2 slices bacon
- 1 small onion, chopped (¼ cup)
- 2 medium potatoes, peeled and cubed
- 2 cups fresh corn cut from cob, or one 10-ounce package frozen whole kernel corn
- 1 stalk celery, chopped (½ cup)
- 2 cups water
- ½ teaspoon salt
- ¼ teaspoon pepper
- 2 tablespoons all-purpose flour
- 2 teaspoons instant chicken bouillon granules
- 2 cups buttermilk

In a 3-quart saucepan, cook the bacon till crisp. Remove and drain, reserving drippings. Crumble bacon and set aside. Cook onion in drippings till tender but not brown. Add potatoes, corn, celery, 1½ cups of the water, the salt, and pepper. Bring to boiling; reduce heat. Cover and simmer 15 to 20 minutes. Blend flour, chicken bouillon granules, and remaining water; add to the vegetable mixture. Cook and stir till thickened and bubbly. Turn heat to low. Stir in buttermilk; heat through, but do not boil. Ladle into Stacking Bowls. Top with crumbled bacon. Makes 6 servings.

MEATLESS MENU

MEATLESS ITALIAN LASAGNA
FRUIT COCKTAIL FREEZE
BREADSTICKS OR CRACKERS
PEANUT BUTTER-FILLED FUDGE
CUPCAKES
(see recipe, page 83)
MILK   COFFEE

FRUIT COCKTAIL FREEZE

- 2 8-ounce cartons orange, strawberry, or peach yogurt
- ⅓ cup sugar
- 1 16-ounce can fruit cocktail, drained
- ½ cup finely chopped celery
    Lettuce

Assemble Jel-N-Serve® mold with design Seal; set aside.
    In a Large Mix-N-Stor® pitcher, stir together yogurt and sugar. Fold in fruit cocktail and celery. Turn the mixture into mold. Apply large Seal; freeze firm.
    Just before serving time, remove Jel-N-Serve mold from the freezer. Immerse mold, large Seal down, in warm water for 20 seconds; remove from water and dry with a cloth. Peel off large Seal. Place serving tray over mold; invert tray and mold together. Slowly remove design Seal. Carefully lift off mold. Arrange lettuce under and around molded salad on tray. Let stand 10 minutes before serving. Makes 8 servings.

MEATLESS ITALIAN LASAGNA

- 1 cup chopped carrots
- 1 cup chopped celery
- 1 cup chopped green pepper
- 1 cup chopped onion
- ¼ cup butter or margarine
- 2 cups sliced zucchini
- 1 16-ounce can tomatoes, cut up
- 1 12-ounce can tomato paste
- 2 bay leaves
- 2 cloves garlic, minced
- ¼ cup snipped parsley
- 1 teaspoon dried basil, crushed
- ¾ teaspoon salt
- ½ teaspoon *each* dried oregano and dried thyme, crushed
- ¼ teaspoon pepper
- 10 lasagna noodles, cooked, rinsed, and drained (about 8 ounces)
- 2 cups cream-style cottage cheese, drained
- 8 slices mozzarella cheese, torn (8 ounces)
- ¼ cup grated Parmesan cheese

In large saucepan, cook carrots, celery, green pepper, and onion in butter till tender but not brown. Add zucchini, undrained tomatoes, tomato paste, bay leaves, garlic, parsley, and seasonings. Simmer, covered, 30 minutes; simmer, uncovered, 15 to 20 minutes more or till thickened. Discard bay leaves.

In 13x9x2-inch baking pan, layer one-third of the noodles, vegetable sauce, cottage cheese, and mozzarella. Repeat twice, ending with mozzarella. Sprinkle with Parmesan. Cover with foil; place on baking sheet. Bake in 350° oven 45 minutes. Uncover; bake 10 minutes more. Let stand 10 minutes before serving. Serves 8 to 10.

BACKYARD PICNIC

BARBECUE FRIED CHICKEN
CREAMY POTATO SALAD
PARTY DEVILED EGGS
SPICED APPLE RINGS
(see recipe, page 137)
CHOCO-BUTTERMILK CAKE
(see recipe, page 79)
LEMONADE   ICED TEA

CREAMY POTATO SALAD

This entire menu is pictured on pages 92-93—

- 6 medium potatoes (2 pounds)
- 1 cup thinly sliced celery
- ½ cup finely chopped onion
- ⅓ cup chopped sweet pickle
- 1¼ cups mayonnaise or salad dressing
- 2 teaspoons sugar
- 2 teaspoons celery seed
- 2 teaspoons vinegar
- 2 teaspoons prepared mustard
- 1½ teaspoons salt
- 2 hard-cooked eggs, coarsely chopped

In a covered saucepan, cook potatoes in boiling salted water for 25 to 30 minutes or till tender; drain well. Peel and cube potatoes. Transfer to a 3-qt. green Wonderlier® bowl. Add celery, onion, and sweet pickle. Combine mayonnaise or salad dressing, sugar, celery seed, vinegar, prepared mustard, and salt. Add mayonnaise mixture to potatoes. Toss lightly to coat potato mixture. Carefully fold in the chopped eggs. Apply Seal and chill thoroughly. Makes 8 servings.

BARBECUE FRIED CHICKEN

- 1 2½- to 3-pound broiler-fryer chicken, cut up
- ¼ cup all-purpose flour
- 2 teaspoons salt
- 2 tablespoons cooking oil
- 1 cup catsup
- ½ cup chopped onion
- ½ cup water
- 1 clove garlic, minced
- ¼ teaspoon pepper
- 3 tablespoons lemon juice

In a Medium Mixing Bowl, combine flour and 1 teaspoon of the salt. Coat chicken pieces with flour mixture. Brown chicken in hot oil over medium heat about 15 minutes, turning to brown. In a saucepan, combine catsup, onion, water, garlic, remaining 1 teaspoon salt, and pepper. Bring to boiling. Simmer for 20 minutes. Blend in lemon juice; add to chicken. Cover; cook over low heat 35 to 40 minutes or till tender. Serve with sauce. Makes 4 servings.

PARTY DEVILED EGGS

- 8 hard-cooked eggs, halved lengthwise
- 4 slices bacon, crisp-cooked, drained and crumbled
- 4 teaspoons prepared mustard
- ¼ teaspoon paprika
- ⅛ teaspoon salt
  Dash pepper
- ¼ cup mayonnaise or salad dressing
  Snipped parsley

Remove egg yolks from whites; arrange whites on Egg Tray inserts. Sieve yolks and combine with remaining ingredients; mix well. Refill egg whites with yolk mixture. Garnish with additional crumbled bacon or paprika or snipped parsley. Makes 16.

THRIFTY FAMILY MEALS

CORNED BEEF DINNER

FRUIT-GLAZED CORNED BEEF
CAULIFLOWER WITH
CHEESE SAUCE
(see recipe, page 50)
MARINATED BEAN SALAD
APPLE PIE
(see recipe, page 86)
MILK   COFFEE

MENU TIP

If it's more convenient, simmer the corned beef ahead of time; cool. Then refrigerate in a Cold Cut Keeper. You'll have only an hour of baking time before serving.

MARINATED BEAN SALAD

½ **cup cooking oil**
2 **tablespoons vinegar**
¾ **teaspoon sugar**
¾ **teaspoon salt**
½ **teaspoon celery seed**
¼ **teaspoon caraway seed**
¼ **teaspoon paprika**
2 **10-ounce packages frozen Italian green beans, cooked and drained**
1 **small onion, sliced and separated into rings**

In Refrigerator Bowl, combine oil, vinegar, sugar, salt, celery and caraway seeds, and paprika. Apply Seal and shake to combine. Combine beans and onion rings in Season-Serve® container; pour oil mixture over all. Apply Seal. Chill 4 to 24 hours, turning Season-Serve container over 2 or 3 times. Serve cold or warm. Makes 6 servings.

FRUIT-GLAZED CORNED BEEF

Cooked corn beef is a good planned-over main dish. Thin slices make tasty sandwiches or can be tossed with greens for a light luncheon salad—

1 **4- to 5-pound corned beef brisket**
   Water
   Whole cloves
1 **orange**
1 **lemon**
½ **cup packed brown sugar**
½ **cup apple cider or apple juice**

Place corned beef brisket in Dutch oven and barely cover with water. Cover pan with lid and simmer till almost tender, 2½ to 3 hours. Remove from heat; cool meat in cooking liquid. While cooling, use Handy Grater to finely grate 2 teaspoons peel from orange; halve orange, squeeze, and measure ⅓ cup juice. Repeat with lemon to make 1 teaspoon peel and 2 tablespoons juice. Drain liquid from meat; place meat in shallow roasting pan; score fat and stud with cloves. Combine grated peels, brown sugar, and dry mustard; pat into meat. Combine cider and orange and lemon juices in Small Mix-N-Stor® pitcher; pour over meat. Bake in 350° oven for 1 hour, basting occasionally. Serve hot or cold. To serve, thinly slice across grain.

JIFFY PORK DINNER

VEGETABLE-PORK CASSEROLES
SPICED MANDARIN MOLD
HARD ROLLS   BUTTER
CHOCOLATE LAYER PIE
(see recipe, page 87)
MILK   COFFEE

SPICED MANDARIN MOLD

1 **11-ounce can mandarin orange sections**
6 **inches stick cinnamon**
½ **teaspoon whole cloves**
¼ **teaspoon salt**
1 **6-ounce package lemon-flavored gelatin**
1 **cup orange juice**
1 **cup cold water**
½ **cup chopped pecans**
   Lettuce

Use 1-qt. Strainer over a Small Mix-N-Stor pitcher to drain orange sections, reserving syrup. Add water to syrup to make 1¾ cups. In saucepan, combine syrup mixture, cinnamon, cloves, and salt. Cover and simmer 15 minutes. Add gelatin to syrup mixture; stir over low heat till gelatin is dissolved. Strain out stick cinnamon and cloves. Add orange juice and cold water. Chill till partially set.

Meanwhile, assemble a Jel-N-Serve® mold with design Seal. Fold drained oranges and pecans into partially set gelatin; turn into Jel-N-Serve mold. Apply large Seal. Chill salad till firm, 4 hours or overnight. Remove large Seal. Dip Jel-N-Serve into warm water for a few seconds. Do not melt gelatin. Invert mold onto Jel-N-Serve tray. Remove design Seal. Lift off mold. Arrange lettuce under and around salad on tray. Makes 8 servings.

VEGETABLE-PORK CASSEROLES

You can substitute one pound of ground pork, thoroughly browned and drained, for the diced cooked pork —

- 4 cups HERB STUFFING MIX (see recipe, page 45)
- 2 tablespoons butter or margarine
- 1 egg
- ½ cup water
- 2 10-ounce packages frozen Chinese-style vegetables
- 2 cups diced cooked pork
- 1 cup cold water
- 4 teaspoons cornstarch
- 1 tablespoon soy sauce

Use Rolling Pin and Pastry Sheet to coarsely crush Herb Stuffing Mix. In a saucepan, melt butter or margarine. Remove from heat; add the crushed Herb Stuffing Mix. In a Small Mix-N-Stor pitcher, beat the egg and the ½ cup water together; pour over the butter-stuffing mixture in the saucepan. Toss mixture well to combine. Press stuffing mixture into bottom and up onto sides of six lightly greased 1-cup casseroles. Bake casseroles in 425° oven for 10 minutes.

Meanwhile, cook the Chinese-style vegetables according to package directions. Add pork. In a clean Small Mix-N-Stor pitcher, blend the 1 cup water, cornstarch, and soy sauce; add to the vegetable-pork mixture. Cook and stir till mixture is thickened and bubbly. Cook and stir 1 to 2 minutes more. Spoon the hot vegetable-pork mixture into the baked stuffing cups. Makes 6 servings.

HEARTY SOUP SUPPER

TURKEY-VEGETABLE SOUP
CITRUS YOGURT SALAD
FRENCH BREAD WITH
PARMESAN SPREAD
(see recipe, page 73)
CARROT CAKE
(see recipe, page 83)

CITRUS YOGURT SALAD

- 1 16-ounce can pear slices or halves
- 1 6-ounce or two 3-ounce packages lime-flavored gelatin
- 2 cups boiling water
- 1 medium banana, sliced
- 1 8-ounce carton lemon yogurt
- Lettuce

Drain pears, reserving syrup. Add cold water to syrup to make ¾ cup liquid. Place gelatin in Small Mix-N-Stor pitcher; add boiling water, stirring to dissolve. Set aside 1 cup of the gelatin mixture; keep at room temperature. Stir reserved syrup into remaining gelatin. Chill till partially set. Chop pears; fold into partially set gelatin along with banana. Pour into Jel-Ring® mold; apply Seal and chill till almost firm. In Small Mix-N-Stor pitcher, beat reserved gelatin-mixture into yogurt. Spoon over layer in mold. Reapply Seal; chill till firm. Dip mold into warm water for a few seconds. Do not melt gelatin. Remove Seal. Invert mold onto lettuce-lined plate; remove mold. Makes 8 to 10 servings.

TURKEY-VEGETABLE SOUP

- 1 cup dry navy beans
- 8 cups water
- 2 teaspoons salt
- 1 meaty turkey frame
- 1 medium onion, chopped
- 1½ teaspoons Worcestershire sauce
- ½ teaspoon poultry seasoning or ground sage
- ⅛ teaspoon pepper
- 1 17-ounce can whole kernel corn, drained
- 2 stalks celery, sliced (1 cup)
- 2 medium carrots, sliced (1 cup)
- 1 medium turnip, chopped (1 cup)
- French bread slices or rolls (optional)

Rinse navy beans in 1-qt. Strainer under running water. In 5-quart Dutch oven, combine beans, water, and salt. Bring to boiling; reduce heat and simmer for 2 minutes. Remove from heat. Cover; let stand for 1 hour. (Or, soak beans in the water overnight in a covered pan.) Do not drain.

Break turkey frame to fit Dutch oven. Add to navy bean mixture. Stir in chopped onion, Worcestershire sauce, poultry seasoning or sage, and pepper. Cover and simmer for 1 hour.

Remove turkey frame; cool slightly. Cut meat off frame; chop meat. Slightly mash beans. Return chopped meat to Dutch oven. Add drained corn, sliced celery, sliced carrots, and chopped turnip. Cover and simmer about 30 minutes more or till vegetables are tender. Serve with thick slices of French bread or rolls, if desired. Makes 8 to 10 servings.

MEALS FOR ONE OR TWO

LIGHT EATER'S LUNCH

TUNA SLAW VINAIGRETTE
BRAN MUFFINS
CHEDDAR CHEESE WEDGE
COFFEE OR TEA

TUNA SLAW VINAIGRETTE

If you omit the tuna, this slaw serves two as a meal accompaniment —

- 1 3-inch wedge cabbage
- 1 4-inch carrot
- 2 tablespoons snipped parsley
- 4 teaspoons vinegar
- 1 tablespoon sugar
- 1 tablespoon salad oil
- ½ teaspoon salt
- 1 3¾-ounce can tuna

Grate cabbage and carrot on coarse side of Handy Grater. Remove grater; add parsley. Apply storage Seal and turn several times to combine; set aside. In a Snack Set cup, combine vinegar, sugar, salad oil, and salt. Apply Seal and shake until sugar and salt are dissolved. Pour over cabbage mixture in Handy Grater; apply Seal and refrigerate several hours or overnight. (To pack in a lunch, include sealed Handy Grater, tuna, can opener, and fork.)

At serving time, open tuna, drain, and combine with slaw mixture. Garnish with carrot curls, if desired. Makes 1 serving.

BRAN MUFFINS

For those who live alone, a recipe for 5 or 6 muffins is way too big. Solve the problem with Seal-N-Serve® containers. A Medium container will store up to 4 muffins, a Super, up to 7 —

- ¾ cup whole bran cereal
- ½ cup buttermilk*
- ½ cup all-purpose flour
- 3 tablespoons brown sugar
- 1 teaspoon baking powder
- ¼ teaspoon baking soda
- ¼ teaspoon salt
- 1 egg
- 2 tablespoons cooking oil
- ⅓ cup raisins or snipped pitted dates (optional)

In Small Mix-N-Stor® pitcher, combine bran cereal and buttermilk; let stand about 3 minutes or till liquid is absorbed.

In Medium Mixing Bowl, stir together flour, sugar, baking powder, soda, and salt. Beat egg and oil into bran mixture; blend into dry ingredients, stirring just till moistened. (Batter will be thick.) Fold in raisins or dates, if desired. Fill paper bake cup-lined muffin pans ⅔ full. Bake in 400° oven for 20 to 25 minutes or till muffins are done. Cool on a wire rack. Makes 5 or 6 muffins.

*Note: If you don't have buttermilk, substitute 1½ teaspoons lemon juice or vinegar combined with enough whole milk to make ½ cup. Let stand 5 minutes before using.

PAN PIZZA FOR TWO

PEPPERONI PAN PIZZA
ASSORTED RELISHES
QUICK TORTONI DESSERT CUPS
(see recipe, page 140)
BEVERAGE

PEPPERONI PAN PIZZA

- 1½ cups WHOLE WHEAT YEAST BUN MIX (see recipe, page 64)
- 1 package active dry yeast
- ⅓ cup warm water (115° to 120°) Yellow cornmeal
- 3 ounces mozzarella cheese, shredded
- 1 small green pepper, chopped (½ cup)
- ½ of an 8-ounce can (½ cup) tomato sauce
- ¼ teaspoon dried basil, crushed
- 2 ounces pepperoni, sliced

In Medium Mixing Bowl, stir together Whole Wheat Yeast Bun Mix and yeast. Add water; mix well. Cover and let rest 10 minutes. Grease a heavy 8-inch skillet with oven-proof handle; sprinkle bottom with a little cornmeal. With greased fingers, pat dough out onto bottom and halfway up sides of skillet. Bake in 400° oven for 10 to 15 minutes or till lightly browned. Sprinkle baked crust with half the mozzarella cheese. In a Small Mix-N-Stor pitcher, combine green pepper, tomato sauce, and basil; pour over cheese-topped crust. Top with pepperoni slices and remaining cheese. Bake in 400° oven about 15 minutes longer. Makes 2 servings.

Tuna Slaw Vinaigrette is a salad lover's delight. It's easily prepared, marinated, and served in the Handy Grater for a light, totable lunch.

MEALS FOR ONE OR TWO

MEATBALL FEAST

MEATBALLS IN MUSHROOM SAUCE
HOT COOKED RICE OR NOODLES
BUTTERED CAULIFLOWER
LIME-APPLE SALAD
BANANA-NUT TURNOVERS
(see recipe, page 87)
MILK   COFFEE

LIME-APPLE SALAD

*The remaining half package of
gelatin will stay fresh for
another salad in a Snack Set cup
or 2-oz. Midget —*

½ of a 3-ounce package
     (3½ tablespoons)
     lime-flavored gelatin
¾ cup boiling water
¼ cup finely chopped un-
     peeled apple
2 tablespoons finely
     chopped walnuts
2 tablespoons dairy sour
     cream
½ teaspoon sugar

In Small Mix-N-Stor® pitcher,
dissolve gelatin in boiling water.
Cover and chill till partially set
(consistency of unbeaten egg
whites). Fold in chopped apple and
walnuts. Pour into 2 Dessert Set
dishes; apply Seals. Chill several
hours or till firm. In Snack Set
container, combine sour cream
and sugar; apply Seal and chill.

   To serve gelatin mixture,
remove Seals. Spoon some of the
sour cream mixture atop each
salad in Dessert Set Dish. Makes
2 servings.

MEATBALLS IN MUSHROOM SAUCE

*Store the remainder of the
tomato sauce in a Snack Set cup
for use in the Pepperoni Pan
Pizza on the preceding page —*

1 7½-ounce can semi-con-
     densed savory cream
     of mushroom soup
½ of an 8-ounce can
     tomato sauce (½ cup)
1 12-meatball container
     FREEZER MEATBALLS
     (see recipe, page 19)
2 tablespoons finely
     chopped onion
2 tablespoons finely chopped
     green pepper
     Hot cooked rice or noodles

In an 8-inch skillet, combine soup
and tomato sauce. Bring to boiling,
stirring occasionally. Add meatballs, onion, and green pepper.
Cover and simmer for 15 to 20
minutes or till meatballs are heated
through, stirring occasionally.
Serve over hot cooked rice or
noodles. Makes 2 servings.

MENU TIP

*No Freezer Meatballs on hand?
Use this tailored-for-two meatball recipe. Combine 1 beaten
egg; 1 slice white bread, torn up;
1 tablespoon catsup; ¼ teaspoon
salt; and a dash pepper. Add ½
pound ground beef and mix well.
Shape into 1-inch meatballs. Add
them with the onion and green
pepper. Simmer a full 20 minutes
or till meatballs are cooked.*

RELAX-WHILE-IT-COOKS DINNER

OVEN CHICKEN WITH VEGETABLES
BERRY FRUIT SALAD
HARD ROLLS WITH HERB BUTTER
(see recipe, page 73)
CHOCO-MINT FREEZE
(see recipe, page 140)
MILK   COFFEE

OVEN CHICKEN WITH VEGETABLES

2 tablespoons fine dry
     bread crumbs
1 tablespoon grated
     Parmesan cheese
⅛ teaspoon dried oregano,
     crushed
2 chicken drumsticks or
     thighs
2 tablespoons butter or
     margarine, melted
1 or 2 carrots
1 medium potato, peeled
     and halved lengthwise
     Dried dillweed

Combine bread crumbs, Parmesan cheese, and oregano. Brush
chicken pieces with some of the
melted butter or margarine, then
roll in bread crumb mixture to coat.
Place chicken, skin side up, in
8x8x2-inch baking pan. Halve
carrots crosswise, then lengthwise. Arrange cut-up carrots and
potato around chicken in pan.
Sprinkle chicken and vegetables
generously with salt and pepper.
Bake in 375° oven for 30 minutes.

   Brush vegetables with the remaining melted butter; bake about
25 minutes longer or till chicken
and vegetables are tender.
Sprinkle potato with dillweed.
Makes 1 serving.

BERRY FRUIT SALAD

- ⅓ cup pineapple yogurt
- 2 tablespoons orange juice
- 2 teaspoons sugar
  Dash ground cinnamon
- ½ cantaloupe, seeded and cut into 2 wedges
  Lettuce leaves
- 1 grapefruit, peeled and sectioned
- ¼ cup fresh blueberries

In one container of Salad Dressing Set, combine yogurt, orange juice, sugar, and cinnamon. Apply Push-Button Seal. Shake well; chill.

Separate melon from shell; cut into bite-size pieces. Return melon pieces to shell. Place on individual lettuce-lined salad plates. Arrange grapefruit and blueberries atop melon. Pour dressing over fruit. Makes 2 servings.

BUYING FRESH VEGETABLES

Fresh vegetables present special problems for small households. Careful shopping and storage in Tupperware® products can avoid waste.

Choose fresh vegetables at a market that prices by piece or pound instead of prepackaged quantities of carrots, potatoes, beans, onions, corn, and tomatoes. Lock in the freshness of large vegetables such as cabbage, cauliflower, and salad greens in a Super Crisp-It® container.

COMPANY MEAT LOAF DINNER

SCOTCH MEAT LOAVES
CURRY CHEESE-SAUCED
BROCCOLI
CHILLED PEACH HALVES
CARROT CAKE
(see recipe, page 83)
MILK   COFFEE

SCOTCH MEAT LOAVES

- 1 beaten egg
- ¼ cup soft bread crumbs
- 2 tablespoons finely chopped celery
- 2 tablespoons finely chopped onion
- ¼ teaspoon salt
- ⅛ teaspoon ground sage
  Dash garlic powder
- ½ pound lean ground beef
- 2 hard-cooked eggs
- ¼ cup chili sauce
- 1 tablespoon snipped parsley
- 1 tablespoon water
- ⅛ teaspoon dried oregano, crushed
- 1 slice sharp American cheese, shredded

In Large Mixing Bowl, combine beaten egg, bread crumbs, celery, onion, salt, sage, and garlic powder. Add ground beef; mix well. Shape half of the meat mixture around each hard-cooked egg, completely enclosing egg. Arrange meat loaves in a 6½x6½x2-inch baking dish.

In Small Mix-N-Stor® pitcher, combine chili sauce, parsley, water, and oregano; pour over meat loaves. Bake in 350° oven for 45 minutes. Spoon chili sauce mixture over loaves; top each with some cheese. Return to oven and heat till cheese melts. Makes 2 servings.

CURRY CHEESE-SAUCED BROCCOLI

Use ½ teaspoon curry powder in the sauce for more bite —

- ½ pound fresh broccoli or one 10-ounce package frozen broccoli spears
- 1 tablespoon butter or margarine
- 1 tablespoon all-purpose flour
- ¼ teaspoon curry powder
- ½ cup milk
- 1 ounce shredded American cheese (¼ cup)
- 1 ounce shredded process Swiss cheese (¼ cup)

Cut fresh broccoli stalks lengthwise into uniform spears, following the branching lines. In covered saucepan, cook fresh broccoli spears in 1 inch of boiling water for 10 to 15 minutes or till crisp-tender. (Or, cook frozen broccoli spears according to package directions.) Drain well.

Meanwhile, in small saucepan, melt butter or margarine; blend in flour, curry powder, and dash salt. Add milk all at once. Cook, stirring constantly, till thickened and bubbly. Cook and stir 1 to 2 minutes more. Stir in American and Swiss cheese. Cook, stirring constantly, till cheeses are melted and mixture is smooth. (Or, in small saucepan, combine ¼ cup Creamy Sauce Mix (see recipe, page 50) and the curry powder; blend in ½ cup cold water. Cook and stir till thickened and bubbly; cook and stir 1 to 2 minutes more. Stir in cheeses till smooth.) Spoon curry-cheese mixture over hot cooked broccoli spears. Makes 2 servings.

MEALS FOR ONE OR TWO

ANYTHING GOES TEX-MEX SUPPER

CHILI-FOR-TWO
or
TACO-SALAD-FOR-ONE

CORN MUFFINS
or
TOASTY GARLIC BREAD
(see recipe, page 133)
VANILLA ICE CREAM WITH
STRAWBERRY SUNDAE SAUCE
or
PINEAPPLE-ORANGE
SUNDAE SAUCE
(see recipes, page 138)

CHILI-FOR-TWO

Create two single-serving meals; or freeze 1 cup of prepared chili in a 10-oz. Servalier® bowl. Use to make Taco-Salad-For-One —

½ pound ground beef
¼ cup chopped green pepper
¼ cup chopped onion
1 clove garlic, minced
1 8-ounce can tomatoes, cut up
1 8-ounce can tomato sauce
1 8-ounce can red kidney beans
1 to 1½ teaspoons chili powder
¼ teaspoon salt
⅛ teaspoon pepper

In a skillet, cook ground beef, green pepper, onion, and garlic till meat is browned. Drain off excess fat. Stir in undrained tomatoes and remaining ingredients. Bring to boiling; reduce heat. Cover and simmer about 20 minutes. Makes two servings.

TACO-SALAD-FOR-ONE

1 cup CHILI FOR TWO, frozen (see recipe, at left)
Torn lettuce
¼ cup shredded sharp American or cheddar cheese
¼ cup jalapeño bean dip
¼ cup corn chips

Place the frozen chili in a small saucepan; cover and place over low heat. Fill a Stacking Bowl with torn lettuce. When chili is warm through, stir in bean dip. Bring to boiling. Spoon over lettuce mixture; top with cheese and chips. Serve immediately. Makes 1 serving.

CORN MUFFINS

½ cup all-purpose flour
½ cup yellow cornmeal
2 tablespoons sugar
2 teaspoons baking powder
¼ teaspoon salt
1 beaten egg
½ cup milk
2 tablespoons cooking oil

In Small Mix-N-Stor® pitcher, stir together flour, cornmeal, sugar, baking powder, and salt. Add egg, milk, and oil. Beat just till smooth. (Do not overbeat.) Spoon batter into 6 greased or paper bake cup-lined muffin tins. Bake in 425° oven for 15 minutes. Cool on wire rack. Store in Super Seal-N-Serve® dish. Makes 6 muffins.

SPECIAL OCCASION DINNER

CHERRY-GLAZED HAM
BAKED POTATOES
TOSSED SALAD WITH
BUTTERMILK SALAD DRESSING
(see recipe, page 137)
RYE ROLLS   BUTTER
FRESH FRUIT CRISP
(see recipe, page 89)

MENU TIP

Take full advantage of your oven by baking potatoes, ham, and dessert together. Scrub potatoes and rub with shortening for tender skins. Prick with a fork. Bake in a 325° oven for 1¼ hours or till potatoes test done.

CHERRY-GLAZED HAM

1- to 1½-pound fully cooked boneless smoked ham or canned ham
¼ cup cherry preserves
2 teaspoons prepared mustard
Dash ground cloves

Place ham, fat side up, on a rack in small shallow baking pan. Score ham in diamonds, cutting only ¼ inch deep. Insert a meat thermometer into center of meat, making sure bulb does not rest in fat. Bake, uncovered, in 325° oven for 30 minutes.

Meanwhile, combine cherry preserves, mustard, and cloves. Spoon fat from pan. Spoon about half the glaze over ham. Continue baking about 15 minutes or till meat thermometer registers 140°, spooning remaining glaze over after 10 minutes.

Whether you're in the mood for spicy Chili or a zesty Taco Salad, serve this thrifty meal for 1 or 2 along with hot Corn Muffins.

Busy-Day MEALS

"There's just no time to cook around my family's busy schedule!" has become a nationwide lament. Well, despite the odds, we've come up with some innovative and easy solutions to your family's time crunch. Discover these practical, tasty, and time-saving recipes that will simplify meal making at your house.

Pictured clockwise from bottom left are: French bread slices with Mustard-Parsley Spread, Buttermilk Salad Dressing Mix, Spaghetti And Meat Rolls, and Quick Tortoni Dessert Cups. (See Index for recipe pages.)

ADVANCE COOKING

The hours before the evening meal are when you'll find most family members together. It's the best time to share the day's events. It's also the time when everyone, including the cook, would like to relax.

How can you have home-cooked meals and enjoy time with the family, too? The key is good planning. Here are some helpful ideas to shorten meal preparation and cleanup.

PLAN TO SAVE TIME

Saving time in the kitchen really begins with menu planning and careful shopping. Smooth meal preparation depends on selecting recipes that are quick and having the right ingredients available. Here are some tips to help you plan fast-to-fix menus.

- Keep an up-to-date calendar of all family activites. Select short-cut menus for hectic times.
- Serve one-dish meals such as meat and vegetable combinations frequently. They save cooking, serving, and cleanup time. To balance one-dish dinners, you can serve simple unmixed side dishes, such as fresh or canned fruit, green salads, and rolls with butter.
- Shortcut salad making by serving lettuce wedges instead of torn salad greens. Make gelatin salads in a hurry by spooning your favorite gelatin mixture into Dessert Set dishes and chilling them in the freezer for 20 to 25 minutes.
- Remember that some of the easiest desserts are nutrition boosters. Choose fruit with cheese, puddings, whole grain cookies, and ice cream.

STORE IT READY TO USE

- Instead of freezing ground meat in 1-pound packages, use the Hamburger Press and Freezer Sets to make and store patty portions. Individual patties thaw in minutes for use in casseroles or meat fillings.
- Wash fresh greens and vegetables before refrigerating in Tupperware® Fresh Vegetable Containers. Clean and cut up celery and carrots so you're ready for an instant relish tray.
- Plan menus ahead and shred the amount of American, Swiss, cheddar, or mozzarella cheese you'll need for a week on the Grater Bowl or Handy Grater. Refrigerate in sealed grater container. Or, keep several varieties in Refrigerator Bowls.

PREPARE FOR AN EMERGENCY

You can turn out a terrific meal on a moment's notice if you've planned ahead for an unexpected time crunch.

Make an "emergency shelf" in the refrigerator, freezer, cupboard, or a combination. Plan a quick but complete menu and stock all the ingredients you'll need. Use a large Tupperware container to set it apart from your regular groceries. Then it's ready to make when you need it most.Once you've used it, replenish the stock so you're ready for the next emergency.

The "Quick Stove-Top Dinner" shown on pages 4 and 5 is an ideal "emergency shelf" meal. Canned tuna and relishes for an antipasto tray, pasta, frozen broccoli, Parmesan cheese and ham for the entrée plus canned pears and dessert topping makes a three-course spur-of-the-moment dinner for four. (For more ideas, check Fast Foods from the Kitchen beginning on page 126.)

If it's more convenient, make a list of what you'll need for a favorite meal from "Fast Foods from the Kitchen." Carry it in your purse or wallet so you can make a quick stop at the supermarket as you head home to face a hungry family.

DOUBLE UP AND SAVE TIME

Save time and energy by preparing foods in double or triple batches and freezing portions for another meal. To avoid tying up your supply of baking pans and casserole dishes, freeze the extra portions in Tupperware containers.

- Select the storage container closest to the size and shape of the appropriate baking dish.
- Pour, layer, or arrange the casserole ingredients in the storage container.
- Apply the Seal carefully to lock in freshness and avoid freezer burn. Store in freezer.
- When you need the ready-to-bake casserole, transfer the frozen mixture to the appropriate baking dish and bake according to recipe instructions. (For examples, see Make-Ahead Main Dishes beginning on page 120).
- If you're storing large volumes of precooked foods, the heat of the food may raise the temperature inside the freezer. To cool hot mixtures quickly before freezing, place saucepan in ice water and stir occasionally. Transfer to Freezer Container and store at 0°.
- Casseroles can be reheated from their frozen state or allowed to thaw in the refrigerator overnight.
- Two-crust fruit pies can be prepared in batches, frozen in 9" or 12" Pie Takers, and baked later. Be sure to use a freezer-to-oven or metal pie plate. To bake without thawing, cut vent holes in top crust. Cover edges with foil. Bake in 450° oven for 15 minutes, then in 375° oven for 15 minutes. Uncover edges and continue baking in 375° oven for 30 to 35 minutes.

REFRIGERATE AHEAD OF TIME

Shift the assembly of many foods to a time of day when you have free time — while children are at school or napping, after supper when today's appetites are satisfied, or during early morning hours.

- Most casseroles can be refrigerated up to 24 hours before baking. It may be necessary to add 15 to 20 minutes to the normal baking time for your recipes. (Refrigerated recipes in this section give accurate timings for refrigerator-to-oven baking.)
- Chilled salads add variety to meals. Select from marinated, molded, or overnight salads.
- Individual dessert servings waiting in the refrigerator are so easy to serve. You can ask a child to be host or hostess for the family. Choose Tupperware bowls or Dessert Sets for puddings, fresh fruit mixtures, or sliced cake. Refrigerate chiffon pie for an elegant final course. Keep sauces and toppers chilled to make simple desserts special.

USE THE FREEZER

Take full advantage of all the freezer space you have available. The greatest time savings will be realized from a supply of make-ahead main dishes. Add breads, salads, and desserts as space permits.

Successful frozen foods depend on proper preparation for the freezer. When preparing main dishes, keep these ideas in mind:

- Cook all vegetables only till "crisp-tender."
- Cook pasta to the "just tender" stage (see tip, page 129).
- For "wet" vegetables such as spinach, drain well in a 1-qt. Strainer, gently pressing out excess moisture.
- Use fat sparingly in sauces. It can separate when reheated. Stirring during baking can help keep the sauce smooth.
- Casseroles that contain uncooked meat that has been previously frozen and thawed, raw vegetables, or uncooked rice should be baked before freezing. Reheat till bubbly.
- Label all foods with date and contents. For best quality, use casseroles within 3 to 6 months.

SKIP PREHEATING THE OVEN

To save energy and get out of the kitchen sooner, omit preheating the oven before baking casseroles and meat dishes. You may need to add a few minutes to the baking time; when a recipe gives a range, use the longer time. But for cookies, cakes, pies, and breads, it's still best to preheat the oven.

MAKE-AHEAD MAIN DISHES

LIME CHICKEN

When summer entertaining time comes, you'll want to try this on your outdoor grill. Serve with traditional potato salad, corn on the cob, and homemade ice cream —

- ½ cup salad oil
- ½ cup lime juice
- 2 tablespoons snipped chives
- ½ teaspoon grated lime peel
- ½ teaspoon salt
- 2 drops bottled hot pepper sauce
- 1 2½- to 3-pound broiler-fryer, cut up

For marinade, in Small Mix-N-Stor® pitcher, thoroughly combine salad oil, lime juice, snipped chives, grated lime peel, salt, and bottled hot pepper sauce. Place chicken in Season-Serve® container. Pour marinade over chicken; apply Seal and marinate in refrigerator for 8 to 24 hours, turning occasionally. Place chicken, skin side down, in broiler pan. Broil 5 to 7 inches from heat till lightly browned, about 20 minutes. Brush chicken occasionally with marinade.

Turn and broil 15 to 20 minutes more or till done. Baste occasionally with marinade. Serves 4 to 6.

BARBECUE MEAT LOAVES

A must for families that eat in shifts. Double bonus: each meat loaf has only 225 calories —

- 1 beaten egg
- ½ cup skim milk
- 1 cup soft bread crumbs (about 1½ slices)
- ¼ cup chopped onion
- 1 teaspoon salt
- ½ teaspoon dried oregano, crushed
- 1½ pounds ground beef
- ⅔ cup catsup
- 1 tablespoon brown sugar
- 1 tablespoon prepared mustard
- 1 tablespoon lemon juice
- 1 tablespoon Worcestershire sauce

In Medium Mixing Bowl, combine egg, milk, bread crumbs, onion, salt, and oregano. Add ground beef and mix well. Divide mixture into 6 portions; shape into small loaves, about 3½x2 inches. Arrange in Thin-Stor® container; apply Seal, label, and freeze.

To bake, place frozen individual meat loaves in 4½x2½x1½-inch baking pans. Bake, uncovered, in 375° oven 40 to 45 minutes or till done.

In small saucepan, combine catsup, brown sugar, mustard, lemon juice, and Worcestershire sauce. Bring to boiling. Spoon 2 to 3 tablespoons over each meat loaf last 10 minutes of baking. Refrigerate any unused sauce in Classic Sheer™ Refrigerator Bowl. Makes 6 servings.

ORIENTAL BEEF SKILLET

- 3 pounds ground beef
- 1 cup chopped celery
- 1 cup chopped onion
- ¾ cup chopped green pepper
- 3 cups water
- ⅓ cup cornstarch
- 1 tablespoon sugar
- ¾ teaspoon ground ginger
- ¾ cup soy sauce
- 2 7-ounce cans bamboo shoots, drained
- 2 6-ounce packages frozen pea pods, thawed
- 2 10-ounce packages frozen peas
- 3 3-ounce cans chow mein noodles

In a Dutch oven, cook ground beef, celery, onion, and green pepper till meat is browned; drain off excess fat. Add water. Combine cornstarch, sugar, and ginger; blend in soy sauce. Add to beef mixture; cook and stir till thickened and bubbly. Stir in bamboo shoots, pea pods, and frozen peas.

To serve without freezing, simmer one third of the mixture in skillet till heated through and vegetables are tender. Serve with chow mein noodles.

To freeze and cook later, turn one third of the mixture into each of 2 Super Seal-N-Serve bowls. Apply Seals; label and freeze. Immerse sealed container in warm water about 5 minutes, just till mixture is thawed enough to remove from container. Invert into a large skillet. Cook, covered, over low heat about 25 minutes, stirring frequently. Serve with chow mein noodles. Makes 3 casseroles, 4 to 5 servings each.

Make Oriental Beef Skillet and freeze two portions in the Super Seal-N-Serve® Set. It'll be handy on busy days when minutes count.

MAKE-AHEAD MAIN DISHES

REUBEN BAKE

- 2 27-ounce cans sauer-kraut
- 1 pound corned beef, thinly sliced
- 1 cup thousand island dressing
- 8 ounces shredded process Swiss cheese (2 cups)
  Rye Biscuits (see recipe at right)

In 1-qt. Strainer over Small Mix-N-Stor® pitcher, drain sauerkraut, reserving ¾ cup liquid. Cut corned beef into bite-size pieces. Combine sauerkraut, the ¾ cup liquid, corned beef, thousand island dressing, and Swiss cheese.

To bake immediately, spread half the mixture in bottom of a 12x7x2-inch baking dish. Bake, uncovered, in 350° oven for 40 to 45 minutes. Increase oven temperatures to 425°. Top with 12 Rye Biscuits. Brush with 1 tablespoon melted *butter or margarine*. Bake 15 minutes or till golden.

To freeze and bake later; spoon half the mixture into a Bacon Keeper. Apply Seal, label, and freeze. Immerse sealed container in warm water about 5 minutes or just till mixture is thawed enough to remove from container. Invert into a 12x7½x2-inch baking dish. Bake, covered, in a 400° oven for 30 minutes; spread mixture evenly in casserole. Bake 30 minutes more. Increase oven temperature to 425°. Uncover; top with 12 Rye Biscuits. Brush with 1 tablespoon melted *butter or margarine*. Continue baking 15 minutes more or till biscuits are golden. Makes 2 casseroles, 6 servings each.

RYE BISCUITS

- 1½ cups all-purpose flour
- 1½ cups rye flour
- 2 tablespoons baking powder
- 1 teaspoon salt
- 1 teaspoon caraway seed
- ⅓ cup shortening
- 1 cup milk

In Large Mixing Bowl, combine flours, baking powder, salt, and caraway seed. Mix thoroughly. Cut in shortening till mixture resembles coarse crumbs. Make a well in center; add milk all at once. Stir just till dough clings together. Turn onto a lightly floured Pastry Sheet. Knead gently 10 to 12 strokes. Use Rolling Pin to roll dough to ½-inch thickness. Cut with a floured 2-inch biscuit cutter. (Reroll as necessary to get 24 biscuits.) Place in Cold Cut Keeper; apply Seal. Freeze. To conserve freezer space, frozen biscuits may be stacked in smaller container such as Square Rounds® containers. Makes 24.

FROZEN VEGETABLE TIP

To partially thaw vegetables such as frozen cauliflower and broccoli, so that the vegetable can be separated and large pieces cut up, use the Multi-Server™ container to make the job easy.

Place the frozen vegetable in the strainer insert inside the serving dish. Pour in enough boiling water to cover vegetable. Cover and let stand on the counter for 5 to 10 minutes. Lift strainer to drain.

CAULIFLOWER TUNA AHOY

- 2 10-ounce packages frozen cauliflower
- 1 cup chopped onion
- 2 tablespoons butter
- 2 11-ounce cans condensed cheddar cheese soup
- 1 4-ounce can mushroom stems and pieces, drained
- ¼ cup milk
- 2 tablespoons snipped parsley
- 1 teaspoon Worcestershire sauce
- ⅛ teaspoon red pepper
- 2 6½-ounce cans tuna, drained and broken into chunks

Place cauliflower in Multi-Server container and partially thaw. (See tip at left.) Cut up any large pieces. In a large saucepan, cook onion in butter. Remove from heat. Stir in soup, mushrooms, milk, parsley, Worcestershire, and red pepper. Fold in cauliflower and tuna.

To bake immediately, spoon half the mixture into a 1-quart casserole. Bake in a 350° oven for 35 minutes. Sprinkle with paprika, if desired.

To freeze and bake later, spoon half the mixture in a 5-cup Classic Sheer™ Jr. Canister container. Apply Seal, label, and freeze. Immerse sealed container in warm water for 3 to 5 minutes, just till mixture is thawed enough to remove from container. Invert into a 1-quart casserole. Bake, covered, in a 400° oven for 40 minutes; stir to spread tuna mixture evenly in casserole. Bake, covered, for 30 minutes. Sprinkle with paprika, if desired. Makes 2 casseroles, 4 servings each.

HAM AND BROCCOLI BAKE

     2 10-ounce packages fro-
        zen chopped broccoli
        Boiling water
     1 8-ounce jar process
        cheese spread
     2 10¾-ounce cans
        condensed cream of
        chicken soup
     ½ cup milk
     ½ cup chopped onion
     2 tablespoons butter or
        margarine
     4 cups diced fully
        cooked ham
     2 cups quick cooking rice
     ½ teaspoon Worcestershire
        sauce

Place broccoli in Multi-Server
container and partially thaw. (See
tip at left.) Meanwhile, in
Fix-N-Mix® bowl, blend cheese
spread, soup, and milk. Cook
onion in butter or margarine till
tender. Add to soup mixture along
with broccoli, ham, rice, and
Worcestershire sauce.

To bake immediately, turn half
the mixture into a 1½-quart
casserole. Bake, uncovered, in
350° oven for 35 to 40 minutes or
till heated through.

To freeze and bake later, place
half the mixture in a 7-cup Classic
Sheer Jr. Canister. Apply Seal,
label, and freeze. Immerse sealed
container in warm water for 3 to 5
minutes or till thawed just enough
to remove from container. Invert
into a 1½-quart casserole. Bake,
covered, in a 400° oven for 1 hour.
Break apart with a fork and stir to
spread evenly in casserole. Bake,
uncovered, 20 to 25 minutes
longer or till heated through.
Makes 2 casseroles, 4 to 5
servings each.

HERBED ROUND STEAK

     1 large onion, sliced
     2 tablespoons cooking oil
     2 pounds beef round steak
     ½ teaspoon salt
     ⅛ teaspoon pepper
    1¼ cups milk
     2 tablespoons all-purpose
        flour
     1 10¾-ounce can
        condensed cream of
        celery soup
     1 teaspoon dried oregano,
        crushed
     ½ teaspoon dried thyme,
        crushed
        Hot cooked noodles

In skillet, cook onion in oil till
tender. Reserve half the onion;
spread remaining onion in bottom
of Deli-Keeper. Cut steak into 8
portions; trim off fat. Season with
salt and pepper. Brown in
remaining oil in skillet. Place four
pieces in 10x6x2-inch baking dish;
spread reserved onions atop.
Place remaining beef portions
atop onion in Deli-Keeper. For
sauce, in saucepan, blend milk
and flour; stir in soup, oregano,
and thyme. Cook and stir till
thickened and bubbly. Cook and
stir 1 to 2 minutes more. Divide the
sauce between meat in baking
dish and Deli-Keeper.

To bake immediately, bake,
covered, in 350° oven for 1 hour.
Place meat atop noodles; stir
sauce to blend and pass.

To freeze and bake later, apply
Seal to Deli-Keeper; label and
freeze. Immerse sealed container
in warm water 3 to 5 minutes till
mixture can be removed easily. Invert into 10x6x2-inch baking dish.
Bake, covered, in 350° oven for
1½ hours. Serve as above. Makes
2 casseroles, 4 servings each.

SPAGHETTI AND MEAT ROLLS

Pictured on page 116—

     3 eggs, beaten
     ¾ cup chopped onion
     ⅓ cup soft bread crumbs
     ¾ teaspoon salt
     ¼ teaspoon pepper
     3 pounds lean ground beef
     4 ounces shredded
        mozzarella cheese
        (1 cup)
     2 2-cup containers ITALIAN
        SAUCE (see recipe,
        page 13)
        Hot cooked spaghetti or
        other pasta

In Large Mixing Bowl, stir eggs,
onion, bread crumbs, salt, and
pepper. Add meat; mix well. Divide
mixture into sixteen portions. On
Pastry Sheet, pat each portion into
a 4x3-inch rectangle. Sprinkle 1
tablespoon mozzarella cheese
lengthwise down center of each
rectangle; fold in half lengthwise to
form a 4-inch-long roll. Seal long
edges; pinch ends together.
Makes 16 rolls.

To bake immediately, place
eight meat rolls in a 12x7½x2-inch
baking pan. Bake in 350° oven
about 25 minutes. Meanwhile, in
covered saucepan, thaw one
2-cup container Italian Sauce over
low heat till bubbly, about 20
minutes; stir occasionally. Place
spaghetti on serving plate; arrange
meat rolls atop. Spoon some of
sauce over; pass remaining. If
desired, sprinkle with additional
shredded mozzarella cheese.

To freeze and bake later, place
eight meat rolls in Bacon Keeper.
Apply Seal, label, and freeze. Turn
meat rolls into a 12x7½x2-inch
baking pan. Bake, covered, in 400°
oven about 30 minutes. Prepare
sauce and arrange over spaghetti
as above.

MAKE-AHEAD MAIN DISHES

SHRIMP-MACARONI CASEROLE

2 7¼-ounce packages macaroni and cheese dinner mix
1½ cups milk
3 10¾-ounce cans condensed cream of chicken soup
1 10-ounce package frozen cooked shelled shrimp
1½ teaspoons Worcestershire sauce
¼ teaspoon pepper
1½ cups crisp rice cereal squares, crushed

Prepare macaroni and cheese dinner mix according to package directions, except substitute 1½ cups milk for the total amounts called for. Stir in soup, shrimp, Worcestershire, and pepper.

To bake immediately, turn one-third of mixture into a 1-quart casserole. Bake, uncovered, in 350° oven for 30 minutes. Stir. Sprinkle with ½ cup of the crushed rice squares. Bake 10 minutes more.

To freeze and bake later, divide remaining two-thirds of the mixture between the Super Seal-N-Serve® Set. Apply Seals, label, and freeze. Immerse sealed container in warm water for about 3 to 5 minutes, just till mixture is thawed enough to remove from container. Invert into a 1-quart casserole. Cover and bake in a 400° oven for 40 minutes; stir to spread mixture evenly in casserole. Bake, covered, for 30 minutes. Uncover and stir. Sprinkle ½ cup crushed rice squares atop casserole. Bake 10 minutes more. Makes 3 casseroles, 4 servings each.

SWISS CHICKEN ROLLS

4 whole large chicken breasts, skinned, boned, and halved lengthwise
2 ounces process Swiss cheese, cut into 8 strips
2 tablespoons crumbled blue cheese
1 cup fine dry bread crumbs
1 tablespoon butter, melted
½ cup all-purpose flour
2 beaten eggs

Place chicken pieces, boned side up, between two pieces of clear plastic wrap. Using the finetoothed side of a meat mallet, pound from center out to form ¼-inch-thick cutlets. Peel off wrap; sprinkle with salt. Place one strip of Swiss cheese at end of each cutlet; sprinkle with a little of the blue cheese. Beginning with short side, roll up jelly roll-fashion, tucking in sides. Press edges together gently with fingers to seal.

Mix crumbs and butter in a Super Seal-N-Serve container. Spread flour on the Duo-Seal® closure. Coat each roll with some flour; dip in eggs. Roll in crumb mixture. Arrange chicken rolls in Bacon Keeper; apply Seal. Refrigerate till well chilled, at least 1 hour or up to 24 hours.

Bake, uncovered, in a 350° oven about 45 minutes or till done. Serves 4 to 6.

SWEET POTATO TURKEY PIE

2 18-ounce cans vacuum-packed sweet potatoes
¼ cup butter, melted
2 eggs
¼ teaspoon ground nutmeg
¼ teaspoon ground allspice
1 cup chopped onion
2 tablespoons butter
1 10¾-ounce can condensed cream of mushroom soup
¼ cup milk
3 cups diced cooked turkey
1 16-ounce can mixed vegetables, drained
2 small tomatoes, peeled and diced
  Cheese triangles

Beat sweet potatoes on medium speed of electric mixer till smooth. Add ¼ cup melted butter, 1 egg, nutmeg, allspice, and ½ teaspoon *salt*. Line two 9-inch pie plates with the sweet potato mixture, building up sides about 1 inch. Cook onion in the 2 tablespoons butter. Combine onion, soup, 1 egg, and milk; mix well. Add turkey, vegetables, and tomatoes. Spoon half into each pie plate.

To bake immediately, cover with foil. Bake in 350° oven for 15 minutes. Uncover; bake 25 minutes. Arrange cheese atop. Bake 10 minutes or till cheese melts.

To freeze and bake later, place in a 9" or 12" Pie Taker. Apply Seal, label, and freeze. Remove from Pie Taker and bake, covered, in 400° oven 30 minutes. Uncover; bake 35 minutes. Arrange cheese triangles atop. Bake 10 minutes. Makes 2 pies, 6 servings each.

The unique "crust" to Sweet Potato Turkey Pie is made out of fluffy sweet potatoes. Make one to bake now, and freeze the other for later.

FAST FOODS FROM THE KITCHEN

FROZEN FISH FEAST

CURRY-SOUR CREAM APPETIZER
FISH FLORENTINE
TOSSED SALAD WITH CHOICE
OF SALAD DRESSINGS
SHORT-CUT CLOVERLEAF ROLLS
(see recipe, page 72)
BUTTER OR MARGARINE
DOUBLE RASPBERRY TORTES
MILK   COFFEE

PREPARATION SCHEDULE

Step 1. Assemble the needed ingredients. In addition to staples found in most kitchens, you'll need:

- 1 pound frozen fish
- 1 10-ounce package frozen spinach or broccoli
  American cheese
- 1 8-ounce can sliced water chestnuts
  Bacon bits
  Dairy sour cream
  Carrots, cucumbers, cherry tomatoes, cauliflower
  Frozen raspberry yogurt
- 1 10¾-ounce loaf frozen pound cake
  Raspberry preserves

Step 2. Prepare the Double Raspberry Torte and freeze.

Step 3. Mix the Curry-Sour Cream Dressing and chill in Dip-N-Serve® bowl. Clean vegetables; arrange on Dip-N-Serve tray.

Step 4. Roll and poach the fish fillets; cook spinach or broccoli and cheese sauce.

Step 5. Combine cheese sauce and vegetables; place on serving plate. Top with fish rolls and cheese sauce.

FISH FLORENTINE

- 1 16-ounce package frozen perch or other fish fillets, thawed
- 1 10-ounce package frozen chopped spinach or chopped broccoli
- 2 tablespoons butter
- 2 tablespoons all-purpose flour
- 1¼ cups milk
- 4 ounces shredded Swiss or American cheese (1 cup)
- 1 8-ounce can sliced water chestnuts
- 3 tablespoons bacon bits
- 2 tablespoons lemon juice

Roll each fish fillet lengthwise to form a pinwheel; secure with a toothpick, if necessary. Place on strainer insert in Multi-Server™ container. Sprinkle with 1 teaspoon *salt*. Add boiling water to cover fillets. Cover container and let stand on counter 10 minutes or till fish flakes with a fork. Cook spinach according to package directions; drain in 1-qt. Strainer and set aside. In same saucepan, melt butter; blend in flour and ¼ teaspoon *salt*. Add milk all at once; cook and stir till thickened and bubbly. Add cheese; cook and stir till melted. Pour ¾ cup of cheese sauce into Small Mix-N-Stor® pitcher; set aside. Stir spinach, water chestnuts, and bacon bits into sauce in saucepan; heat through. Place spinach mixture on heated serving dish. Arrange fish rolls atop; drizzle with lemon juice. Reheat reserved cheese sauce; pour over fish rolls. Garnish with halved lemon slices and dillweed, if desired. Makes 4 servings.

CURRY-SOUR CREAM APPETIZER

- ½ cup dairy sour cream
- ½ cup mayonnaise or salad dressing
- 1 teaspoon curry powder
- ¼ teaspoon prepared horseradish
- ⅛ teaspoon onion powder
  Dash garlic powder
  Assorted fresh vegetable dippers

In a Small Mix-N-Stor pitcher, combine all ingredients except vegetables. Transfer to Dip-N-Serve bowl; apply Seal. Chill till serving time. Serve with fresh vegetables arranged on Dip-N-Serve tray. Makes 1 cup.

DOUBLE RASPBERRY TORTES

- ½ pint frozen raspberry yogurt
- 1 10¾-ounce loaf frozen pound cake
- ¼ cup raspberry preserves
- 1 tablespoon orange juice
  Whipped cream

Cut eight ½-inch-thick slices from pound cake. Return unused cake to freezer. Stir together raspberry preserves and orange juice. Spread some of the preserves mixture over 4 slices of cake. Spread the frozen yogurt over. Top each with another slice of cake and some preserves mixture. Store individual tortes in Snack-Stor® container in freezer while cooking fish entrée. Garnish with whipped cream. Makes 4 servings.

You can sit down to this elegant fish feast in less than 1 hour. And we'll show you how with our step-by-step preparation schedule.

FAST FOODS FROM THE KITCHEN

EASY OVEN DINNER

MEXICAN-STYLE QUICHE
MIXED BEAN SALAD
EASY FRUIT COBBLER
MILK   COFFEE

PREPARATION SCHEDULE

Step 1. Preheat oven to 350°. Assemble the needed ingredients. In addition to staples found in most kitchens, you'll need:

- 4 **6-inch flour tortillas**
  Monterey Jack cheese with peppers
- 1 **3-ounce can French-fried onions**
- 2 **16-ounce cans three-bean salad or Marinated Bean Salad (see recipe, page 108)**
- 1 **21-ounce can fruit pie filling**
- 1 **11-ounce can mandarin orange sections**
- 1 **package (6) refrigerated biscuits**

Step 2. Assemble and put Mexican-Style Quiche in the oven to bake.

Step 3. Assemble and put Easy Fruit Cobbler in oven to bake.

Step 4. For Mixed Bean Salad, open the two 16-ounce cans of three-bean salad. Turn canned salad or Marinated Bean Salad into a 2-qt. lemon Servalier® Bowl. Top with red or green pepper rings. Chill.

MEXICAN-STYLE QUICHE

Flour tortillas make these crusts easier than pie —

- 4 **6-inch flour tortillas**
- 4 **ounces Monterey Jack cheese with peppers, sliced**
- 1 **3-ounce can French-fried onions (1⅔ cups)**
- 4 **eggs**
- 2 **cups milk**
- ½ **teaspoon salt**
- ½ **teaspoon chili powder**
- ¼ **teaspoon dry mustard**
  Pickled peppers (optional)
  Parsley (optional)

Gently press one flour tortilla in each of four individual au gratin casseroles; top with cheese slices and about three-fourths of the onion rings; reserve remaining onions for garnish.

In a saucepan, heat milk almost to boiling. In a Large Mix-N-Stor® pitcher, beat eggs; gradually add milk, blending well. Stir in salt, chili powder, and mustard. Place casseroles in shallow baking pan; place on oven rack. Divide egg mixture evenly between the casseroles.

Bake in 350° oven for 25 minutes. Sprinkle reserved onions atop. Bake 5 minutes more or till knife inserted near center comes out clean. Let stand at room temperature 5 minutes before serving. Garnish with pickled peppers and parsley, if desired. Makes 4 servings.

EASY FRUIT COBBLER

- 1 **21-ounce can apricot, blueberry, cherry, or French apple pie filling**
- 1 **11-ounce can mandarin orange sections, drained**
- 2 **tablespoons sugar**
- ¼ **teaspoon ground cinnamon or ground nutmeg**
- 1 **package (6) refrigerated biscuits**
- 2 **tablespoons butter or margarine, melted**

In medium saucepan, heat pie filling till bubbly; stir in orange sections. Turn mixture into 8x8x2-inch baking dish. Place sugar and cinnamon or nutmeg in a Six Little Wonders™ bowl; apply Seal and shake to blend. Dip tops of biscuits in melted butter or margarine, then in sugar-cinnamon mixture. Arrange atop fruit. Bake in 350° oven for 20 to 25 minutes or till heated through. Serve in Dessert Set dishes. Makes 4 to 6 servings.

TORTILLA TIP

Serve warm rolled-up flour tortillas instead of bread as a meal accompaniment. On one side only, lightly spread each tortilla with butter or margarine. Sprinkle lightly with sugar, if desired. Gently roll up each tortilla and wrap them in foil. Heat in a warm oven to serve with the meal.

QUICK STOVE-TOP SUPPER

AD-LIB ANTIPASTO
HAM AND PASTA
BREADSTICKS
ORANGE-SAUCED PEARS
MILK   COFFEE

PREPARATION SCHEDULE

Step 1. Start water boiling for pasta. Assemble the needed ingredients. In addition to staples found in most kitchens, you'll need:

- 1 6½-ounce can tuna
  Olives, pickled beets, cherry tomatoes, pickles
- 8 ounces pasta
- 1 10-ounce package frozen cut broccoli
  Parmesan cheese
  Dairy sour cream
- 4 ounces smoked ham
  Breadsticks
- 1 29-ounce can pear slices
  Frozen whipped dessert topping

Step 2. Prepare Orange-Sauced Pears. Let stand until serving time before spooning into Parfait dishes and adding topping.

Step 3. Arrange Ad-Lib Antipasto in Egg Tray.

Step 4. Cook pasta and broccoli for Ham and Pasta. Cut up ham; make sour cream sauce.

Step 5. Combine Ham and Pasta ingredients in sealed Servalier Bowl.

ORANGE-SAUCED PEARS

- 1 29-ounce can pear slices
- ¼ cup orange juice
- 3 inches stick cinnamon
- ½ of a 4-ounce container frozen whipped dessert topping, thawed
  Stick cinnamon or ground cinnamon (optional)

Use 1-qt. Strainer over Small Mix-N-Stor® pitcher to drain pears, reserving 1 cup pear syrup. In medium saucepan, combine the reserved syrup, orange juice, and 3 inches stick cinnamon. Bring to boiling; add sliced pears. Cook, uncovered, 1 to 2 minutes or till heated through. Let stand till serving time; remove stick cinnamon.

To serve, spoon pears and syrup into Parfait dishes. Top with dessert topping. Garnish with stick cinnamon and sprinkle with ground cinnamon, if desired. Makes 4 servings.

AD-LIB ANTIPASTO

Lettuce leaves
- 1 6½-ounce can chilled tuna, drained and broken into large chunks
  Ripe olives
  Sliced pickled beets
  Pimiento-stuffed olives
  Cherry tomatoes
  PICK-A-DILLIES (see recipe, page 103) or other pickles

In Egg Tray with inserts removed, arrange lettuce to form four to six cups. Fill one lettuce cup with tuna. Select from ripe olives, pickled beets, pimiento-stuffed olives, cherry tomatoes, and pickles to fill each of remaining lettuce cups. Makes 4 to 6 servings.

HAM AND PASTA

- 8 ounces spaghetti or linguini
- 1 10-ounce package frozen cut broccoli
- ¼ cup butter or margarine
- ½ cup dairy sour cream
- ¼ cup milk
- 1 4-ounce package thinly-sliced smoked ham, cut into 1-inch strips
- ¾ cup grated Parmesan cheese

Cook pasta in a large amount of boiling salted water about 10 to 12 minutes or till tender. Meanwhile, cook broccoli in boiling salted water till crisp-tender; drain and keep warm. Melt butter in saucepan; blend in sour cream and milk. Stir in broccoli and ham; heat through. Drain pasta well in 1-qt. Strainer (do not rinse). Transfer to 2-qt. lemon Servalier bowl; pour vegetable mixture over. Apply Instant Seal and turn several times to coat pasta. Sprinkle with Parmesan cheese. Serve immediately. Makes 4 to 6 servings.

PERFECT PASTA TIP

To make perfect pasta every time, start with three quarts cold water and one tablespoon salt for each eight ounces of pasta. Bring water to a rolling boil. Add one tablespoon cooking oil to prevent pasta from sticking together.

Add the pasta when the water boils vigorously. Cook uncovered. After three or four minutes, taste test for doneness. Pasta should be firm but tender with no starchy taste. Continue testing every minute till just tender.

Drain immediately; do not rinse.

129

FAST FOODS FROM THE KITCHEN

OFF-THE-SHELF SUPPER SALAD

This salad is tasty any time of year, but when summer heat overtakes the kitchen, you'll appreciate it doubly —

- 6 cups torn mixed salad greens
- 2 6¾-ounce cans chunk ham or two 6½-ounce cans tuna, drained and broken up
- 4 ounces shredded cheddar or mozzarella cheese (1 cup)
- ½ cup pitted ripe olives and/or pimiento-stuffed olives
- 1 3½-ounce jar sliced mushrooms, drained
  Broccoli buds
  Cauliflower flowerets
  Carrot sticks or curls
  Tomato wedges or cherry tomatoes
  Radish slices
- 1 cup HERB STUFFING MIX (see recipe, page 45) or packaged croutons
  Russian Dressing
  Buttermilk Salad Dressing

Place salad greens, ham or tuna, cheese, and olives in large Decorator Salad Bowl. In a Small Mix-N-Stor® pitcher, measure 2 cups of any combination of remaining vegetables. Add to salad greens mixture along with Herb Stuffing Mix. Toss thoroughly. Serve in individual Salad Bowls with choice of dressings. Makes 4 to 6 servings.

Keep basic salad-making ingredients on hand when minutes matter so all you have to do is toss together your favorite combination of fresh vegetables, cheese, and salad greens to make Off-The-Shelf Supper Salad.

ORANGE-PINEAPPLE DESSERT-IN-A-MUG

- 2 8-ounce cartons orange yogurt
- 1 8¼-ounce can crushed pineapple
- ½ cup milk
- 2 to 3 ice cubes (½ cup)
  Sugar

In blender container, place yogurt, undrained crushed pineapple, and milk. Cover and blend until smooth. Add ice cubes, one at a time, blending after each addition till chopped. Sweeten to taste with sugar. Pour into 4 Multi-Mugs® beverage servers; top with coaster/covers. Chill while preparing remainder of meal. To serve, garnish with fresh mint, if desired. Makes 4 servings.

RUSSIAN DRESSING

In a Salad Dressing Set Container, combine ⅓ cup *salad oil*, 3 tablespoons *catsup*, 2 tablespoons *sugar*, 1½ tablespoon *lemon juice*, 1 tablespoon *Worcestershire sauce*, 1 tablespoon *vinegar*, 1 tablespoon *water*, 1 teaspoon *onion salt*, and ¼ teaspoon *paprika*. Apply Push-Button Seal and shake well. Chill; shake again before serving. Makes ¾ cup.

NO-COOK SALAD SUPPER

OFF-THE-SHELF SUPPER SALAD
RUSSIAN DRESSING
BUTTERMILK SALAD DRESSING
(see recipe, page 137)
RYE ROLLS   BUTTER
ORANGE-PINEAPPLE
DESSERT-IN-A-MUG

PREPARATION SCHEDULE

Step 1. Assemble the necessary ingredients. In addition to staples found in most kitchens, you will need:

- 2 cans ham or tuna
  Cheddar or mozzarella cheese
- 1 3½-ounce jar sliced mushrooms
  Broccoli, cauliflower, carrots, tomatoes, radishes
  Herb Stuffing Mix or croutons
  Buttermilk Salad Dressing Mix
  Fresh herbs
- 2 8-ounce cartons orange yogurt
- 1 8¼-ounce can crushed pineapple

Step 2. Blend Orange-Pineapple Dessert-In-A-Mug.

Step 3. Shake together Russian Dressing and Buttermilk Salad Dressing.

Step 4. Mix Off-The-Shelf Supper Salad in Decorator Salad Bowl.

131

FAST FOODS FROM THE KITCHEN

SPEEDY STIR-FRY SUPPER

HAWAIIAN SAUSAGE STIR-FRY
FRESH SPINACH SALAD
AVOCADO-YOGURT DRESSING
INSTANT PEACH-ALMOND
SHERBET
FORTUNE COOKIES
MILK   COFFEE

PREPARATION SCHEDULE

Step 1. Assemble the necessary ingredients. In addition to staples found in most kitchens, you will need:

Instant orange-flavored breakfast drink powder
2 **10-ounce packages frozen peaches**
Fresh spinach
1 **small avocado**
1 **cup plain yogurt**
Bottled teriyaki sauce
Unsweetened pineapple juice
1 **6-ounce package frozen pea pods**
1 **12-ounce package smoked sausage links**
1 **10-ounce package frozen Hawaiian-style vegetables**
Chow mein noodles

Step 2. Blend the Instant Peach-Almond Sherbet. Freeze until serving time. Clean blender container (see tip, page 21).

Step 3. Blend Avocado-Yogurt Dressing.

Step 4. Tear spinach for salad.

Step 5. Cook the Hawaiian Sausage Stir-Fry; spoon onto a bed of chow mein noodles.

HAWAIIAN SAUSAGE STIR-FRY

A blend of bottled teriyaki sauce, pineapple juice, and brown sugar lends a Cantonese flavor —

3 **tablespoons bottled teriyaki sauce**
4 **teaspoons cornstarch**
1¼ **cups unsweetened pineapple juice**
1 **tablespoon brown sugar**
1 **6-ounce package frozen pea pods**
1 **12-ounce package smoked sausage links, cut crosswise into thirds**
1 **10-ounce package frozen Hawaiian-style vegetables**
Chow mein noodles

In Small Mix-N-Stor® pitcher, blend teriyaki sauce into cornstarch. Stir in pineapple juice and brown sugar; set aside. Place pea pods in 1-qt. Strainer. Run hot tap water over to thaw. Drain and set aside. In large skillet or wok, stir-fry sausage about 5 minutes or till browned. Stir the teriyaki mixture; stir into skillet or wok along with the frozen Hawaiian-style vegetables. Cook and stir till mixture bubbles, breaking vegetables apart as they begin to thaw. Cover and cook 2 minutes longer; stir in pea pods. Cover and cook 1 minute longer. Serve at once over chow mein noodles. Makes 4 servings.

INSTANT PEACH-ALMOND SHERBET

½ **cup water**
2 **tablespoons instant orange-flavored drink powder**
2 **10-ounce packages frozen peaches**
¼ **teaspoon almond extract**

Place water and breakfast drink powder in a blender container. Break up frozen peaches with a fork; add to blender along with almond extract. Cover and blend on high till smooth and sherbet-like in texture. If necessary, stop blender and push ingredients toward blades with rubber spatula. Spoon into Dessert Set dishes; apply Seals. Store in freezer till serving time. Garnish with shredded coconut, if desired. Makes 4 servings.

AVOCADO-YOGURT DRESSING

1 **small avocado**
1 **cup plain yogurt**
¼ **cup milk**
1 **tablespoon honey**
½ **teaspoon garlic salt**

Peel, seed, and cut up avocado. In blender container, combine avocado, yogurt, milk, honey, and garlic salt. Cover and blend till mixture is smooth. Add additional milk, if needed, to make of desired consistency. Transfer to Refrigerator Bowl to store. Makes 1⅓ cups.

PIZZA PORK CHOPS

Sliced olives make good toppers, too —

- 4 pork chops, cut ½ inch thick
- 3 ounces mozzarella cheese
- ¼ cup chili sauce
- 4 thin green pepper rings
- 1 2-ounce can mushroom stems and pieces, drained
   Toasty Garlic Bread (see recipe below)

Place chops on rack in broiler pan; sprinkle with salt and pepper. Broil chops, 3 to 4 inches from heat, for 8 to 10 minutes. Turn chops; broil 8 minutes more or till nearly done.

Meanwhile, shred cheese on Handy Grater or Grater Bowl. Brush chops with chili sauce; sprinkle each with one-fourth of cheese. Place one green pepper ring and one-fourth of the mushrooms atop each chop. Broil for 1 to 1½ minutes more or till cheese melts. Serve atop or with hot slices of Toasty Garlic Bread. Makes 4 servings.

TOASTY GARLIC BREAD

Next time, sprinkle the bread with your favorite crushed dried herbs —

- 4 slices French or sourdough bread, cut 1 inch thick
   Butter or margarine
   Garlic salt

Spread bread with butter or margarine. Sprinkle lightly with garlic salt. Place bread slices on broiler pan with chops; broil on one side 3 to 4 inches from heat for 1 to 1½ minutes. Serves 4.

ITALIAN POTATO SALAD

- 1½ cups frozen loose-pack California-style mixed vegetables or other frozen vegetable combination
- ¼ cup bottled creamy Italian salad dressing
- ¼ cup plain yogurt
- 1 16-ounce can sliced potatoes, drained
- 2 cups torn salad greens

Cook frozen vegetables, covered, in a small amount of boiling, salted water 2 to 3 minutes. Remove from heat; drain. Cover vegetables in pan with very cold water. Place pan in freezer. In a Small Mix-N-Stor pitcher, combine Italian dressing and yogurt; fold in drained potatoes. Cover; chill. Place salad greens in 2-qt. lemon Servalier® bowl; chill. Just before serving, thoroughly drain vegetables. Add to greens; top with potato mixture; toss. Makes 4 servings.

STRAWBERRY ICE

- 2 10-ounce packages frozen strawberries
- ½ of an envelope (1½ teaspoons) unsweetened lemonade soft drink mix
- 1 cup ice cubes

Break up frozen berries with a fork; place in blender container along with drink mix. Cover and blend for ½ to 1 minute or till smooth. Add ice cubes, one at a time. Blend ½ to 1 minute more or till mixture is sherbet-like in texture. Spoon into Dessert Set dishes; apply Seals. Store in freezer till serving time. Garnish each serving with a sprig of fresh mint, if desired. Makes 4 servings.

PRONTO ITALIAN DINNER

PIZZA PORK CHOPS
ITALIAN POTATO SALAD
TOASTY GARLIC BREAD
STRAWBERRY ICE
MILK   COFFEE

PREPARATION SCHEDULE

Step 1. Assemble the necessary ingredients. In addition to staples found in most kitchens, you'll need:

- 4 pork chops
   Bottled chili sauce
   Mozzarella cheese
   Green pepper
- 1 2-ounce can mushroom stems and pieces
   French or sourdough bread
   Frozen loose-pack vegetables
   Creamy Italian dressing
   Plain yogurt
- 1 16-ounce can sliced potatoes
   Lettuce or other salad greens
- 2 10-ounce packages frozen strawberries
- 1 envelope unsweetened lemonade soft drink mix

Step 2. Blend Strawberry Ice.

Step 3. Cook vegetables for Italian Potato Salad; combine Italian dressing, yogurt, and potatoes. Prepare greens.

Step 4. Start broiling Pizza Pork Chops. Prepare Toasty Garlic Bread for broiling.

Step 5. Complete Italian Potato Salad. Place topping on chops; broil chops and bread.

133

STANDBY SALADS AND SIDE DISHES

TOMATO SOUP MOLD

- 1 10¾-ounce can condensed tomato soup
- ½ cup water
- 2 envelopes unflavored gelatin
- ¼ teaspoon salt
- 1 cup cream-style cottage cheese
- ½ cup mayonnaise or salad dressing
- 1 cup chopped celery
- ½ cup chopped green pepper
- ½ cup chopped radishes
- ½ cup chopped walnuts or pecans
- 2 tablespoons sliced green onion
  Lettuce
  Whole pimiento
  Green pepper

Assemble Jel-N-Serve® mold with tulip design Seal; set aside. In medium saucepan, stir together soup, water, gelatin, and salt; let stand 10 minutes to soften gelatin. Stir over low heat till gelatin dissolves. Pour into Large Mix-N-Stor® pitcher; add cottage cheese and mayonnaise or salad dressing. Cover and chill till partially set (the consistency of unbeaten egg whites). Fold in celery, green pepper, radishes, walnuts or pecans, and green onion. Turn into Jel-N-Serve mold. Apply large Seal; refrigerate, with the design Seal down, overnight or till firm. Carefully unmold onto Jel-N-Serve tray and surround with lettuce leaves. Garnish by cutting pimiento and green pepper to fit tulip design Seal; arrange on mold. Makes 8 to 10 servings.

BEAN SALAD ASPIC

- 1 6-ounce package lemon-flavored gelatin
- 1 cup boiling water
- 1 2-cup container ITALIAN SAUCE, thawed (see recipe, page 13)
- 2 tablespoons vinegar
- 1 15-ounce can garbanzo beans, drained
- 1 8-ounce can red kidney beans, drained
- 1 2½-ounce can sliced mushrooms, drained
- ½ cup finely chopped celery
- ½ cup finely chopped green pepper
  Lettuce

In a Large Mix-N-Stor pitcher, dissolve gelatin in boiling water. Stir in the Italian Sauce and vinegar. Cover and chill till partially set (consistency of unbeaten egg whites), stirring occasionally. Fold beans, mushrooms, celery, and green pepper into gelatin mixture. Apply inner Seal to Jel-Ring® mold. Pour gelatin mixture into Jel-Ring mold. Apply large Seal and chill till firm.

If desired, leave mold at room temperature for 10 to 15 minutes. With large Seal down, immerse in warm water 15 seconds, taking care not to melt gelatin. Remove from water; peel off large Seal. Place plate over mold and invert. Slowly release inner Seal and carefully remove. Lift off mold. Surround with lettuce leaves. Makes 10 to 12 servings.

UNMOLDING GELATIN

1. Immerse mold in warm water for 15 seconds; remove large Seal. Place Jel-N-Serve tray or serving plate upside down over mold and invert together.

2. Carefully release design or inner Seal; remove. Lift off mold.

3. Lift gelatin with spatula; slide edges of salad greens under.

Standby Tomato Soup Mold is decoratively shaped in the Jel-N-Serve. The tulip design pictured here is filled with pimiento and green pepper.

135

STANDBY SALADS AND SIDE DISHES

24-HOUR FRUIT SALAD

Don't throw out the egg whites. Make Surprise Meringue Kisses (see recipe, page 76) or add them to scrambled eggs —

- 1   20-ounce can pineapple chunks
- 3   slightly beaten egg yolks
- 2   tablespoons sugar
- 2   tablespoons vinegar
- 1   tablespoon butter or margarine
    Dash salt
- 1   17-ounce can pitted light sweet cherries, drained
- 3   oranges, peeled, sectioned, and drained
- 2   cups tiny marshmallows
- 1   cup whipping cream

Use 1-qt. Strainer over Small Mix-N-Stor® pitcher to drain pineapple; reserve 2 tablespoons syrup. To make custard, in small heavy saucepan, combine reserved pineapple syrup, egg yolks, sugar, vinegar, butter or margarine, and salt. Cook and stir over low heat about 6 minutes or till mixture thickens slightly and coats a metal spoon. Cool to room temperature.

In 3-qt. green Wonderlier® bowl, combine pineapple, cherries, oranges, and marshmallows. Pour custard over; mix fruit mixture gently. In Medium Mixing Bowl, whip the whipping cream till soft peaks form. Fold whipped cream into fruit mixture. Apply Seal and refrigerate 24 hours or overnight. Makes 10 to 12 servings.

FRUIT MELANGE

- 1   15¼-ounce can pineapple chunks (juice pack)
- 1   11-ounce can mandarin orange sections
- 2   cups honeydew melon balls
- ½   cup orange marmalade
- ¼   cup hot water
- 1   teaspoon finely chopped candied ginger

Use 1-qt. Strainer to drain pineapple chunks and orange sections. Combine with melon balls in a burnt orange 1-qt. Servalier® bowl. Stir together the marmalade, hot water, and ginger; spoon over fruit. Apply Seal and chill up to 24 hours. Serves 4 to 6.

JUBILEE SALAD MOLD

- 1   16-ounce can pitted dark sweet cherries
- 1   10-ounce package frozen red raspberries, thawed
- 1   6-ounce package red raspberry-flavored gelatin
- ¼   cup lemon juice

Use 1-qt. Strainer over Small Mix-N-Stor pitcher to drain cherries, reserving ½ cup syrup. Halve cherries; set aside. Return 1-qt. Strainer to Small Mix-N-Stor pitcher and drain raspberries, adding all raspberry syrup to ½ cup cherry syrup. In Large Mix-N-Stor pitcher, dissolve gelatin in 1¾ cups boiling *water*. Stir in lemon juice and reserved syrups. Cover and chill till partially set. Fold in cherries and raspberries. Pour into a Jel-Ring® mold; apply Seal. Chill. Unmold. (See tip, page 135). Makes 8 servings.

GRAPEFRUIT PARFAITS

This salad is a good choice for brunch —

- 2   medium grapefruit
- 1   3-ounce package lemon-flavored gelatin
- 2   tablespoons milk
- 1   8-ounce package cream cheese, softened
- ½   cup chopped walnuts
- 3   lemon slices, halved

Place 1-qt. Strainer over Small Mix-N-Stor pitcher; section grapefruit into Strainer; set fruit aside.

Add enough water to juice to make 2 cups liquid. Heat half the juice to boiling; add to gelatin and stir till dissolved. Add remaining juice mixture; cool. Add grapefruit. Spoon ¼ cup gelatin mixture into bottom of six Parfait Dishes. Chill Parfaits in slanted position till almost firm. Let remaining gelatin stand at room temperature. Blend milk into cream cheese. Remove 3 tablespoons to Snack Set cup for garnish; refrigerate. Add nuts to remaining mixture and spread over gelatin in Parfait Dishes. Pour remainder of gelatin mixture over cream cheese. Apply Seals and refrigerate till firm.

To serve, remove reserved cream cheese from refrigerator about 30 minutes before serving time and let stand to soften. Pipe through a pastry tube onto parfaits. Garnish with lemon slices. Makes 6 servings.

CABBAGE SALAD

- ½ of a small head cabbage
- ½ cup small-curd cottage cheese
- ⅓ cup mayonnaise or salad dressing
- 2 tablespoons chopped onion
- ¼ teaspoon celery seed
- ¼ teaspoon salt
  Dash pepper

Shred cabbage on shredder/slicer of Grater Bowl. Add cottage cheese, mayonnaise or salad dressing, onion, celery seed, salt, and pepper to cabbage. Apply storage Seal and turn several times to blend. Makes 6 servings.

FROZEN LIME-MINT SALADS

You can also serve this for a refreshing, light dessert —

- 1 29½-ounce can crushed pineapple
- 1 3-ounce package lime-flavored gelatin
- 1 6-ounce package tiny marshmallows (about 4 cups)
- 1 cup butter mints, crushed
- 1 9-ounce container frozen whipped dessert topping, thawed
  Lettuce leaves

In Large Mixing Bowl, combine undrained pineapple, dry lime gelatin, marshmallows, and crushed mints. Apply Seal and refrigerate for several hours or till marshmallows soften and melt. Fold in dessert topping. Spoon mixture into 18 paper bake cup-lined muffin pans. Cover and freeze till firm. Transfer to a 12" Pie Taker.

To serve, peel off paper and serve on lettuce-lined plates. Makes 18.

COTTAGE POTATO SALAD

- 2 cups cubed, cooked potatoes
- 2 hard-cooked eggs, chopped
- ¼ cup dairy sour cream
- 2 tablespoons Italian salad dressing
- 2 cups cream-style cottage cheese
- ½ cup chopped celery
- ⅓ cup sliced radishes
- ⅓ cup pitted ripe olives, sliced
- 3 tablespoons sliced green onion
- ½ teaspoon salt

In a 2-qt. peach Wonderlier Bowl, combine potatoes and chopped eggs.

Combine sour cream and Italian salad dressing; pour over potato mixture. Apply Seal to bowl and turn gently to coat. Combine cottage cheese, chopped celery, sliced radishes, sliced pitted ripe olives, green onion, and salt. Toss with potato mixture; apply Seal to bowl; chill well. Serves 6 to 8.

CRANBERRY-ORANGE RELISH

- 1 pound fresh cranberries
- 2 cups sugar
- ½ cup water
- 1 teaspoon grated orange peel
- ½ cup orange juice
- ½ cup slivered almonds

In saucepan, combine cranberries, sugar, water, orange peel, and orange juice. Cook, uncovered, about 10 minutes or till cranberry skins pop. Stir once or twice. Remove from heat; stir in almonds. Cool to room temperature. Refrigerate in 1-qt. yellow Wonderlier bowl. Makes 4 cups.

BUTTERMILK SALAD DRESSING MIX

Can't find dry buttermilk? Use nonfat dry milk powder and add 1 teaspoon lemon juice to prepared dressing —

- 1 cup dry buttermilk powder
- ¼ cup sugar
- 4 teaspoons dried basil, crushed
- 4 teaspoons minced dried onion
- 2 teaspoons dry mustard
- 1 teaspoon garlic powder
- 1 teaspoon salt

Place all ingredients in a 16-oz. Square Rounds® container. Apply Seal; shake till thoroughly combined. In one Salad Dressing Set container, combine 2 tablespoons *dry mix* and 2 tablespoons cold *water*. Apply Seal and shake. Spoon in ½ cup *mayonnaise or salad dressing*. Apply Seal and shake vigorously till blended. Chill; shake well before serving.

SPICED APPLE RINGS

- 2 cups water
- ½ cup sugar
- ¾ cup honey
- 2 tablespoons lemon juice
- 6 inches stick cinnamon, broken
- 6 whole cloves
- 3 pounds cooking apples

In a large saucepan, combine first 6 ingredients. Heat syrup, stirring to dissolve sugar. Wash apples; core, and cut into ⅜-inch rings. Add one-fourth the rings at a time to syrup. Cook, covered, 5 to 10 minutes or till apples are almost tender. Repeat with remaining rings. Pack rings and syrup in two 30-oz. Square Rounds containers, leaving ½-inch head-space. Cool. Apply Seals, label, and freeze. Makes two containers.

137

DESSERTS ON CALL

BANANA SPLIT PUFFS

- **6 Cream Puffs, thawed (see recipe at right)**
- **3 small bananas, sliced**
  Strawberry ice cream
  Vanilla ice cream
  Chocolate ice cream
  Strawberry Sundae Sauce
  Chocolate Fudge Sauce (see recipe, page 140)
  Pineapple-Orange Sundae Sauce
  Chopped nuts

Place half of a split Cream Puff in each of six Cereal Bowls. Fill each puff half with half a sliced banana and a small scoop each of strawberry ice cream, vanilla ice cream, and chocolate ice cream. Ladle sauces over. Garnish with chopped nuts. Cover with top of puff. Makes 6 servings.

Strawberry Sundae Sauce: In saucepan, combine 2 tablespoons *sugar* and 1 tablespoon *cornstarch*. Stir in ¼ cup light *corn syrup*. Add one 10-ounce package frozen sliced *strawberries*, thawed. Cook and stir over medium heat till thickened and bubbly. Cook and stir 1 to 2 minutes more. Cool. Transfer to a Condimate® Set bowl. Store in refrigerator. Makes about 1⅓ cups.

Pineapple-Orange Sundae Sauce: In saucepan, combine 1 tablespoon *brown sugar*, 1 teaspoon *cornstarch*, and ½ teaspoon grated *orange peel*. Blend in ¼ cup *orange juice*. Stir in one 8¼-ounce can crushed *pineapple*, undrained. Cook and stir over medium heat till thickened and bubbly. Cook and stir 1 to 2 minutes more. Cool. Transfer to a Condimate Set bowl. Refrigerate. Makes about 1¼ cups.

CREAM PUFFS

- **½ cup butter or margarine**
- **1 cup boiling water**
- **1 cup all-purpose flour**
- **¼ teaspoon salt**
- **4 eggs**

In saucepan, melt butter in boiling water. Add flour and salt all at once; stir vigorously. Cook and stir till mixture forms a ball that doesn't separate. Remove from heat; cool 10 minutes. Add eggs, one at a time; beat after each addition till smooth. Drop batter onto a greased baking sheet, using about ¼ cup batter for each. Space puffs about 3 inches apart. Bake in 400° oven 30 to 35 minutes, till golden and puffy. Remove from oven. With serrated knife, split warm puffs in half horizontally, removing any soft dough inside. Cool thoroughly on wire rack. Makes 10 to 12 puffs.

Arrange in a Cold Cut Keeper; apply Seal, label, and freeze. To thaw, remove from container and let stand at room temperature about 1 hour.

CREAM PUFF TIP

Cream puffs can be filled with sweetened whipped cream, your favorite pudding, or fruit filling, as well as ice cream. For a traditional cream puff dessert, fill them with Cream Cheese Filling (see recipe, page 79) or Vanilla Cream Filling (see recipe, page 80). Frost tops with Chocolate Butter Frosting (see recipe, page 76) and dust lightly with powdered sugar.

STRAWBERRY-LEMON FREEZE

- **1 quart low-fat strawberry frozen yogurt**
- **1 pint low-fat lemon frozen yogurt**
- **1 8-ounce can crushed pineapple (juice pack), drained**

Assemble Jel-N-Serve® mold with design Seal and place in freezer to chill. In Medium Mixing Bowl, soften the strawberry yogurt by using a wooden spoon to stir and press it against the sides of bowl. Soften just till pliable. Quickly spread the softened yogurt up the sides of the Jel-N-Serve mold, making an even layer on sides and bottom of the mold. (If yogurt slips down, refreeze in mold until workable.) Seal and freeze till firm.

In a Large Mix-N-Stor® pitcher, soften the lemon yogurt in the same manner as strawberry. Gently fold in drained pineapple. Spoon lemon-fruit mixture into center of mold. Apply Seal and freeze until very firm.

Just before serving time, remove Jel-N-Serve mold from freezer. Immerse mold, large Seal down, in warm water for 20 seconds; remove from water and dry mold with a cloth. Peel off large Seal. Place Serving Tray over mold and invert tray and mold together. Slowly remove design Seal. Carefully lift off mold. Let stand 10 minutes before serving. Garnish with fresh strawberries and mint, if desired. Makes 8 servings.

You can indulge in dessert and count calories at the same time. Use the Jel-N-Serve mold to enjoy Strawberry-Lemon Freeze at only 125 calories per serving.

DESSERTS ON CALL

CHOCO-MINT FREEZE

- 1 4-serving-size package *regular* vanilla pudding mix
- ½ cup sugar
- 2 cups milk
- ¼ teaspoon peppermint extract
- ½ cup semisweet chocolate pieces
- 1 cup whipping cream

Combine pudding mix, sugar, and milk. Cook and stir till thickened and bubbly. Remove from heat; stir in extract. Cover surface with waxed paper; chill till partially set. Stir in chocolate pieces. In Medium Mixing Bowl, whip cream to soft peaks; fold into pudding. Turn into Bacon Keeper; apply Seal. Freeze firm. Spoon into Dessert Set dishes. Makes 6 servings.

QUICK TORTONI DESSERT CUPS

Pictured on page 116 —

- 1 quart vanilla ice cream
- ½ cup toasted slivered almonds
- ½ cup milk chocolate pieces
- 2 tablespoons chopped maraschino cherries
- ¼ teaspoon each grated orange and lemon peel

In Medium Mixing Bowl, soften ice cream. Stir in remaining ingredients. Spoon into six Dessert Set dishes. Apply Seals; freeze firm. Let stand at room temperature 10 minutes before serving. Garnish with shaved chocolate, additional cherry halves, and almonds, if desired. Makes 6 servings.

ICE CREAM SUNDAE RING

Two-layered ice cream treat with chocolate sauce —

- ¼ cup flaked coconut, toasted
- 1½ teaspoons almond flavoring
- 1 quart vanilla ice cream, softened
- 1 quart coffee ice cream, softened
- ¼ cup slivered almonds, toasted
  Chocolate Fudge Sauce (see recipe below)

Stir coconut and almond flavoring into vanilla ice cream; turn into Jel-Ring® mold. Apply Seal and freeze firm. Stir together coffee ice cream and almonds; spoon into mold atop vanilla layer. Freeze about 5 hours or till firm.

Unmold onto serving plate. Drizzle with Chocolate Fudge Sauce; sprinkle with additional almonds, if desired. Pass remaining sauce. Makes 10 to 12 servings.

CHOCOLATE FUDGE SAUCE

In saucepan, combine one 6-ounce package semisweet *chocolate pieces* and ⅔ cup light *corn syrup*. Cook and stir over low heat till chocolate melts. Remove from heat; cool. Gradually stir in one 5⅓-ounce can *evaporated milk.* Transfer to a Condimate® Set or 20-oz. Servalier® bowl. Makes 1½ cups.

RASPBERRY LADYFINGER CAKE

- 2 envelopes unflavored gelatin
- ¾ cup sugar
- 2 cups milk
- 3 slightly beaten egg yolks
- 1 cup dairy sour cream
- 2 teaspoons vanilla
- 12 ladyfingers, split
- 3 stiff-beaten egg whites
- ½ cup whipping cream
  Raspberry Sauce

In medium saucepan, combine gelatin, sugar and ¼ teaspoon *salt*. Stir in milk and egg yolks. Cook and stir over low heat till mixture coats spoon. Remove from heat; stir about 1 cup of the hot mixture into sour cream; return mixture to saucepan; add vanilla. Chill till partially set. Meanwhile, arrange 6 ladyfinger halves, spoke-fashion, in bottom of Stacking Canister; line sides of Canister with remaining. Fold egg whites into gelatin mixture. Whip cream; fold into gelatin mixture. Spoon into Canister. Apply Seal. Chill several hours till firm. Unmold Canister onto 10″ Cake Taker base. Drizzle with some Raspberry Sauce; pass remaining. Garnish with additional raspberries, if desired. Serves 10 to 12.

Raspberry Sauce: In a saucepan, crush one 10-ounce package frozen *raspberries,* thawed; stir in 1 tablespoon *cornstarch* and ½ cup *currant jelly.* Cook and stir till bubbly; cook 1 minute more. Strain by placing 1-qt. Strainer over Small Mix-N-Stor® pitcher. Cover and chill sauce.

Elegant Raspberry Ladyfinger Cake starts with delicate ladyfingers. Serve this easy dessert with its luscious Raspberry Sauce.

INDEX

A - B